Charles Bill Kimbell

**History of Battery A - First Illinois Light Artillery Volunteers**

Charles Bill Kimbell

**History of Battery A - First Illinois Light Artillery Volunteers**

ISBN/EAN: 9783337250140

Printed in Europe, USA, Canada, Australia, Japan

Cover: Foto ©ninafisch / pixelio.de

More available books at **www.hansebooks.com**

'Tis the Star Spangled Banner!
O, long may it wave
O'er the land of the free
And the home of the brave!

# HISTORY

OF

# BATTERY "A"

FIRST ILLINOIS

LIGHT ARTILLERY

VOLUNTEERS

———

CHARLES B. KIMBELL

———

CHICAGO:
CUSHING PRINTING COMPANY
1899

A beautiful Monument, in memory of the Battery's dead, was erected in Rose Hill Cemetery in 1874. The cost with the stone curbing, foundation and filling was $3,052.75, $2,000 of which was generously donated by Capt. Smith for that purpose in his will. The balance was paid by subscriptions from members and friends. A monument committee having the matter in charge consisted of the following members: C. B. Kimbell, Olof Benson, J. W. Rumsey, S. W. Butterfield and John L. Stockton. The Battery Veteran Association has a FULL PAID UP contract with the Rose Hill Cemetery Company for the PERPETUAL CARE of the lot and Monument. As many of the members as can do so, meet every year on Decoration Day at the Monument.

BATTERY "A," CHICAGO LIGHT ARTILLERY MONUMENT,
ROSE HILL CEMETERY, CHICAGO, ILL.

# PREFACE.

TO RECORD the history and achievements of noted military organizations, is a desire both natural and commendable. The reasons are too various and obvious to the thoughtful mind to require any apology for so recording. The attempt has been made in this work to narrate, as fully as practicable, from all the reliable data obtainable, a clear, concise and continuous tale of the work of our cherished Battery in doing its part in assisting to put down the War of the Rebellion from 1861 to 1865, and to give brief biographical sketches of its individual members, so as to make it both useful and interesting for all future reference.

This history I would dedicate to my dear comrades of Battery "A," who stood manfully by each other during the trying times of war; and having as steadfastly continued to do so in the "piping times of peace," I am encouraged in this effort to reproduce the main and important incidents connected with the Battery's long active and eventful career. It is not strange that old comrades, who for months and years, shared the dangers and privations of army life, in camp, on the march and battlefield; many having suffered sickness and hunger, in hospitals and prison pens, should desire to keep alive the memories and associations of those trying times. We are all hastening on to our final muster-out. In all human probability most of our surviving comrades will have answered the last roll call, by the close of the next decade, and will assemble on the parade ground of eternity.

A conscious feeling that I have done what was within my feeble power to keep alive and strengthen the fraternal feelings which have always bound together the members of old Battery "A," and to perpetuate the memory of the living and our noble dead, prompts me to undertake, before too late, the task of recording our history.

In writing the history of the Battery it is not the design of the writer to furnish a history of the War in the west, or of the Army of the Tennessee, to which the Battery belonged, nor will any attempt at doing so be made, only so far as the humble part taken in the great struggle by our gallant Battery is connected with it. In fact, the history of the Army of the Tennessee is but a history of our Battery, for it was in nearly all the great battles of the west, and the records of the war are full of its achievements, and this would be sufficient for the public at large, and for general history. But the Battery was like one large family, and all its members were proud of and loyal to it. All were tried in the balance and not found wanting in fidelity to each other, in patriotism and valor, which bound them together with no ordinary ties. The object of this history is to condense and perpetuate the achievements of the Battery, with the daily details and prominent incidents, which were of so much interest to its members, but would find no place in the general history of the war, and make it of personal value to each individual member and all its friends, bringing us more closely in touch with one another during the few remaining years of our lives, and make it an heirloom worthy of being handed down to future generations of our descendents.

I wish to return my sincere thanks to the many comrades and friends who have contributed in various ways to the completeness and accuracy of this history. Conscious that the entirely successful accomplishment of this task is more than could reasonably be promised or expected, I ask as mild criticism of my labor as possible, trusting that my efforts may be appreciated in the same fraternal spirit in which they are made.

Fraternally,

C. B. KIMBELL.

# HISTORY

OF

# Battery "A" First Illinois

LIGHT ARTILLERY VOLUNTEERS

---

## CHAPTER I.

"IN THE beginning" of Chicago, or a few years thereafter, the public-spirited and patriotic citizens of that embryo city, formed several military militia companies, among them the Chicago Light Artillery, afterwards Battery "A," Chicago Light Artillery, and, still later, Co. "A" 1st Illinois Artillery Vols., as it was officially known when in the U. S. service during the War of the Rebellion. The first militia organization in the city was a company of mounted volunteers, which was mustered into service May 23, 1832, and was mustered out June 23 of the same year. Various companies afterward sprung up and had their day. In discussing the military situation at that time, the *Chicago American* says: "The formation of a dragoon company would be much too expensive, for each member would be required to furnish himself with a good horse. An artillery company would not meet our wants, it being an arm of the service that moves with the heaviness of its own eighteen or twenty-four pounders," etc. This is the first mention we find regarding artillery in the history of Chicago. The next mention is in the *Chicago Democrat*, "Long John" Wentworth's paper, of Nov. 13, 1847, which says: "At a meeting of citizens at the office of R. K. Swift for the purpose of organizing a company of cavalry and flying artillery, Mr. Rankin was chairman and C. F. Howe, secretary. Committee on constitution, Capt. J. B. F. Russell, R. K. Swift, John R. Orr, James Smith and C. F. Howe. Committee on uniform, R. K. Swift and Dr. Boardman." November 23d the same paper says: "Captain Swift's cavalry company, accompanied by a piece of artillery, and a band of music paraded the streets yesterday. They made a fine appearance, and created an unusual stir in the city. After parading the streets the company retired without the city limits and continued firing some time. We should judge from the time between each report that the gun was well handled." Again, a later issue, in the same month, says: "The cavalry and flying artillery will meet to-day at the old garrison ground. We hope all who take an interest in military affairs will be in attendance. The artillery will be escorted by a band of music outside the city limits, where there will be some practice in gunnery."

For a long season after the close of the Mexican War, peace ensued, and until the breaking out of the Civil War, in 1861, the military companies were not called out for any work more serious than to quell some local disturbances, notably the famous "lager beer riot," or to add to the gorgeousness and impressiveness of some holiday parade. At the close of 1860 all the military organizations of the city, even those who had maintained but a nominal organization, aroused by the peril threatening the country, and assuming fresh vitality from the spontaneous wave of patriotism that was sweeping over the country, answered to its call with solid ranks, filled with the best young blood of the land, and marched with more enthusiasm to the battlefield, than ever in the quiet days of peace to the holiday parade or drill. The Chicago Hussars and Light Artillery were organized as before stated, in November, 1847, as follows: Captain, R. K. Swift; 1st Lieut., James Smith; 2d Lieut., Nelson Buchanan; 3d Lieut., C. F. Howe; Cornet, John A. Reichert. R. K. Swift was continued as captain until May 5, 1854, when the Chicago Light Artillery was organized with Capt., James Smith; 1st Lieut., Ezra Taylor; 2d Lieut., E. W. Hadley; Commissary, H. S. Speers. The battery records now in existence, show that the organization was a small but healthy and active one between 1854 and the spring of 1861.

On the 11th of April, 1861, Gen. Beuregard, commanding the rebel forces at Charleston, demanded the surrender of Fort Sumter. The demand not being complied with, fire was opened upon it on the 12th, and its evacuation followed on the 14th. Immediately after the firing on the Fort over which floated the national flag, President Lincoln called for 75,000 volunteer troops for 90 days. Gen. Grant, in his memoirs, says: "If the shot at

CAMP SMITH, CAIRO, ILL., JUNE 1861.

Ft. Sumter was heard around the world, the call for 75,000 men was heard throughout the Northern States. There was not a State in the North, of one million inhabitants, that would not have furnished the entire number." Chicago, as in everything else, was foremost in her efforts to furnish her quota of troops, and in less than three days, more men had offered themselves than could be taken in the city militia organizations, which were filled to their maximum number, and their services offered immediately to the Governor, gallant old " Dick " Yates, one of the noblest war governors among the loyal States. Their offer was accepted, and on the night of Sunday, April 21, the first body of troops in the war, left the city on the Cairo expedition.

The Battery's first appearance in public was at the grand muster by Gen. R. K. Swift on that ever memorable Sunday morning, April 21st, 1861, on the streets of this city. The infantry consisted of two companies of the old Ellsworth Zouaves, the Chicago Turn-Gemeinde company, and Captains Mihalotzky's and Harding's companies. After the muster they were confined to their quarters in the armory, and communication with the outside world cut off. Preparations for immediate transportation South were commenced and the final departure via the I. C. R. R. took place at 9 P. M. amid the tears and shouts of the thousands who thronged the lake shore to bid them farewell.

President Lincoln's first call for troops found the Battery organization a ready nucleus for forming a first-class battery on very short notice. It was recruited to the maximum number in less than twenty-four hours after the rolls were opened, and many more recruits offered themselves than could be accepted. Many of the old members enrolled themselves, headed by Capt. James Smith. Among them were, E. P. Tobey, Edward Mendsen, W. L. Southworth, John R. Botsford, and many others. Among its members were some of the most prominent business men of the city. Its outfit was a full field battery of four guns, with caissons, battery wagon, forge, harness, etc. It was stationed in the old armory building on the corner of Adams and Franklin streets. Capt. James Smith was an old and efficient artillery officer, then a member of a prominent lumber firm. The company was organized under the militia laws of the State, and was called into service by Governor Richard Yates in response to the first call of President Lincoln. Nearly all its members were young men, many of them born or raised in this city and educated in her schools, and they were, therefore, fully entitled to the name they bore, a name that became as famous throughout the army as the name of our city has since become throughout the world, for its great strides in commercial and industrial progress.

There was the wildest excitement among the entire populace of the city, and the greatest enthusiasm among the soldier boys, who were eager to avenge the insult offered to our flag at Ft. Sumter. Little did they dream that it would be many months before they would have the dire experience of a regular battle, and instead of closing out the rebellion in 90 days, that over four years of terrible warfare would ensue before the declaration of peace. It was well for them perhaps that they could not foresee the future.

The roster of Company A, Chicago Light Artillery as it left Chicago, Sunday 10:30 P. M., April 21st, 1861, via Ill. Cen. R. R., arriving at Cairo, Ill., Monday 11 A. M., April 22nd, is as follows:

Captain, James Smith; Sr. 1st Lieut., Chas. M. Willard; Jr. 1st Lieut., Francis Morgan; Sr. 2nd Lieut., John R. Botsford; Jr. 2nd Lieut., Peter P. Wood; 1st Sergt., A. R. Abbott; Quarter Master Sergt., Edgar P. Tobey; Chiefs of Pieces, (Sergeants), Ed. Mendsen, Samuel Beers, Chas. C. Briggs, John W. Rumsey, Thos. E. Taylor, Horace S. Foote, Corporals (gunners) J. L. Thompson, Thaddens S. Clarkson, Hoxie L. Hoffman, Jacob Clingman, Henry H. Handy, Wm. L. Southworth. Chiefs of Caissons, Harry Morgan, Arthur M. Kenzie, George E. Adams, Sam. F. Childs, Adam C. Hall, Geo. McCagg. Commissary, Horace W. Chase; Assistant Commissary, Chas. W. Poole. Farrier, James Taylor.

Privates: Abbott L. Adams, Alex. Anderson, W. Ames, M. W. Axtel, Henry Bennett. Henry E. Brewster, Wm. H. Bailey, Peter Bostwick, Jerome P. Briggs, Geo. M. Brown, J. E. Bissell, Martin A. Bartleson, Olof Benson, Caleb S. Burdsal, Thomas Burton, C. A. Bridges, Ed. Baggot, John T. Connell, Horace M. Chapman, Chauncey R. Crandall, Fred E. Church, Nathan T. Cox, Judson R. Crary, Benjamin L. Cleaves, George E. Cooper, Geo. Childs, Samuel C. Durkee, John D. Dyer, F. S. Dean, Martin Dollard, J. Fred. Dunlap, W. S. Fonda, Orrington C. Foster, Wm. Furness, Daniel R. Farnham, J. L. Flanigan, Samuel M. Fargo, Allen W. Gray, G. R. Green, Ferdinand V. Gindele, Wm. C. Greene, Otto C. Heimburger, J. L. Hazlett, Edward S. Hills, Harvey Hart, Geo. T. Hebard, Jas. Hennessy, H. Hinch, Henry Hobart, Ed. D. Howland, John D. Holmes, Thos. Halpin,

LIEUT. JOHN R. BOTSFORD.

John R. Irwin, J. E. Johnson, Lewis F. Jacobs, Thomas A. Kearnes, Theodore W. Kennedy, Geo. King, Harrison Kelley, Charles B. Kimbell, Wm. Kirk, Cornelius Kendall, George Kennicott, Wm. H. Lepperr, Charles A. Lamb, N. A. Lull, Tim. W. Lynch, Wm. Lowe, Cass. F. Maurer, Augustin P. Maddock, John Marder, Geo. A. Mariner, J. L. Morrison, Lewis B. Mitchell, C. C. Nelson, Jerry D. Powell, Stephen N. Pease, Wm. M. Pratt, Thos. Powell, Aurelius V. Pitts, S. Parsons, John M. Peters, E. H. Russell, O. R. Richardson, E. Richardson, Harvey B. Risley, J. F. Stackhouse, Joseph Sproules, John Steele, John S haffer, Frank B. Smith, O. F. Shead, W. C. G. L. Stevenson, James Sergeant, Edward S. Sherrill, S. J. Sherwood, Jno. Tack, S. H. Tallmadge, Wm. B. Vernon, J. T. Vigers, George L. Whittier, D. R. Wilson, J. A. White, Willard I. Wilcox, F. C. Wilson, E. S. Warner, J. L. Whittaker, Wilber J. Wilcox, Frederick W. Young.

The departure from home and the long dusty ride to Cairo, will not soon be forgotten. After passing Big Muddy bridge in safety, where many of us expected we would be attacked by rebel sympathizers, we reached Cairo in the night of the 22d. One gun, under Lieut. C. M. Willard, with the Ellsworth Zouaves, was sent back to Big Muddy bridge and left there as a guard in charge of Sergeant Ed. Mendsen, for several days. The next morning the most of us beheld for the first time, the mighty and muddy Mississippi, and the blue Ohio, with the shores of two slave States on the opposite sides. Our reception by the citizens was not the most cordial, and it was plainly evident that they would have been better pleased if the occupying forces had come from the opposite direction. However, we were there first, and there to stay, as it afterward proved, for nearly five months. Many of our soldier boys, after the close of the war, remained or returned to various points throughout the South, where attractions of some nature allured them. But it is not on record that a single one of them ever located permanently in Cairo alive. The croaking frogs, double-barreled, long-billed musquitoes, the deep mud, and the smell of rank weeds and swamps around it, were sufficient to dispel any thoughts of locating there permanently. The many names applied by the boys to Cairo, would do to mention in the early part of the war, but would not bear repetition in a history like this.

The battery was assigned the duty of bringing to all downward bound boats, which were required to be inspected for contraband goods, before

"IN BATTERY" CO. "A" CHICAGO LIGHT ARTILLERY, CAMP SMITH, JUNE 1894.

going down the river. On the 24th of April the steamer "Baltic," in passing Cairo, disregarded the blank shot summoning her to land, when a solid shot was fired across her bow which had the desired effect. These shots fired by "squad one," under command of Lieut. J. R. Botsford, were the first fired from a field piece in the war for the Union, and the first on the banks of the mighty river. Their echoes were heard its entire length, and their reverberations were carried down its currents, figuratively speaking, even to the city of New Orleans, bringing forth a challenge to our Battery to mortal combat, from the famous Washington Light Artillery of that city. The challenge was accepted, but not until the terrible battle of Shiloh did the trial take place, which was decided in our favor.

The second act was the capture of the steamer "C. E. Hillman," from St. Louis, loaded to the guards with contraband goods of war. This was accomplished by Capt. James Smith in person, with one gun and a small detachment of infantry, on the steamer "Swallow!"

The "Hillman" hugged the Missouri shore and tried to escape, but overtaken by Capt. Smith, she ran ashore, and the officers and a portion of the passengers took to the woods. She was brought over to Cairo and found to have on board about $300,000.00 worth of war material. Several rebel flags were taken from the remaining passengers on the boat.

After about a week's stay at Cairo, during which time large reinforcements arrived, we were on the following Sunday ordered to take a position about two miles up stream on the Mississippi river bank. This position was christened "Camp Smith," in honor of our commander, and was occupied by the Battery nearly five months. The arduous guard and picket duty imposed upon the command, and the labor of clearing a dense forest of about ten acres for drill grounds, with almost incessant wet weather for two months, caused quite a number to succumb under the severe strain, and many were unwillingly discharged and sent home. Many of our young men had their first experience in hard work here, as many a lame back and blistered hand, could testify.

Arduous camp and picket duty, relieved only by the regular daily drills, was the order of each day during our stay at Camp Smith. Being in close communication with "God's Country," as the boys reverently spoke of home, we fared much better, with the addition to our supplies of the good things received almost daily from the loved ones at home, than after we proceeded farther south, and our extra supplies were cut off.

Under the instructions of our efficient officers, the Battery soon became so thorough in drill and evolution, that when it appeared on parade at Cairo it was supposed by military men, unacquainted with the facts, to be a regular battery, notably so by General McClellan, who thought it wonderful for volunteers to attain such proficiency in so short a time.

The expectation and desire to be called to the east were great, after this inspection, and in fact we were under orders several days, but happily for us, positive orders never arrived. Early in July a section was ordered by Gen. Fremont to St. Louis, from whence they proceeded along the North Missouri road to St. Charles and Mexico, Mo. After several weeks of hard service, the section rejoined the Battery.

A majority of the members in the three months service, who did not reinlist, formed an association with a number of prominent and patriotic friends of Chicago, for the purpose of supplying the Battery with many of the necessaries and even luxuries of which they were deprived by army rations, and looking after the sick and wounded of the Battery. Among the most active in this service were Capt. James Smith, E. P. Tobey, W. L. Southworth and John L. Stockton. Many a sick and wounded member of the Battery had cause to remember them with great gratitude. Private citizens threw open their homes to receive the sick and wounded on their arrival in the city, until they could be sent to their homes. A notable instance of this kind was when Mr. S. B. Walker took four wounded members, after the battle of Shiloh, on their cots, into his parlor on Michigan Avenue, and kept them several days. The association passed a hearty vote of thanks to Mr. Walker and his family, which consisted of his wife and three patriotic daughters, for ministering to the care of their comrades in so hospitable a manner. The eldest daughter, Chastina B. Walker, afterward served as volunteer nurse for several months on a Mississippi River Hospital Steamer, and any soldier from Chicago, especially those of Battery "A", was the object of her special care.

The Battery, for various reasons, did not muster into the United States three months service, but when the question of entering for the three years or during the war, came up, a large majority decided to do so, and 85 members were mustered in July 16, 1861, as Battery "A" First Regiment Illinois Light Artillery. The members mustered in received a ten days' fur-

Harry Morgan, Jo. Morrison, F. G. Dean, John M. Peters, Jas. Dexter,
W. L. Southworth, Frank B. Smith, John R. Irwin, Ed. S. Sherrill.

lough to visit their homes, while those not reinlisting held the camp until their return.

While stationed at Cairo, the Battery was presented with a beautiful silk flag by Miss Katie Sturgis, of Chicago. This flag was carried by the battery through all its subsequent campaigns. It was destroyed by the great fire of October 10, 1871, in the rooms of the Chicago Historical Society, where it had been placed for safe keeping.

## CHAPTER II.

ON the 16th of July, 1861, at Cairo, Ills., eighty-seven members of Company "A," Chicago Light Artillery, were mustered into the United States service by Colonel Pitcher, as Battery "A" First Illinois Light Artillery Volunteers. The Battery was stationed at "Camp Smith," about two miles above Cairo, on the east bank of the Mississippi, where they were comfortably established in good quarters, which they had been nearly three months in acquiring. The members re-enlisting were given a ten days' furlough to visit their homes and friends, and the members who did not re-inlist held the camp till their return. July 18, three additional members were mustered in, and on July 28th, seventy-two recruits were added, among them being several of the three months men.

Enlistments to fill vacancies caused by discharges, promotions, and deaths, continued till the close of the war, the total number of enlistments, (exclusive of the consolidation of Batteries "A" and "B" in 1864)

were...................................................... 212
Those enlisting in the Battery for three months only............ 50
Making total number of enlistments during the war............ 262
The survivors known at this date (1899) are..................... 115
Leaving unknown, killed, dead, and missing................... 147

The following is a list of members of Battery "A" First Illinois Light Artillery enlisting into the United States service, July 16, 1861, and subsequently. Those who were in the three months service, enlisting April 19, 1861, are marked 1:

| NAMES. | Date of Muster. In | Date of Muster. Out | Enlisted. Rank. | Remarks and Address, 1900. |
|---|---|---|---|---|
| James Smith 1 | July 16, 1861 | Sept. 27, 1861 | Captain. | Resigned. Died, California, May 1, 1872. |
| Charles M. Willard 1 | " | Jan. 16, 1863 | Sr. 1st Lieut. | Major. Dead. |
| Francis Morgan 1 | " | May 24, 1862 | Jr. 1st Lieut. | Captain. Died, August, 1887. |
| Peter P. Wood 1 | " | July 23, 1864 | Sr. 2nd Lieut. | Captain. Died, Dec. 13, 1865, Chicago. |
| Edgar P. Tobey 1 | " | Feb. 3, 1862 | Jr. 2nd Lieut. | Resigned. Died, June 28, 1894. |
| Abial R. Abbott 1 | " | | 1st Sergeant | Promoted Lieut. Battery E. Died, Jan. 9, 1891. |
| George McCagg 1 | " | | Q. M. Serg't | " " Dead. |
| John W Rumsey 1 | " | July, 1864 | Sergeant | " " Seattle, Washington. |
| Samuel Beers 1 | " | Mch 24, 1862 | " | Discharged for Disability. Dead. |
| Charles C. Briggs 1 | " | Jan. 17, 1863 | " | To United States Navy. Pittsburgh, Pa. |
| Harry Morgan 1 | " | | " | Discharged for Disability. Died, July 23, 1893. |
| Thaddeus S. Clarkson 1 | " | Nov. 27, 1861 | " | Promoted 1st Lt. 13th Ill. Cavalry. Omaha, Neb. |
| Jeremiah D. Powell 1 | " | | Corporal | Killed, Battle of Shiloh, April 6, 1862. |
| William M. Pratt 1 | " | | " | Promoted Jr. 2nd Lieut. Prisoner of war. Dead. |
| Jacob Clingman 1 | " | July 23, 1864 | 1st Sergeant | Died, December 3, 1888. |
| Hoxie L. Hoffman 1 | " | Jan. 17, 1863 | Corporal | Resgn'd Jr, 2d Lt. Soldiers Home, Los Angeles Co. [Cal. |
| Ed. S. Sherrill 1 | " | July 23, 1864 | Corporal | Sergeant. Wounded, Jackson, Miss. |
| Chauncey R. Crandall 1 | " | " | " | Wounded, Shiloh. Dead. |
| Frank B. Smith 1 | " | | " | Promoted 1st Lieut. 2nd Illinois Artillery. |
| Wilber J. Wilcox 1 | " | July 23, 1864 | " | Killed July, 1863. Jackson, Miss. Sergeant. |
| Wm. Lowe 1 | " | | " | Chicago. |
| Fred. W. Young 1 | " | July 27, 1865 | " | Jr. 2nd Lieut. Died, April 19, 1892. |
| Adam C. Hall 1 | " | | " | Wounded, Shiloh. Prisoner. Des Moines, Iowa. |
| George L. Whittier 1 | " | July 23, 1864 | " | Sergeant. Killed, Vicksburg, May 23, 1863. |
| Orrington C. Foster 1 | " | " | " | Chicago. |
| Everett H. Rexford | July 28, 1861 | | Bugler | Blue Island, Ill. |

DINING HALL, SQUAD 6. CAMP SMITH, JUNE 1861.
Geo. L. Whittier, Wallace Ames, W. L. Southworth, Chauncey R. Crandall.
(Roof made from shell of decayed sycamore tree.)

| NAMES. | DATE OF MUSTER. In | DATE OF MUSTER. Out | ENLISTED RANK. | REMARKS AND ADDRESS, 1900. |
|---|---|---|---|---|
| James F. Stackhouse 1... | July 16, 1861 | April 22, 1862 | Farrier | Discharged. Disability. Dead. |
| PRIVATES. | | | | |
| Anderson, Alex. 1....... | July 28, 1861 | | Private | Died, Hospital, Memphis, June 23, 1862. Chicago. |
| Arnold, Charles L....... | " | July 23, 1864 | " | Corporal. |
| Allen, Frank S.......... | " | " | " | Promoted 2d Lt. 2d La. Col'd Art'l'y. Died Jan. 24 '94 |
| Austin, Frank D......... | " | Dec. 28, 1862 | " | Discharged for Disability. |
| Alston, James........... | 1861 | Mch. 9, 1863 | " | Discharged for Disability. Dead. |
| Adams, Ashley.......... | | July 10, 1865 | " | |
| Brown, Geo. M. 1....... | July 16, 1861 | July 23, 1864 | " | Corporal. Conneaut, Ohio. |
| Brown, Wm. G. 1....... | " | Aug. 7, 1862 | " | Wounded, Shiloh. Died. |
| Brown, John P.......... | July 28, 1861 | Mch. 10, 1863 | " | Discharged for Disability. Florin, California. |
| Bissell, John E. 1....... | July 16, 1861 | | Sergeant | Killed, Chattanooga, December 8, 1863. |
| Bartleson, Martin A. 1... | " | July 23, 1864 | Private | Nogales, Arizona. |
| Benson, Olof 1.......... | " | " | " | Chicago. |
| Burton, Thomas 1 ...... | " | " | " | Serg't. 1st Lieut. Battery "M." Dead. |
| Briggs, Jerome P. 1..... | " | July 23, 1864 | " | Died, April, 1862, Galveston. Yellow fever |
| Bangs, George.......... | July 28, 1861 | Feb. 29, 1864 | " | Dead. |
| Bailey, Alex. J.......... | 1861 | Aug. 11, 1862 | " | Wounded, Shiloh, April 6, 1862. |
| Butterfield, Samuel W... | July 28, 1861 | 1862 | " | Discharged for Disability. Died April 7, 1887. |
| Beach, George B........ | " | July 23, 1864 | " | Died December 2, 1892. |
| Burdick, Henry.......... | 1862 | July 10, 1865 | " | Woodstock, Ill. |
| Beach, Laurin H........ | July 28, 1861 | June 12, 1865 | " | Chicago. |
| Bailey, William H. 1.... | " | July 10, 1865 | " | Chicago. |
| Bowman, Charles A..... | | " | Sergeant | Chicago. |
| Betts, James............ | 1862 | | Private | |
| Burdick, Barnett........ | Oct. 12, 1861 | July 10, 1865 | Corporal | Died, Hospital, Str. Mamphis, Feb. 9, 1863. |
| Chase, Horace W. 1.... | July 16, 1861 | July 23, 1864 | Commissary | Waterloo, Kansas. |
| Chase, George M....... | " | " | Private | Died, September 6, 1893. |

| NAMES. | Date of Muster. In | Out | Enlisted. Rank. | Remarks and Address, 1900. |
|---|---|---|---|---|
| Connell, John T. | July 16, 1861 | July 23, 1864 | Corporal. | Grand Island, Nebraska. |
| Church, Fred. S. | " | " | " | New York City. |
| Cox, Nathan T. | " | Dec. 28, 1862 | Private. | Denver, Colorado. |
| Chittenden, Morris A. | July 28, 1861 | July 23, 1864 | " | Atchison, Kansas. |
| Cleaves, Benjamin L. | " | " | " | Dead. |
| Chambers, Anthony G. | 1861 | " | " | Died, April 5, 1862. |
| Cooper, Thomas B. | July 28, 1861 | Dec. 22, 1861 | " | Discharged for Disability. |
| Clark, Charles E. | " | July 23, 1864 | " | Chicago. |
| Colby, Enoch, Jr. | Aug. 3, 1861 | July 10, 1865 | " | 1st Lieutenant Chicago. |
| Clark, Edward D. | Oct. 12, 1861 | Oct. 12, 1864 | Sergeant. | Died, February 15, 1895. |
| Clark, John H. | " | Oct. 11, 1864 | Private. | Wounded. Prisoner. Died, June 15, '90. |
| Crocker, James F. | August, 1861 | Aug. 30, 1864 | " | Soldiers' Home, Danville, Ill. |
| Cowlin, William H. | Feb. 3, 1862 | June 12, 1865 | " | Prisoner. Wounded. Woodstock, Ill. |
| Canfield, Thomas B. | " | Feb. 6, 1865 | " | Lost arm, Atlanta. Dead. |
| Church, Clarence L. | Feb. 3, 1862 | April 6, 1865 | " | Prisoner of War. Wellington, Ohio. |
| Durkee, Samuel C. | July 16, 1861 | July 23, 1864 | " | Wounded. |
| Dyer, John D. | " | " | " | Ravenswood, Ill. |
| Dunlap, Fred. J. | " | June 11, 1862 | " | |
| DeKay, Henry A. | " | July 23, 1864 | " | Bedford, N. Y. |
| Day, John B. | July 16, 1861 | Sept. 1, 1863 | " | Discharged for Disability. Dead. |
| Dooling, Michael. | July 28, 1861 | April 24, 1864 | " | |
| Dusenberry, James M. | July, 1861 | April 13, 1865 | Sergeant. | San Francisco, California. |
| Dezang, Robert M. | August, 1862 | June 3, 1865 | Private. | |
| Daly, Daniel. | Aug. 22, 1861 | Feb. 29, 1864 | " | Dead. |
| Dixson, Albert. | Feb. 3, 1862 | Feb. 21, 1865 | Corporal. | Rochester, N. Y. |
| Eastwood, James G. | Aug. 1, 1862 | July 10, 1865 | " | Dead. |
| Emory, Fred. A. | | | | Magnolia, Virginia. |
| Edwards, George P. | | | Private. | |
| Fonda, William S. | July 16, 1861 | July 19, 1864 | Corporal. | No Record of Muster. |

| NAMES. | DATE OF MUSTER. In | DATE OF MUSTER. Out | ENLISTED. RANK. | REMARKS AND ADDRESS, 1900. |
|---|---|---|---|---|
| Furness, William | July 16, 1861 | July 28, 1862 | Private. | Discharged for Disability. Ogdensburg, N. Y. |
| Farnham, Daniel R. | " | " | " | Killed, Shiloh, April 6, 1862. |
| Flanigan, John J. | " | " | " | " " " |
| Foote, Horace S. | " | July 28, 1864 | " | Milwaukee, Wis. |
| Fandish, Samuel | " | " | " | Died Anders'ville prs'n June 26, '64, grave No. 2435 |
| Fish, Edward P. | July 28, 1861 | July 25, 1864 | " | Pueblo, Colorado. |
| Follansbee, Wm. Pitt | " | " | " | Dead. |
| Earl, John | Oct. 18, 1861 | | " | Killed, Atlanta, Ga., July 22, 1864. |
| Fitch, Wm. A. | Feb. 3, 1862 | | " | Died, St. Louis, May 12, 1864. |
| Funch, Frank | " | | " | Died, Belleville, Ill., December 12, 1863. |
| Gray, Allen W. | July 16, 1861 | Feb. 9, 1862 | " | Lieutenant 51st Ill. Infantry. Chicago. |
| Green, Greely R. | " | July 23, 1864 | " | Wounded, Shiloh. Died, May 21, 1862. |
| Green, Wm. C. | July 28, 1861 | | " | Died, Chicago, 1890. |
| Gates, George | " | July 23, 1864 | " | |
| Godley, John C. | " | " | " | Discharged for Disability. Brest, Michigan. |
| Gould, Meric. | " | " | " | Chicago. |
| Gindele, Fred. V. | August, 1862 | Jan. 28, 1862 | " | To 8th Illinois Cavalry. |
| Gamble, George H. | " | May 26, 1865 | " | Wounded, Shiloh. Died May 16, 1862. |
| Heimberger, Otto C. | July 16, 1861 | Nov. 25, 1864 | " | Discharged for Disability. Atlanta, Ga. |
| Hills, Edward S. | " | Jan. 9, 1863 | " | |
| Hart, Harvey I. | " | July 23, 1864 | " | No Record of Muster. |
| Hebard, George T. | " | " | " | |
| Hobart, Henry | July 18, 1861 | " | " | To United States Navy. Died, Cairo. |
| Holmes, John D. | July 16, 1861 | Jan. 9, 1862 | " | |
| Howard, Everett R. | July 28, 1861 | July 23, 1864 | " | Wounded at Donelson. |
| Hawks, Moses | " | " | " | Dead. |
| Hatch, Walter | | July 10, 1865 | " | Discharged for Disability. Dead. |
| Henry, John P. | | Dec. 29, 1861 | " | Died, Soldiers' Home, Leavenworth, Kans., '93. |
| Henry, Cyrus C. | | June 16, 1862 | " | |

| NAMES. | DATE OF MUSTER. | | ENLISTED RANK. | REMARKS AND ADDRESS, 1900. |
|---|---|---|---|---|
| | In | Out | | |
| Hughes, Edward......... | July, 1862 | Jan. 4, 1864 | Private. | Prisoner sixteen months. Chicago. |
| Irwin, John R. ......... | July 16, 1861 | July 23, 1864 | Corporal. | Chicago. |
| Jacobs, Lewis F. ....... | " | " | Private. | Died, Chicago, October 21, '89. |
| Johnson, Edward........ | July 28, 1861 | July 11, 1862 | " | Hospital Clerk, Soldiers' Home, Leavenworth. |
| Johnson, Wm. H........ | Aug. 6, 1862 | May 25, 1865 | " | Alpena, Mich. |
| Kearnes, Thos. A. ...... | " | Jan. 9, 1863 | " | Discharged for Disability. |
| Kennedy Theo. W. ..... | July 16, 1861 | July 23, 1864 | " | Soldiers Home, Milwaukee. |
| King, George ........... | " | " | " | Dead. |
| Kimbell, Chas. B ....... | " | " | Sergeant. | Died, July 14, '98. |
| Kirk, William .......... | " | " | Private. | Disc'ged, Wounded, Shiloh, April 6, '62. Chicago. |
| Kennedy, Samuel ....... | July 28, 1861 | July 24, 1864 | " | Died, June 21, '63, Vicksburg, |
| Kimbell, Spencer S ..... | Aug. 2, 1862 | July 10, 1865 | 2nd Lieut. | Moline, Ill. |
| Krupp, Daniel .......... | 1862 | " | Private. | Chicago. |
| Kepler, Eugene.......... | 1863 | " | Wagoner. | Died, Chicago, July 17, '97. |
| Kantzler, Fred. M....... | " | Jan. 12, 1865 | Private. | Dead. |
| Lepperr, Wm. H. ....... | July 16, 1861 | July 23, 1864 | " | Prisoner sixteen months. |
| Lamb, Charles A. ...... | " | " | " | Dead. |
| Lull, Norman A. ....... | " | " | " | Died, September 23, '93. |
| Lynch, Timothy ........ | " | May 10, 1865 | " | Dead. |
| Leavitt, Fred. B........ | July 28, 1861 | July 23, 1864 | Sergeant. | Arm lost at Atlanta, Ga. Austin, Ill. |
| Lord, John B............ | " | " | Private. | |
| Loog, James H. ........ | Febru'y 1862 | Feb. 23, 1865 | " | Chicago. |
| Lowell, George A....... | " | July 10, 1865 | " | |
| Maurer, Cass F. ........ | July 16, 1861 | July 23, 1864 | " | Chicago. |
| Maddock, Augustin P. .. | " | June 24, 1862 | " | Wounded, Prisoner. Died, Chicago, May 16, '85. |
| Meath, John W. ........ | " | " 3, 1865 | " | Dead. |
| Maloney, Jeremiah ...... | August, 1862 | July 10, 1865 | " | Died, Chicago, 1887. |

| NAMES. | DATE OF MUSTER In | DATE OF MUSTER Out | ENLISTED RANK. | REMARKS AND ADDRESS, 1900. |
| --- | --- | --- | --- | --- |
| McCleavey, Richard | | July 10, 1865 | Private. | Dead. |
| Mitchell, David E. | | | " | Disappeared April 13, '62. Reported Deserted. |
| Matthews, Andrew J. | | | " | Dropped from Rolls September 12, '62. |
| Muir, George W. | August, 1862 | July 1, 1865 | " | Discharged for Disability. |
| Nelson, Conant C. | July 16, 1861 | June 12, 1862 | " | Wounded, Shiloh. Washington, D. C. |
| Nickerson, Lemuel | July 16, 1861 | July 23, 1864 | " | Dead. |
| Pease, Stephen N. | " | " | Sergeant. | Chicago. |
| Pitts, Aurelius V. | " | " | Private. | Wounded, Shiloh. Died March 1, '95. Chicago. |
| Peters, John M. | | | | Memphis, Tennessee. |
| Pratt, George | | Mar. 24, 1862 | " | Discharged for Disability. |
| Phillips, James | July 28, 1861 | July 23, 1864 | " | Died, Chicago, March 27, '93. |
| Pond, Harry H. | " | " | " | Chicago. |
| Paddock, James O. | | | | |
| Poole, Charles W. | July 16, 1862 | Ju'y 23, 1864 | Sergeant. | Died, Wounds, Savannah, Tenn., April 13, '62. |
| Phillips, Walter S. | July, 1861 | Aug. 10, 1864 | Bugler. | Chicago. |
| Phillips, Wm. B. | " | Aug. 16, 1864 | Private. | Dubois City, Pa. |
| Pendleton, Alfred W. | Aug. 6, 1862 | July 10, 1865 | Sergeant. | Marion, Iowa. |
| Pratt, George A. | " | Mar. 10, 1863 | Private. | Chicago. |
| Powell, Perry P. | " | Aug. 7, 1863 | " | Fort Atkinson, Wis. |
| Page, John H. | July, 1861 | Sept. 22, 1861 | " | Chicago. |
| Page, William R. | | | | Second Lieutenant, Third U. S. Infantry. |
| Redmond, John J. | July 21, 1861 | July 22, 1864 | " | To Benton Cadets, Mo. Chicago. |
| Russell, Edward H. | July 16, 1851 | | | Died, Chicago, June 8, '90. |
| Richardson, Oscar K. | " | | Corporal. | Killed, Shiloh, April 6, '61. |
| Risley, Harvey B. | " | July 23, 1864 | Private. | Disappeared July 27, '61. |
| Rexford, Roscoe E. | July 28, 1861 | | " | Died at Calumet, April 25, '62. |
| Renfro, Wm. H. | " | Aug. 24, 1864 | " | Seattle, Washington. |
| Reynolds, Wallace | Feb. 3, 1862 | Mar. 8, 1865 | " | Blue Island, Ill. |
| Roberts, Harrison | Sept. 1862 | July 10, 1865 | 1st Lieut. | Died, Pennsylvania, 1868. Seneca Falls, New York. |

| NAMES. | Date of Muster. In | Out | Enlisted. Rank. | Remarks and Address, 1900. |
|---|---|---|---|---|
| Ramsey, Albert | | July 10, 1865 | Private. | |
| Russell, Sherman W | Oct. 16, 1861 | Mar. 3, 1862 | " | Discharged for Disability. Evanston, Ill. |
| Rice, William O | July 16, 1861 | July 10, 1865 | Sergeant, | Discharged for Disability. Osseo, Wisconsin. |
| Sproules, Joseph | " | July 23, 1864 | Private. | Dead. |
| Steele, John I | " | " | " | Wounded, Missionary Ridge. Chicago. |
| Schaffer, John | " | " | " | Wounded at Shiloh. Chicago. |
| Shead, Oliver F. | " | Oct. 10, 1862 | " | Wounded at Shiloh. " |
| Sargent, James I | July 18, 1861 | | " | Died, March 22, 1862, Paducah. |
| Sprong, Robert | July 28, 1861 | July 23, 1864 | " | Dead. |
| Snow, Oscar N | " | | " | Died, March 1, 1863, Cincinnati, Ohio. |
| Stewart, Adam | July 28, 1861 | July 23, 1864 | " | National Soldiers' Home, Virginia. |
| Slosser, Mac | " | " | " | Chicago. |
| Stiger, Silas C | July 18, 1862 | " | " | Wounded. Asbury Park, New Jersey. |
| Smith, Charles E | July 28, 1861 | " | Corporal. | Cincinnati, Ohio. |
| Sherman, Jeremiah N | " | | Private. | Soldiers' Home, Quincy, Ill. |
| Sherwin, Charles G | " | | " | Died, November 20, 1861, Paducah. |
| Sawtell, David W | " | | " | Died, October 5, 1861, Paducah. |
| Speer, William W | " | July 23, 1864 | " | |
| Spaulding, Henry A | 1861 | Aug. 24, 1864 | " | Riverside, Ill. |
| Scott, George M | June 16, 1862 | May 23, 1865 | " | Traverse City, Michigan. |
| Shrigley, James H | Aug. 15, 1862 | May 25, 1865 | " | Died, December 17, 1888, Chicago. |
| Sweenie, Francis T | 1862 | July 10, 1865 | " | |
| Snyder, Frank | " | | " | Discharged for Disability. |
| Smith, John J | | Dec. 25, 1862 | " | Chicago. |
| Stockton, William E | Aug. 13, 1861 | Feb. 23, 1863 | " | Syracuse, New York. |
| Tack, John I | July 16, 1861 | July 23, 1864 | " | Burned, Prairie Fire, Kansas. |
| Town, Henry M | July 28, 1861 | " | " | Dead. |
| Thompson, Thos. C | " | | " | |
| Taylor, Thomas E. I | July 16, 1861 | Aug. 10, 1864 | " | Chicago. |

| NAMES. | DATE OF MUSTER. In | DATE OF MUSTER. Out | ENLISTED. Rank. | REMARKS AND ADDRESS, 1900. |
|---|---|---|---|---|
| Vernon, Wm. B. | July 16, 1861 | July 10, 1865 | Private. | Died, Chicago, July 23, 1864. |
| Wilcox, Willard I. | " | Jan. 28, 1862 | Sergeant. | Died, San Francisco, California, 1885. |
| Walker, Jesse K. | July 28, 1861 | July 23, 1864 | Private. | Discharged for Disability. |
| Williams, Ed. E. | " | Feb. 21, 1865 | " | Wounded, Shiloh. New York City. |
| Whitson, Fred. O. | Feb. 3, 1862 | May 29, 1865 | Corporal. | Dead. |
| Williams, Silas G. | " | June 12, 1865 | Private. | Died, Chicago, January 15, 1895. |
| Wilcox, Thomas | Aug. 12, 1861 | June 10, 1865 | " | Died, Remington, Indiana, 1895. |
| Wilson, Adelbert J | | Jan. 7, 1865 | " | Discharged for Disability. |
| Williams, Henry | | | " | Died, Rear Vicksburg, July 2, 1863. |
| Woodbury, George | | | | Died, Bolton, Mississippi, July 24, 1863. |
| Wycoff, George H. | | May 23, 1865 | Private. | Discharged for Disability. |
| Willard, Clarence B. | July 28, 1861 | July 18, 1865 | " | Prisoner sixteen months. Chicago. |
| Young, William H. | | | | |

List of names of members assigned from Battery "B," and serving in new or "Consolidated" Battery "A," which existed from July 26, 1864, to July 10, 1865:

| | | |
|---|---|---|
| Ashbrook, Thomas | Hadlock, Samuel. | Roadhuizen, Dirk W. |
| Anderson, John S. | Henry, John. | Sattler, John D. |
| Briggs, Wm. D. | Hathaway Valcourt E. | Simpson, Walter. |
| Beidelman, Alex. H. | Hess, George J. | Stranberg, John F. |
| Beck, John. | Heartt, Wm. L. | Siller, Charles G. |
| Brown, John A. | Hall, Melville. | Scupham, Wm. C. |
| Bradbury, Wm. H. | Hesseiniuns, Fred E. | Sauter, Charles J. |
| Bower, Michael. | Johnson, Godfred. | Stickney, Charles W. |
| Burns, George B. | Johnson, Peter M. | Speight, Henry. |
| Chapple, Harmon T. | Jackson, Wm. F. | Smith, Robert C. |
| Cobb, Henry B. | Kingsbury, John | Thomas, John E. |
| Chalmers, John R. | Lines, Henry F. | Taylor, Wm. |
| Coe, Schyler, P. | Lynch, Michael. | Terry, Edward |
| Clark, Charles H. | Lake, Louis F. | Turner, William. |
| Crampton, Franklin. | Marion, Francis N. | Upton, Timothy, Jr. |
| Crampton, Nelson. | McBride, Ora. | Watts, Isaac. |
| Cameron, Francis D. | Morrison, Peter. | Wentworth, Samuel F. |
| Dealman, Jacob. | Newton, Samuel D. | Wilcox, Albert. |
| Dudley, Henry W. | Porter, James W. | Wilcox, Edward P. |
| Dutch, James B. | Peasle, Ira. | |
| Ellis, Thomas. | Powell, John W. | DETAILED FROM OTHER COMMANDS. |
| Echert, Charles H. | Palmer, Andrew J. | |
| Frazer, John W. | Ross, Miron C. | |
| Finney, Robert N. | Reed, Horace. | Beecham, W. E. |
| Graham, John. | Rising, Henry C. | McNnight, Thomas. |
| Garringer, Isaac. | Rudd, Henry. | |

It is stated in the preface, that the Battery was like one large family To show that it was distinctively a *family* Battery, it will be seen by a glance at the rosters there were among its members three brothers each of the Kimbell and Wilcox boys, two brothers each of the Adams, Beach, Childs, Henry, Kennedy, Morgan, Page, Phillips and Rexford boys, the Burdicks, father and son, besides several cousins. Many were boys and schoolmates together, and had always known or known of each other. Since the war the members have scattered into nearly every State of the Union, though quite a large proportion of them remain in Chicago and vicinity.

The Battery remained in Camp Smith until the early part of September, practicing daily in drilling, with frequent target shooting on the river, guard duties and parades, initiating the raw recruits, as the new members were called, into the arts and mysteries of war. One section of the Battery was stationed for a few weeks at Bird's Point, on the Missouri shore south of Cairo. Earth works were thrown up on the point where the Ohio and

Mississippi rivers meet, and named "Fort Defiance." Heavy guns were mounted in them, commanding both rivers. These guns were manned by boys detailed from the Battery, for a week or ten days. On September 6, Gen. Grant who had assumed command at Cairo two days before, succeeding Gen. B. M. Prentiss, ordered a movement on Paducah, Ky., forty-five miles up the Ohio river at the mouth of the Tennessee. The Battery broke up camp with alacrity, and all were delighted with the certainty of breaking the long season of inactivity which had began to grow monotonous. Two regiments of infantry and the Battery embarked on transports, and before midnight we started up the river, and daylight found us in front of Paducah. It seems the rebel general Jeff Thompson had started from Columbus, Ky., with a force of about 10,000 with the intention of occupying and fortifying Paducah, which could easily have been done, greatly to our disadvantage, but the prompt action of Gen. Grant saved the place to us. The troops were stationed to guard the main roads leading into the city and several wooden gun boats were left to guard the rivers. The Battery was camped on the main street leading west from the city, where we remained till February 1862. Earth works were thrown up and after a few days we began to build comfortable quarters for ourselves and horses, after it became apparent that we were likely to remain for some length of time. The day we arrived at Paducah a portion of the battery with a part of the 9th Ill. Infantry, marched out about ten miles and burned a railroad bridge. The Battery took part in the various expeditions from Paducah under command of Generals Lew Wallace and C. F. Smith, among which was the feint on Columbus, Ky., simultaneous with Gen. Grant's attack on Belmont. In making the feint on Columbus, the expedition marched forty-five miles in twenty-four hours, which for green troops was a creditable record.

On this march, we lost our six mule team by running off a bridge in the night. They were left behind at an old confederate's place and were all stolen except one balky old mare mule, which could not be induced to move.

The only bloodshed on this expedition was when comrade Foster charged on a flock of turkeys in a plantation yard, and lopped off an old gobbler's head with his saber, and bore him off in triumph in spite of the protestations of the female owner.

In returning, some of the infantry straggled badly, so Gen. Smith, who was a regular army officer, and as fine and true a soldier as ever lived, determined to give us a taste of marching in earnest, and took nearly the whole command and accomplished what was ever afterward famous in the history of Battery "A" as the "Calloway March," and the later recruits of the Battery were often regaled with remarkable tales and adventures of this march, which they were unfortunate enough not to be connected with.

Another notable expedition in which some sixty members participated, being mounted as cavalry, was the raid on Mayfield, Ky., October 22, for the purpose of capturing a rebel recruiting officer and breaking up the station. We reached the city in the night and took possession at daylight, but the bird had flown, having had an intimation of our approach. We secured some books and papers, a rebel flag and some old small arms which were left behind. We started back for Paducah after noon and arrived before midnight, tired and sore from our unaccustomed saddle exercise.

It was fortunate for us that we left Mayfield as we did, as in less than two hours, a train from Columbus brought in a rebel force of several hundred, which would probably have captured us, or wiped us out if we had stood them a fight.

On Saturday, October 5, 1861, the first death occurred in our company. David W. Sawtell, a genial and universally liked member, died suddenly in the Paducah Hospital of congestion of the brain. The boys raised a fund of $70.00 and procured a metallic coffin, in which the body was enclosed and forwarded to his friends at home.

On the 1st of November, we received all of our new harnesses and two new howitzers, and were now a full six gun Battery.

On the 20th of November the second death in the company occurred. Charles G. Sherwin, one of the youngest members, died in hospital of typhoid fever and homesickness. His body was also sent home by the boys, in a metallic casket.

Paducah was a very pretty and old city, and contained many aristocratic, and at one time, wealthy families. The male portion of the population was largely rebels, and, of course, the sympathies of the female portion were naturally on the same side. The Battery boys had been deprived of ladies' society to a great extent during our five months stay at "Camp Smith," and many of them used their best endeavors to "do the agreeable," and make the acquaintance of some of the ladies. Their musical talent was utilized to a great degree, and serenading parties were out nearly every evening, doing their best to win favor. At first they were either ignored or received very coldly; but, after a while, met with better success, and when Foster, Sam Kennedy, Charley Smith, Johnny Peters, and the Rexfords, returned one evening from a serenade at the residence of old Col. Wolfolk, and announced that the ladies had invited them to partake of cake and wine during the serenade, they were looked upon as heroes who had scored a great victory, as all former efforts to secure recognition in that family had been unsuccessful. This family had previously had some experience with the "Yankees," in which the latter came out ahead, and made the family the special mark for the soldiers' attention. It was generally known that a rebel flag had been flying from a flagstaff on the house up to the very day our troops took possession of the city. On the 25th of November some of the 11th Indiana Infantry, Gen. Lew Wallace's regiment, thought the place looked lonesome without a flag, and proposed to put one up. Their offer was refused, so they determined to put one up without consent. Gen. C. F. Smith, who was in command of the post, heard of the contemplated action, and forbid its being done. Fifty of the Battery boys thought this order did not cover the ground outside of the house; so they secured a pole and flag, and went one evening intending to set the pole in *front* of the house and raise the flag. On their arrival they found a flag had been raised and was "floating proudly to the breeze;" so, further action was unnecessary.

A number of the boys, who were printers, utilized an abandoned rebel printing establishment and issued several numbers of a Battery paper, called the "Picket Guard." They got up a very creditable sheet, and it furnished quite a little amusement and diversion for camp life. A few copies of the paper have been preserved and are still in existence, and they are very interesting relics of the war.

The boys received their first regulation uniforms at Paducah Dec. 22, 1861. Early in February 1862, our work began again in earnest. We were taken up the Tennessee river by steamer and landed below Fort Heiman, which place with Fort Henry on the opposite side of the river was captured by our gunboats on February 6. Most of the garrison escaped across the country to Fort Donelson, so this was a bloodless victory for us.

When we took possession of the rebel camp which had just been evacuated about two hours before, we found several of their camp fires burning and hot corn bread and pea coffee cooking on some of them. Their tents had not been disturbed, and as the boys were tired and hungry, the find was a great treat, and very acceptable and refreshing to them. Feb. 11, 1862, 2nd Lieut. P. P. Wood assumed command of the Battery, and remained in command almost continuously until its muster out July 16, 1864, Capt. Smith having previously resigned on account of illness.

We occupied the camp at Fort Heiman until the 13th, when we received orders at midnight to march to Fort Donelson. At one o'clock on the morning of the 14th we left Fort Heiman, and did not get across the river till after daylight, having to wade in water over knee deep to reach the steamer. After landing we started across the country, escorted by a single company of infantry, Co. "A" 32nd Illinois. We reached the left wing of our army on the outskirts of Fort Donelson after dark of the same day, in a heavy snow storm, which turned into a rainy sleet during the night. The weather was bitterly cold, and we had orders to build no fires. As we were wet, tired and hungry, most of us managed to get our feet near some live coals on our side of some large trees that were down, and after a bite of hard tack and bacon, rolled up in our ponchos under "shebangs" made of evergreen boughs, and had a sound and refreshing sleep. On the next morning, the 15th, we were ordered at daylight to start for the right in a hurry, where heavy firing had begun. The right section arrived in time to have a lively brush with the enemy, and prevented them from turning the right flank of our line. This was our first experience under fire. The wounded were being carried by us to the rear on stretchers, the sight of which was somewhat trying to our nerves, but not a man flinched. The section fired fifty-five rounds of cannister and shrapnel, most of the time using double charges. We were not in the engagement over thirty minutes, but succeeded in repelling the last decisive charges of the enemy as they came pouring out of the fort, trying to cut their way through and escape. Our only casualty was one man wounded. Moses Hawks, being hit on the arm with a spent ball. The fort surrendered the next day, Sunday the 16th, with about 21,000 prisoners, under Gen. Simon B. Buckner. This surrender was made under the memorable demand of General Grant to General Buckner stating that "No terms except an unconditional and immediate surrender can be accepted. I propose to move immediately upon your works." White flags were flying all along the rebels' fortifications, and our troops were inside the fort and mixing up and conversing with their captives, in a very short time. Permission was given the rebels to go outside and gather up and bury their dead, which was done. Many of our boys secured trophies of all kinds, which were carried until the first favorable opportunity of sending home.

On Monday, the 17th we marched back to Ft. Heiman, where we again went into camp, and remained until March 6.

On the 3rd of March we received a vote of thanks, passed February 17th by the Chicago Board of Trade, for the part we bore in the actions of Belmont and Donelson, which was as follows:

BOARD OF TRADE ROOMS,
CHICAGO, ILL., February 17, 1862.

At a meeting of the Board, held on change this day, at 12 M., the following resolutions were unanimously adoped :

*Resolved*, That this Board has heard with pride and heartfelt thanks the glorious news of the success of our troops in the capture of the rebel stronghold, Fort Donelson ; That we tender the thanks of this Board, also of all loyal citizens of our city, to the commanding officers and their comrades for their triumphant effort to plant the stars and stripes over the same ; and that we do particularly thank our gallant Batteries, Companies "A" and "B," Chicago's Light Artilery, for their daring and successful courage displayed on the fields of Belmont, Frederickstown and Fort Donelson.

*Resolved*, That the President of this Board be requested to forward these resolutions to the commanding officers of the expedition and a copy to Lieut. P. P. Wood and Capt. Ezra Taylor, commanding Chicago Light Artillery Companies, "A" and "B."

SETH CATLIN, Sec'y.     STEPHEN CLARY, Pres.

It is generally conceded that for some unknown reason, Battery "A" never received its proper official credit for the part it bore in the Ft. Donelson fight, but its valuable service was known and appreciated by all the neighboring commands. Gen. Livingston, in speaking about the history of the great battles of the rebellion, in the Plattsmouth, (Neb.) *Journal* of February 17, 1885, says :

"Lieut. Wood, who commanded a section of Battery "A," Chicago, Illinois, Light Artillery at the Donelson fight, never received the meed of praise he deserved. At the right time he threw his guns into action, when Buckner had massed his troops and was charging the right of our line, and his guns were shotted to the muzzle, and great winrows of the enemy fell at every discharge of his accurately aimed guns. And it was the work of that Battery and the terrible volleys sent into the ranks of the advancing foe by the first Nebraska that drove back the enemy, and the next morning Buckner surrendered. Wood was the hero of that hour, but he never was properly remembered for his heroism."

On the 6th of March, we broke up camp, and, bidding good bye to Ft. Heiman, where we had spent two very comfortable weeks, we started on the grand advance up the Tennessee.

We disembarked at Crump's Landing, and took part in an expedition with the cavalry in an attempt to destroy the south-western railroad connections with Corinth.

March 27th we moved to Pittsburg Landing, and were transferred from Gen. Lew Wallace's Division to Gen. C. F. Smith's Division, 2nd Brigade, Gen. McArthur. We were sorry to part with our old comrades of the 8th Missouri, and 11th Indiana, but were put in the same brigade with the 9th and 12th Illinois, which quite reconciled us to the change.

We encamped nearly a mile straight west from the landing, where we were on the morning of the memorable April 6th.

Sunday morning, April 6, 1862, dawned upon us clear, warm and bright. The trees were putting forth their leaves, peach trees and other early fruits, were in full bloom, and all nature seemed to rejoice in putting on spring attire, utterly oblivious to the fact that this was to be the bloodiest day in the history of our nation. Our camp was up and astir at the usual early hour. The postilions had taken the horses to drink in a creek near by, and were letting them nibble at the new grass on their way back to camp. The sound of skirmish firing suddenly was heard and in short order the crack of musketry and the booming of artillery followed. We knew this meant business, and our horses were soon harnessed, the ammunition chests filled, and knapsacks packed ready to move. After taking our positions, numbers of wounded began passing our camp, reporting their regiments "*all* cut to pieces." We ridiculed them and shamed some of them to turning back to the front. We soon had orders to move to the front, and we went into position with the 9th and 12th Illinois on our left. A few shells burst around us as we neared the line, causing us to involuntarily start a little, and then to laugh at each other for it. We were put in position as a reserve, and began to receive a severe shelling which we could not return. Two horses were killed under their riders, and brave, handsome Sergeant Jerry Powell had his right arm taken off by a shell and was injured severely in the ribs. He was taken to the hospital where he died within half an hour.

After remaining in reserve about a half an hour, Gen. Hurlburt gave us orders to support him, and about 9 o'clock A. M. we were placed in a new position on the left, still in range of the enemy's shells, which burst around us without effect. Shot fell thick and fast around us here; but, being inactive, we availed ourselves of what protection we could get behind the trees. We were soon moved forward into position, and opened fire on the rebel battery that had been firing at us, and, after about fifteen minutes of lively firing with solid shot and shell, we silenced it completely, compelling it to withdraw to another position. Seeing troops crossing a field near by, we gave them a few shots, and a short time after, engaged another battery. After a brisk fight we managed to pile up this battery, when we immediately opened on another, in a different position. It took us some time to quiet this new position, but it was finally done, and we moved to our original position, to engage the enemy's infantry, they having advanced and taken position on the ridge, next to the one we were on. Here we fought for more than an hour, when they got their battery up to drive us out; but they did us no damage, their range being too long to be effective. This Battery, we afterward learned, was the famous Washington Artillery of New Orleans mentioned in the early part of this history.

At the same time, a part of our Battery was having a duel with them, and the balance were keeping back their infantry. Our boys did most excellent shooting, hitting the mark almost every time, and exploding our shells in their very midst. This was about 2 P. M. We were getting short of ammunition. The infantry supporting us had been lying in the hollow, now charged forward with a yell. They delivered one volley which was returned with terrible effect, causing them to fall back. This gave the rebels courage, and they made a charge for our guns. Things looked rather dubious, but we continued firing as long as prudence allowed, and then limbered up and fell back to a new line which had been formed. Here, after a short fight, we were obliged a second time to fall back. In this stand we suffered severely. Poor Ed. Russell was shot through with a six pound ball and lived but a short time. He was carried to the rear and his last words were, "tell them I died like a man at my post."

Brave Christian man, Daniel R. Farnham was shot through above the heart and killed; James L. Flanigan, a merry hearted Irishman, and the intimate friend of Ed. Russell, was shot through the mouth, and went with his chum to the better world.

Our last stand was made about three hundred yards in the rear of the one just occupied. Here we opened as fierce a fire as we could send, but could not succeed in checking the charge of the enemy. Our right was so turned that their firing was directly in our rear, and we took shot from both front and flank. Lieut. Wood had urged Gen. Hurlburt to relieve us with another Battery, while we replenished our empty ammunition boxes, but it was too late. We were fighting the rebels' whole line of battle on the left, and taking their entire fire. This part of the battle ground was afterward designated as the "Hornet's Nest," by which it is still known.

It was now evident that the tide of battle was going against us, although up to this time our Battery had not been driven to the rear one inch. Our infantry support was all broken up into squads and were fighting desperately, while we were firing solid shots and a few shells, having exhausted our cannister. But with a solid line opposed to us, we could not, in the nature of things, resist much longer, and a little after 4 o'clock the enemy had succeeded in turning our left, and on they came from front and left flank, in solid line to scoop us in. Then Lieut. Wood's voice rang out clear and strong, "Limber to the rear." "Get your guns out of this." Then there was a scramble, No. 1, 3, 4 and 6 guns fell back at once. Not so with 2 and 5. Squad 5 had but three cannoniers and gunner Sherrill left. Dolan and Stiger and Crocker having gone with Flanigan to an ambulance. Four of their horses, including Bailey's Gray Eagle, were badly wounded. The three cannoniers were unable to run up the gun and hook it on A. C. Hall, alias "Garibaldi," jumped off his horse, and putting his shoulder to the wheel, helped to run it up, the others holding up and pulling on the trail. Just at this time Charley Kimbell came hopping on one leg from squad 2 gun, having been badly wounded in the other, and he was caught and tossed on the foot-board of the limber. "Garrie" remounted his horse, and just as the gun was started, he was hit in the head with a shot and knocked off.

Little Bailey, the lead driver, was also dismounted, shot through the hip. Jack Redmond, the swing driver, prudently dismounted and grabbed the near lead horse by the bit, Foster, the near swing horse, and Colby, the near wheeler, and away we started on a run, the rebels less than a hundred yards from us, making a desperate effort to capture at least the two guns that were delayed in getting away. Poor "Garrie" and Bailey were left behind to the tender mercies of the rebels, as we supposed, but Garrie recovered his senses just as they were about to gather him in, and picking himself up, skipped away and escaped to the landing. At the same time Stiger and Dolan came through the woods hunting for the Battery, and found Bailey sitting against a tree, and each catching him by the arm, escaped safely with him to the landing, thus saving all our wounded from being captured.

At the time the order was given, "Limber to the rear," squad two was in worse shape than squad five. The off wheel horse was the only one remaining. The squad, having disengaged all but him, attempted to haul off the gun, which they could easily have done with his help, but he obstinately refused to move. Matters were growing desperate. The rebels were so close their brass buttons could plainly be seen. Minnie balls were rattling like hail, five of the seven men at the gun were hit within five minutes. Lieut. Wood ordered several men from the other guns to come back and help them, which they did promptly.

Just as they reached the gun a minnie ball struck the horse squarely in the root of the tail, and it effectually performed an instantaneous cure for balking.

With Commissary Chase acting as nigh wheel horse, the gun with its wounded, was rushed back about a quarter of a mile, where the other guns were in battery on a small hill ready to cover our retreat, which they did in good shape, and thus was averted what at one time seemed to be inevitable, the losing of a gun-squad and gun.

The rebels were just as determined to have squad two's gun as we were to save it, and did not cease their shower after shower of balls upon us until we were safely back to the next line of support. Three of our dead were left upon the field, as we did not have enough sound men to take care of both dead and wounded, so, of course, the living were cared for in preference. One of our empty caissons from which four out of six horses had been shot, became stuck in crossing a little brook, and was abandoned. It was afterwards recovered.

At about five o'clock we fell back to the landing, and going down to the lower landing, we refilled our ammunition chests with shell and grape. Then we went forward to the small hill we had left and went into battery to the left of and in line with the 32-pounders that Gen. Webster had planted during the day.

Here, together with several other batteries, and about 15,000 infantry, who had been fighting all day, and were still full of fight, we had a line of battle over half a mile long, connecting with the Tennessee River on the south, to a bayou on the north, as solid as a rock, and we will maintain till the crack of doom, that the enemy could not have broken it, if Buell had been hundreds of miles away.

In the meantime, our boats had been rushing a part of Buell's force across the river, so that when the attack was made, our side had about five thousand new troops in line. During the day, also, some heavy siege guns were landed and placed in position. We were in position to see the boat loads of his troops ferried across, and cheer after cheer went up as they landed and filed out on our left.

It was about 5:30 o'clock when the enemy made their last attack on our lines, which was easily repulsed with the aid of two wooden gunboats, which were anchored abreast of a ravine, which was between us and the rebels.

Our line of artillery was about a mile of front, and, in this cordon, we could not find room to operate, so we had to stand, take our chance of being shot, and do nothing. This was harder than fighting, but the boys took it all quietly, patiently waiting the result. We had not long to wait, for the skirmishers opened, then a gun, another and another,—the rebels answering about as lively as ourselves. Then came the rebel charge. Our mile of front was a living sheet of fire, more than a hundred guns were belching forth. The crash of musketry rolled from one end of the line to the other. The rebels faltered, fell by the hundred, gave back a little; our newly arrived troops made a dash, turned the fall back into a retreat, and night drew her sable mantle over the weary and thankful host.

During the last charge, Gen. Grant and his staff were sitting on their horses a little to our left and rear. A Captain on his staff, Kit Carson, was killed within ten feet of the General, being shot in the head, which was completely mashed. The General moved his position a little and sat chewing his cigar as imperturbably as though on dress parade. Some critics have written that the General was not under fire on this day. We of the Battery know better.

Thus ended the first day's fight. The Battery was engaged over eight hours, firing 838 rounds with a loss of four men killed outright, twenty-six wounded, several mortally, and forty-eight horses killed and disabled, without the loss of a gun, or man taken prisoner.

On account of the death of Gen. W. H. L. Wallace in the first day's fight, we had no reported position that day, and an Iowa Battery received the credit that belonged to us in the fight at the "Hornet's Nest" in the official account. Geo. M. Brown, of squad one, fired the shot from a 12-pound howitzer that killed Gen. Albert Sidney Johnson about 4 o'clock in the afternoon, at the "Hornet's Nest." The heads of Gen. Johnson's mounted escort could be seen plainly and drew our fire. A rapid commotion among the troops after the third shot showed that it had been effective, and it was learned afterward that Gen. Johnson was killed at that time and place.

Shortly after dark it commenced raining, and rained almost all night. We had found shelter for our wounded, and they were as comfortable as men could be under the circumstances, but the poor fighting men had to take it as it came. We slept on our arms that night, the sleep of the tired, if not of the just. Although it rained hard nearly all night, we cared little for it. All through the night once in about ten minutes flashes lighted up the sky, followed by the boom of the heavy guns of the gun boats. A dreary night dragged by slowly.

The next morning at 8 o'clock, Maj. Taylor ordered us to the front, across a deep ravine, and into an open field. We went into battery with four guns, two being left in camp on account of loss of men and horses to handle them.

We were ordered to shell the heavy timber, across a ravine in which our infantry lay, about 800 yards away. We fired for half an hour and ceased. Our infantry then charged out of the ravine and gained a good foot-hold in the timber. Lieut. Wood was laying on the ground so sick he could hardly hold up his head, but when we were ordered forward into line with the infantry, he sprang into his saddle, and we rushed forward on a gallop with three guns to the assistance of the infantry, who were struggling to hold the advantage they had already gained.

Here, for the first time, we came under command of Gen. W. T. Sherman, and we make the following quotation from his "Memoirs," p. 239, vol. I.: "Taylor had just got to me from the rear, where he had gone for ammunition and brought up the three guns, which I ordered into position to advance by hand-firing. These guns belonged to Company "A," Chicago Light Artillery, commanded by Lieut. P. P. Wood, and did most excellent service. Under cover of their fire we advanced till we reached the point where the Corinth Road crosses the line of McClernand's Camp."

Hard fighting continued at intervals through the day, the rebels making a most stubborn resistance and losing heavily till about 3 o'clock P. M. We had driven them out of our farthest encampment, occupied by Sherman on Sunday morning. We went into battery about fifty yards to the right of Shiloh Church, and gave the flying rebels a few parting shots. This ended our part of the great fight. We did not lose a man or a horse on this day, and found from our feelings there was a vast difference between whipping and being whipped.

General Sherman rode up to Lieut. Wood and publicly praised him and thanked the Battery for the service it had rendered.

There has been some controversy as to the time when Gen. Prentiss was captured. We of old Battery "A" have good reasons for knowing that it was not before 5 o'clock on Sunday P. M.

Capt. Wood's official report of the battle of Shiloh is as follows:

HEADQUARTERS COMPANY "A," C. L. A.,<br>PITTSBURG LANDING, TENNESSEE, April 9, 1862.

THOMAS J. NEWSHAM,
  *Assistant Adjutant General:*

SIR :—I have the honor of reporting to you the part taken in the actions of the 6th and 7th inst., by Company "A," Chicago Light Artillery. After the commencement of the firing on the 6th, as ordered, I reported with command to Maj. Cavender, and was shortly afterward ordered into a position to support the Division of Gen. Hurlburt on the left. We opened fire about 9 A. M., and was successful in silencing the enemy's batteries twice, with two changes of position, when we immediately moved, taking position on a ridge near the extreme left, and opened on the enemy's infantry, posted on a ridge opposite, about 500 yards distant. This position we held for over an hour, fighting both infantry and artillery, when our support was retired, and we were forced to follow to avoid being flanked and cut off. Taking position again 300 yards in the rear, we were again, after a short fight, forced back, our support this time leaving in disorder. A new line being formed, we went into battery, opened, were entirely abandoned by our new support, and were obliged, reluctantly, to fall back on the reserve, taking one of our guns off with but one horse and the cannoniers. An empty caisson was left for want of horses to draw it off, and afterwards recovered.

Retiring inside the reserve, I marched the Battery to the Steamer "Rocket" for a supply of ammunition, filled the boxes, returned to the line and reported for duty, before the last desperate attack on our position was made, but was not again ordered into service on that day.

We were engaged during the day seven successive hours, firing 838 rounds of ammunition, with a loss of four men killed and twenty-six wounded, and a loss of killed and disabled horses of forty-eight.

On the morning of the 7th, as ordered, I reported to Gen. Sherman, with three pieces, all I had men to serve; was given a position on his left; engaged a battery, silenced it; shelled the enemy's line of battle until they gave way; advanced with our troops, opening during the advance four times and remained in the engagement until the enemy broke and fled; fired during the day 334 round of ammunition. On this day we met with no loss.

To you, sir, and all who know the men, few words of mine are necessary in praise of the coolness and gallantry of Lieuts. J. W. Rumsey, Geo. McCagg and F. W. Young, Staff Sergeants Briggs and Poole, and every non-commissioned officer and man in the command. In war, he is blessed who has such men to command.

     Very respectfully,
       Your obedient servant,
 (Signed)       P. P. Wood, First Lieut.
    Commanding Company "A." Chicago Light Artillery.

I annex hereto a list of casualities and losses. Killed, Sergeant J. D. Powell, Corporal E. H. Russell; Privates, D. R. Farnham, John L. Flanigan. Dangerously wounded, Privates Jas. O. Paddock, E. E. Williams. Seriously wounded, Corporal Charles B. Kimbell; Privates, C. C. Nelson, W. G. Brown, John Schaffer, A. J. Bailey, O. C. Heimberger, T. W. Lynch, W. C. Green. Slightly wounded, Lieut. Geo. McCagg, Corporals, C. R. Crandall, Thomas Burton, F. B. Smith, W. J. Wilcox; Privates, A. V. Pitts, L. F. Jacobs, J. F. Crocker, S. C. Durkee, W. I. Wilcox, M. Dooling, John Earl, Moses Hawks, H. H. Pond, G. L. Whittier, A. C. Hall.

On the 9th we were relieved from duty and allowed to return to Camp. The rebels had retreated in disorder, destroying everything which could impede our progress; the road for miles, toward Corinth, was strewn with the ruins of artillery, tents, stores and everything pertaining to an army. The only things left were the wounded, and they numbered by the thousand. Their loss was immense and ours not small; five thousand men will not cover our losses, and theirs must have been a half more. For numbers engaged, fierceness and losses, it will exceed any fight on this side of the Atlantic.

On the afternoon of the 7th, a portion of our wounded were placed upon a hospital steamer and taken down the river to Mound City, Illinois, and placed in hospital there. They remained here nearly two weeks, when the high water of the Ohio river filled the lower story of the hospital and forced its abandonment. M. K Kimbell came from Chicago with the wife of Wm. G. Brown, and they assisted and cared for the boys of the Battery, which, in addition to the regular hospital nurses, made them much more comfortable than those who had only the ordinary care. The wounded of the Battery here, were Wm. G. Brown, C. C. Nelson, C. B. Kimbell, Wm. C. Green, O. C. Heimberger and A. J. Bailey. These were placed on cots and taken out of the second story windows of the hospital and placed on a flat boat, which was poled to the high land at Villa Ridge which was as far as the cars could run. Mr. Kimbell engaged a special car of the I. C. R. R. and the boys were shoved through the end windows, on their cots, and placed on top of the backs of the seats, and thus taken to Chicago, where their friends met them and conveyed them to their different homes.

Heimberger and Bailey died soon after, and the only survivors at this date are C. B. Kimbell and C. C. Nelson. While in the hospital at Mound City the surgeons decided to amputate Kimbell's leg, but his vigorous protest delayed the attempt at the operation until the arrival of his father, whom he had telegraphed at Paducah. His timely arrival, and decided protest, carried the day, and the surgeons reluctantly decided to postpone the operation, and the final result was his recovery with a fairly sound leg.

On the 15th of April, we received a stand of colors from "friends at home," accompanied by this letter :

CHICAGO, April 7th, 1862.

TO THE MEMBERS OF COMPANY "A," CHICAGO LIGHT ARTILLERY:

*Gallant Men and Brave Soldiers :*—When you left us, your friends and fellow citizens, on that solemn Sunday night one year ago, we felt sure that when, in the vicissitudes of war your hour of trial came, you would not flinch or be found wanting, and we have not been disappointed. You have done *your whole duty on the field of battle*, and no greater praise than this can be said of any soldiers. We are proud of you all, and your whole city is proud of you, and the State and Nation are proud of you. Your fame has filled the land, and you have deserved it all.

Receive this *Flag* and *Banner*, then, brave men, as slight tokens of the gratitude, the admiration and the unwavering confidence of your Chicago friends. On the glorious blue of the banner we have inscribed the words, "Fort Donelson," because there you covered yourselves with glory, and, by driving back by deeds of valor, an enemy flushed with the certainty of victory, you won in that memorable conflict the applause and the approbation of a grateful Nation. And with the Flag and Banner receive also the assurance of our firm belief that you will never dishonor them; as well as our sincere prayer that the God of Battles will protect you and give triumph to the right.

YOUR FRIENDS AT HOME.

[REPLY.]

PITTSBURG, TENNESSEE, April 16, 1862.

TO OUR FRIENDS AT HOME:

Words of cheer, ever welcome to the absent soldier, have this week been showered upon us by those at home, who, one year ago—on our departure to take part in our country's struggle—bade us as heartily, "God bless and care for you." We are to-day proud that we were among the first to leave home; proud that by our efforts we have won your praise and confidence, and proud in the knowledge that, after peace shall have blessed our now distracted and unhappy country, we may say, "We helped to gain it."

Gentlemen—With many thanks, we receive the Flags, assuring you that never by deed of ours shall they be disgraced, but triumphantly borne aloft unto the end.

May we ever be deserving of your respect and admiration, by unwavering and zealous endeavors to do our whole duty. And in the coming struggle may God defend the right.

COMPANY "A" CHICAGO LIGHT ARTILLERY.

When the forward movement to Corinth commenced, we were placed back in General Lew Wallace's division, which was held in reserve on Pea Ridge till after the evacuation of Corinth. Here Mort. Pratt was taken prisoner while foraging with Willard (old man) Wilcox, who came into camp with three buckshot under his skin.

Pratt was held as prisoner several months. He, with two others, made their escape once and were at liberty two or three days endeavoring to make their way to Memphis to rejoin their commands. They traveled by night, being fed and directed in their course by friendly negroes, and remained in hiding during the day. They were pursued and tracked by blood hounds, and recaptured, and taken back to the rebel prison from which they escaped, where they received more inhuman treatment than the other prisoners, on account of their efforts to escape. He was finally sent with a large number of others on a steamer up the Mississippi river to Cairo for exchange. In passing Memphis the boat made a short stop and anchored out near the middle of the river, to prevent any of the boys from coming ashore. Coal barges were sent out from the wharf with coal for the steamer.

Among the spectators in the large crowd of soldiers on the wharf, were a number of the Battery boys. Mort. was so overjoyed to see them, that, regardless of the consequences, he jumped overboard, swam under the steamer and a barge and came out on the opposite or shore side, and was taken by the boys to the Battery camp unmolested. His condition was pitiable in the extreme, but his peculiar grin of happiness at being once more a free man, made it comical. His clothing, what little he had, was a complete mass of shreds, and being wet from his plunge and swim, clung to his body as though glued there. He was granted a furlough home, and shortly after his return, was appointed Captain of a colored Battery, and served with it till the close of the war.

After remaining in camp a few weeks at Pea Ridge, the march toward Memphis was begun. Our route was by easy stages via Purdy, Somerville and Bolivar, Tennessee, where we remained two or three days, thence on to Union Station, near Memphis. Gen. Lew Wallace went on to Memphis, which had surrendered a few days before. He found the rebel civil officers of the city were ruling the place to suit themselves, and, without waiting for any red tape orders, marched us into the city on the 17th of June, arriving at midnight during one of the hardest rain storms we ever experienced. The rebel police seemed to take special delight in persecuting any of the darkies connected with the Union Army. Two of our officers' servants were arrested without cause the first day of our entry to the city. The next morning Lieutenants Wood and Rumsey, with nearly half of the boys of the Battery, went to the Police Court and compelled the Judge to release them, and informed him that a repetition of such doings would necessitate the tearing down of his "temple of justice," and the police would be arrested and flogged. It is needless to say the colored servants were not molested again.

During our march to Memphis, Alex. Anderson, one of our old members, and the life of the Battery, was taken alarmingly sick, and immediately on our arrival at Memphis, was placed in the Gayoso Hospital, which was in charge of the Sisters of Mercy. He became violently insane, and, breaking away from the attendants, jumped from the fourth story window, landing on the hard pavement below. He was so severely injured that he lived but a short time.

It was on this march that Jo Sproule uttered a remark which made him famous, being so original and full of Irish wit. The night was as dark as could be made. A number of the boys sat down in front of an old cotton shed in which all the others had stretched themselves out to have a smoke by a smoking, smoldering fire. It was so dark the boys could not see their hands before them. Jo was sucking away at his pipe, trying to light it. After taking several strong puffs, he broke out with, "Be Jasus, it is poor satisfaction smoking whin you can't see your own bhlast." The roar that followed made the boys forget their discomforts for awhile, and Jo's expression became a by-word in the Battery.

We passed a very comfortable summer in camp at Memphis. We had frequent company drills and occasionally a march through the streets of the city, which we thought was done to make an impression on the minds of the natives. The Battery received recruits until we had the maximum number. Early in September C. B. Kimbell returned to the Battery, bringing nine recruits with him, his brothers, Julius W. and Spencer S., among them. Occasional expeditions into the country served to relieve the monotony of camp life, the principal ones being the Hernando or cold water march, and the Tallahatchie march.

While stationed at Memphis, three of the members, Charley Arnold, Wm. Kirk and Harry Hobart, had an experience which made a lasting impression on their memories, and served as a guide to their future course through life. They were not particularly proud of the part they took, but as Charley Arnold explains in extenuation of his part, he was young, and, with both the others, was innocent of any wrong doing. But there was quite an element of spice and adventure about it that made it rather interesting, and as the survivors have been called upon many times to narrate it, they will not object to having it permanently and correctly recorded. It began on one of the expeditions out from Memphis, and is best told in

Charley Arnold's own words: "While on the Hernando march, one of the horses in our squad had terribly galled shoulders and was to me an object of extreme solicitude. At one of our stops on the road, Bill Kirk, Harry Hobart and myself took kettles and went in search of water. We came across some horses hitched to trees, that we concluded at once were rebel horses and legitimate prey. I had suggested that one of them might make a good substitute for that poor, galled horse; whereupon we decided to take one for that purpose, with the understanding that we should take turns riding the galled horse. This worked all right till we got back to Memphis, and we were happy. A week or so after we had got into camp at Memphis again, Kirk and Hobart had been down town on passes, and, coming back, informed me that they could sell our horse to a friend of theirs, a former Chicagoan, who was in the wagon making business in Memphis. I agreed, and the following day they took the horse down town and came back with $60 in cash. They gave me $20 and kept $20 each. We had a high time for a few days, and thought not of a day of reckoning; but it came. A Provost Guard of three appeared in camp a week or so thereafter, with orders to arrest Harry Hobart and William Kirk. We were all three in one tent at the time, and when the guard announced their errand Hobart answered promptly, but Kirk turned over in his bunk, hiding his face, apparently very much frightened. Seeing his condition and realizing that I was equally culpable with him, (the squad having explained cause of arrest), I announced that I was the man they wanted, and, taking Kirk's place, Hobart and myself were marched to the Irving block and put in with the other prisoners, both Federal and Confederates. The immediate cause of the arrest and the reason my name was not in the order, was this: Some time previous to the Hernando march a bunch of Federal Cavalry had been in the same locality where we got the horse, and one of them *forcibly* traded the horse he was riding (and owned), for a much better one than his own. (It will be recalled that cavalry men generally owned their own horses.) It seems that the very horse *he left* was the one *we took*, and, when the cavarly man, by chance, saw his old horse in the possession of the blacksmith in Memphis, he claimed him, and, because the blacksmith wouldn't give him up, claiming he had bought and paid for him, the trooper had the old man arrested, and the whole story came out, how the blacksmith had bought the horse of Kirk and Hobart, etc. He didn't know anything about my part in the deal, and I might have escaped all that followed if I had not pitied Kirk. The cavalry man, by his action, run his head into a noose, too, for, while the horse he left in the country was *his own* the horse he took became *a government* horse, same as the one *we* took, became a government horse, and not private property, a fact that we were soon to learn in a very summary and lasting manner. He lost his horse and we paid for our fun, while the blacksmith was liberated. Kirk escaped, for we said nothing about him, while Hobart and myself were confined and court martialed. I don't recollect just how long we were in the Irving block, but only a few days, for we *escaped* one night, taking a perilous chance to get away from our undesirable associates and their *vermin*. It was a 'thrilling esenspe.' We had, in a day or two, got acquainted with an inmate by the name of Kelly, a member of the 6th Missouri, who suspected by our appearance, I presume, that we needed sympathy and aid if we could get it. Not being accustomed to such surroundings, he took us aside and quietly unfolded a plan for our escape. He said he had a rope up the chimney leading from the fireplace and that he could let us down during the night into the alley; said he had helped out quite a number, but there was danger; that a day or two before a warning had been read to the prisoners; that if any more escapes were attempted, the guard had orders to shoot without halting. We felt a little nervous over this, so Kelly proposed that at midnight he would fix up a "dummy" to test the sincerity of the order. We had gunny sacks to sleep on. Kelly took some of these and stuffed them into a pair of pants and tied a pair of boots to the bottom of the pants. Hitching a pair of suspenders to this, he approached the window and let it down. All was silent for awhile. Then Kelly rattled the boots against the side of the wall when—bang went a gun and a bullet whistled by. Immediately there was an alarm, and we heard the tramp of hurrying feet up the stairs. Every man tumbled on the floor and feigned sleep. Kelly had taken the stuffing out of his dummy. Soon the door opened and in rushed the guard and an officer, wanting to know who had escaped. Of course, we were all ignorant of anything of the sort. So the roll was called, and every man answered to his name. The officer remarked, 'It must be up-stairs,' and they filed out. They did not find anybody missing, and the mystery remained unexplained. This same day I had found an opportunity to talk with the officer of the guard, and in explaining our predicament, had gained his sympathy, so he gave Hobart and me the privilege of the corridor, which extended the whole length of the building. This fact gave us an opportunity to carry out a plan that we decided on the next morning. The disgusting food and filthy surroundings, decided us to take our chances that night to get to camp again, at least to get a square meal or two and change of clothing. Hobart was to watch the guard at the front or street side, while I was to watch the rear alley, and when both guards were away from the side alley where we expected to escape, we were to make the attempt. This moment arrived about one o'clock in the morning, and Kelly had everything ready. We slid into the alley and walked boldly out on to the lighted street, and quickly made our way to camp without further incident, going to the creek for a bath and change before we turned in.

"Capt. Wood and the boys were very much surprised to see us in line, at roll call the next morning. After roll call the Captain called us up for an explanation. We told him all about it. He advised us to go back and report to the officer in command. 'I won't send a guard with you; go yourselves, and tell the whole story,' said he. So we went back and did so. The commander was surprised that we had no guard, and I could see that he was also amused. We told him we wanted a bath, a change of clothing and something good to eat. He gave us better quarters than we had before. I suppose Kelly lost his rope. That day Capt. Wood came to see us, bringing with him Major Willard, who was the Provost Marshal of Memphis. They talked very seriously to us, saying that we had, willingly or unwillingly, committed a crime, and that they could do nothing for us; their business was to enforce discipline, and that the law should and must take its course. They said, however, they had succeeded in getting Gen. Sherman to permit us to go to camp and there remain under arrest until the court martial convened. Whereupon we went to camp and a special tent was erected for our accommodation, where we remained several weeks with nothing to do—under guard, of course, but quite at liberty. The boys thought we were having a good time and wanted to be under arrest, too.

"Finally, we were summoned for trial, and again we went without guard and reported to the court. The first question was, 'where is your guard.' 'We haven't any.' 'Well, well, this is surprising,' said the Judge Advocate. 'Who is your counsel?' was next asked. 'We haven't any.' We were ushered into the building and the court solemnly convened, and we were alone without counsel or a friend in sight. Things looked serious to us. The charges were about to be read, when in walked Major Willard and Capt. Wood. Major Willard immediately announced that he appeared for the defendants. The charges and specifications were formidable, and I didn't see how we were going to escape being shot; but, by the adroit management of Major Willard (who was a good lawyer), and the influence of both the Major and Captain Wood, the charges were cut down to 'a breach of good order and military discipline, and conduct unbecoming a soldier.' On this we were convicted, and fined two month's pay. The horse we gobbled, and supposed to be ours, was really Uncle Sam's, and we had legally committed a serious crime; but it was made plain enough that we did not realize it, and, owing to our previous good record and conduct, we were let off lightly." It is needless to say that neither of the three boys ventured in any uncertain deals during the remainder of their army service.

Our next move was the advance on Vicksburg, by the way of the Yazoo at Chickasaw Bayou and Haines Bluff. We embarked on the steamer "City of Memphis," December 20, and went down the Mississippi to the Yazoo. On the night of Friday, December 26, we debarked from the steamer, landing against a steep bank, up which we had to drag our guns by hand, camping there that night, and moving into line of battle the next day, when fighting was begun, mostly by the infantry, Frank Blair's men making a brilliant charge through the mud. We masked our Battery and remained quiet till Sunday morning, when we marched forward to Chickasaw Bayou. Our movements at this point are fully detailed in Capt. Wood's official report, which follows:

HEADQUARTERS, COMPANY "A," FIRST ILL. ARTILLERY,<br>
ON BOARD STEAMER PLANET, January 16, 1863.

DEAR SIR:—

I have the honor of reporting to you the part taken by the Battery under my command in the actions before Vicksburg, on the 27th, 28th, 29th, 30th, and 31st ult., and the 1st inst.

Battery debarked from steamer, City of Memphis, on the night of Friday the 26th ult., on the right bank of the Yazoo, about one mile above the old river. On Saturday morning, with Division, moved toward the front, bivouacing for the night near the Vicksburg road.

On Sunday morning, moved forward to Chickasaw Bayou; went into Battery about 11 A. M., and opened a sharp fire on the Levee Rifle Pits,

# BATTLE OF CHICKASAW BAYOU, MISS.

## DECEMBER 29 TH, 1862.

Showing 1st Battalion 13th U. S. Infantry as sharpshooters, behind trees and logs, on right; 6th Missouri Infantry crossing Bayou; and Battery "A" Chicago Light Artillery on left of picture.

---

Drawn by Wm. B. Daniels, Albion, Boone Co., Neb., who was a private in Co. "C," 1st Battalion, 13th U. S. Infantry, and participated in the above engagement.

---

13th Infantry commanded by Major D. Chase.
Battery "A" C. L. A. commanded by Captain P. P. Wood.
Brigade commanded by Colonel Giles A. Smith.
Division commanded by General Morgan L. Smith.
Army commanded by General W. T. Sherman.

---

REFERENCES: "Sherman's Memoirs," pages 438, 439 and 441, volume 1.
Greeley's "American Conflict," page 291, volume 2.

---

EXTRACT FROM GEN. SHERMAN'S MEMOIRS, VOL. 1, PAGE 320:

"Meantime the Sixth Missouri Infantry, at heavy loss, had also crossed the bayou at the narrow passage lower down, but could not ascend the steep bank; right over their heads was a rebel battery, whose fire was in a measure kept down by our sharpshooters (Thirteenth U. S. Infantry) posted behind logs, stumps and trees, on our side of the bayou. The men of the Sixth Missouri actually scooped out with their hands caves in the bank, which sheltered them against the fire of the enemy, who, right over their heads, held their muskets outside the parapet vertically, and fired down. So critical was the position, that we could not recall the men till after dark, and then one at a time."

BATTLE OF CHICKASAW BAYOU.

and a Battery opposite, it is supposed with some effect, as soon after opening, two regiments and some field pieces of the enemy moved rapidly to a more covered position. We were engaged about three hours.

On Monday, from same position, were ordered to cover the advance of the 6th Missouri Regiment, which we did, firing rapidly for about one hour, (for fear of endangering the infantry in front, we used our explosives with uncut fuse), retained our position, after our fire was ordered ceased until dark, when we were retired, being relieved by Battery "B," Capt. Barrett. We were under fire this day about four hours.

Tuesday night we were ordered by Major Taylor into an intrenchment (thrown up by the 55th Illinois under direction of Col. Malmborg), in and over a ravine on the right of Division, the position enfilading enemy's pits, and covering or cross-firing Ford, attempted by the 6th, on the preceding day. Had but four guns in this position. Fired none on Wednesday.

On Wednesday night, with two detachments of command, assisted in placing in position, (to the right of Light Battery), two 30 pound Parrott guns.

Thursday afternoon, the enemy amused themselves trying to unmask us, but, as ordered, we returned no compliments.

At 8 P. M. on Thursday, received orders to withdraw with command to boats; started about 10 P. M.; arrived at boat and embarked during the night in good order. Loss in men—none; horses, four wounded. Rounds of ammunition expended during the two days, the 28th and 29th, shell, 22 pounder howitzer, 117; spherical case, 12 pounder howitzer, 108; spherical case, 6 pounder gun, 286; solid shot, 6 pounder gun, 296. Total rounds, 807. Very respectfully,

P. P. WOOD, Captain,
Commanding Company "A," Chicago Light Artillery.

When the order came, Thursday night, to quietly hook up and withdraw to the boats we were all greatly surprised; but we learned the reason for it afterward. Gen. Grant had failed to connect there, owing to the destruction of his base of supplies at Holly Springs.

Gen. McClernand took command of the expedition here, and with it we came back to the mouth of White River, up which we proceeded to the "cut off," when we went up the Arkansas River to Arkansas Post.

We were engaged in battle here on the 10th and 11th of January, 1863, without the loss of a man and with one horse killed and four wounded. Toward the latter part of the fight we occupied a very exposed position within two hundred yards of the enemy's works, where we went instantly to work, sending half second shells among their works so rapidly the rebels found it impossible to return the fire. This was kept up until our ammunition was entirely exhausted, when we were relieved by Battery "B," about fifteen minutes before the fort surrendered with its 6,000 prisoners and 10,000 stand of arms. Capt. Wood received a severe sprain of the ankle during this engagement, which, though very painful, did not keep him from duty.

Our boys will never forget the trip up the Arkansas River, on the steamer "Von Puhl." The weather was very cold, wet and disagreeable, the rain freezing as it fell. Several darkies crawled under the boilers to keep warm, and smothered during the night. They were "buried" in the river the next day. One of the boys, Charley Arnold, found a place to sleep on a box about six feet long and two feet wide. He noticed a disagreeable odor during the night which he could not account for. The next morning, when he rolled up his blankets, he found marked on the box the name of a Captain who had been killed at Chickasaw, whose body had been enclosed in the box. Another soldier, not one of the Battery, who was a little "full," crawled in with a dead soldier who lay on the upper deck under a blanket.

The details of this fight are given in Captain Wood's subjoined report :

HEADQUARTERS COMPANY "A," ILLINOIS FIRST ARTILLERY,
ON BOARD STEAMER "PLANET," January 16, 1863.

DEAR SIR :—I have the honor of reporting to you the part taken by the Battery, under my command, in the action at the Post of Arkansas on the 10th and 11th inst.:

We debarked about three miles from the Fort on the morning of the 10th inst., and immediately moved forward with 1st Brigade, (under quite a heavy fire from the fort), into the woods, inside of the enemy's second line of works. During the night moved further to the front and right, and, on Sunday morning, were ordered into position by Gen. Sherman, in cleared space on the left of the Division, and north of Fort. At half-past 12, opened fire on batteries and pits, which fire was kept up with but little intermission, until our infantry advanced, when we were ordered forward on road leading directly into the Fort. From this position were again advanced to within five hundred yards of the works, where we remained, keeping up a steady but not rapid fire. Our ammunition getting short, I ceased the fire from two sections, keeping up this fire until our chests were empty. I retired the guns singly to our first position, where finding thirty rounds of 6 pounder projectiles, I sent one gun forward, where it remained but a moment before being relieved by Battery "B." A few moments after, word was brought of victory.

Loss in men—none; horses, one killed, four wounded. (Horse belonging to Lieut. McCagg, killed.) Rounds of ammunition expended, shell, 12 pounder howitzer, 98; spherical case, 12 pounder howitzer, 96; spherical case, 6 pounder gun, 371; solid shot, 6 pounder gun, 139. Total rounds, 704.

Of Lieutentants McCagg and Young, and the men in the command, it is needless to use words of praise. Suffice it, that every man in the command feels we did what we always strive to do, our whole duty.

Very respectfully,

P. P. WOOD, Captain.

Commanding Battery "A," Chicago Light Artillery.

In this last fight we had a wheel shot away, and one man knocked over by round shot. The man was unhurt.

"The rebels are wasting considerable ammunition this morning, but do us no damage whatever."

The man referred to was Julius W. Kimbell. He was helpless several days from the effects of the injury.

Squad one, Geo. M. Brown, gunner, fired the signal gun that commenced the attack on this Fort. Our boys, were glad to see the white flag go up on the Fort. It had hardly been raised when a number of the Battery boys ran for the fort and jumped over the rifle pits into it. Inside they saw a rebel soldier with both legs shot off, alive and holding the stumps in his hands and swearing like a trooper. Just then a rebel artillery Major came up and, shaking hands with our boys, asked if they belonged to the Battery down the road. Upon being answered in the affirmative, he said, "You raised hell with us," and pointed to his guns and the dead and wounded men and horses lying about. He said they had shot most of the horses themselves; the horses were nearly all dead.

Our boys walked about to see the results of our victory, and saw many horrible sights. One casemented gun that had exploded or been knocked to pieces by the gunboats, had a number of dead and terribly mangled gunners inside the casement. The iron rails of the casement had been doubled and twisted all out of shape by the terrific fire of the heavy guns.

Altogether it was a great victory, and compensated for the failure at Chickasaw Bayou, although the withdrawal from that place was a masterly retreat, and the best and only thing to do under the circumstances.

From here we were moved to Young's Point, opposite Vicksburg, and went into camp just inside the levee, where we laid all winter, while the long preparations for the final Vicksburg siege were made. This was a dull winter for the Battery, and the boys do not have any very pleasant recollections of these camps; there was so much sickness and so many deaths. The old levee was full of dead soldiers, although our Battery fared very well in this respect. In addition to their regular duties, they manned two 30-lb. Parrott guns, while Butler's canal was being dug. The canal would persist in overflowing and flooding our camps. On one of these occasions some of the Battery boys went hunting for ducks in a boat, and were upset. Fred Church, who was one of the party, illustrated it the next day, in his own inimitable manner, and furnished a great deal of amusement to the camp out of their misadventure. Few stirring incidents occurred during the winter.

On the 24th of January, the rebel transport "Vicksburg," ran the blockade, receiving three 30-lb. shots from the guns manned by our boys. On the 26th two more transports attempted the same feat, but were driven back.

In the latter part of the winter our right section went with Colonel Giles A. Smith up the Sunflower River and Black Bayou to the relief of Porter's gunboats, which was most timely, as the Admiral was preparing to blow them up to save them.

On the night of April 13, we were fortunate spectators of the grand sight of our gunboats running past the rebel batteries at Vicksburg.

Soon after we went with Sherman up the Yazoo, and made a feint on Haines' Bluff. The design was to cause Pemberton to reinforce the Bluff instead of sending troops to interfere with Grant's crossing at Grand Gulf. It had the desired effect.

We were hurried back out of the Yazoo, and overtook the rest of the army at Raymond on the night of May 15. The next day the battle of Champion Hill was fought, where we were in position and under fire, but were not engaged. May 17, we marched to the Big Black at a place called Bridgeport, where one rebel Lieutenant and twelve men kept our Division under command of Gen. F. P. Blair, from laying in pontoons from 10 o'clock until 3. At that time Gen. Sherman arrived at the river, and seeing only a rifle-pit about fifty feet long, ordered Capt. Wood to open on it with one of our guns. We fired three shells when the rebels surrendered, and the pontoon was built and we crossed over that night. On the 18th we advanced on the works around Vicksburg.

On the 19th of May, the three corps being in line, a charge was made, which the rebels easily repulsed, as they had the best natural fortifications that could be desired, rifle pits, heavy earthworks at the angles, with innumerable large trees felled down the steep hillside with branches sharpened to a point. On the 22nd another charge was made, which resulted like the first.

Several days after this last charge, a truce was declared to bury the dead. They had laid long in the hot sun, and were all swollen and black as negroes, and so decomposed that they would not bear removal and were covered where they lay.

After this we settled down to a regular siege of digging, sapping and mining, occasionally giving them a taste of our artillery all along the line. We manned, besides our own guns, three 30-lb. Parrott guns with which we did some good work, notably in the rear of Fort Hill, when Gen. Logan blew it up. Here the rebels had massed their troops to repel Logan, who was fiercely struggling to enter the breach, we kept landing 30-lb. shells among them till dark, commencing about 4 o'clock. The siege lasted until July 4, 1863, when Vicksburg surrendered with 33,000 troops.

Immediately after the surrender, before the guard was placed, our boys were over the works, and had a chance to circulate among the prisoners, even down to the rebel headquarters in the city, and the batteries on the river front. The prisoners were in a wretched state for food and clothing, as were the citizens, women and children. They were living in caves dug into the street, embankments and elsewhere.

The Battery Glee Club had some interesting and amusing experiences during the siege, and by their singing, engendered a friendly feeling in the hearts of the "Johnny Rebs."

Whenever firing ceased our boys would crawl up on the works on our side, and the rebels would do the same, and there our boys sang and talked with the enemy. When the time came to obey an order for action, our boys would yell out, "down, rebs," and they would yell back, "down, Yanks." Here George Whittier was killed by a sharpshooter. He was washing his hands in a stooping posture behind the works. Getting some soap in his eyes, he called for a towel and holding out his hands, he raised himself a little too high and a rebel bullet went through his heart. Charley Arnold cut his name upon the board that marked his resting place, which like service he did for many of the other boys. Billy Kirk died at this point, it was thought, chiefly from the fear of death, of which he had a presentiment.

On the morning of July 5, our Division was ordered to march to Jackson, the Capital, where Joe Johnston was entrenched. This was in many respects the worst march the Battery ever took, and fairly eclipsed the famous "Calloway March." The road was about six inches deep with fine dry dust, and men and horses were of the same color as the ground. The weather was hot and dry. We were in the rear of the Division, and the cisterns were all drained dry when we came along. But we survived the trip and went into earthworks, which we built ourselves by sinking our guns into a pit, and throwing the dirt in front of a breastwork, making an embrasure of cotton bales. These were the safest works we ever occupied, as being low down, the rebels invariably shot over us.

We besieged the city from the 10th to the 17th of July, when it was evacuated. While in camp here for a few days, eight of our men, Harry Young, Ed. Hughes, John Clark, Clarence Church, Sam Fandish, William Fitch, Fred. Kautzler and A. P. Maddock, were taken prisoners, and were held in captivity sixteen months, and Sergeant Wilber J. Wilcox was killed while foraging for corn for our horses.

The story of the sixteen months of imprisonment which followed the capture of these men, is told by one of the survivors, William H. Young. It is in such simple, earnest language that its truthfulness is indelibly impressed upon the mind of the reader, and the wonder is that any human beings could have endured what they did and be alive and comparatively robust and healthy, to tell the story, thirty-six years afterward. The narrative is best told in his own graphic words, and is in full as follows:

### "HELD BY THE ENEMY." 1863—1864.

"After the second battle of Jackson, Mississippi, in July, 1863, Lieut. Ramsey being in command of the Battery, finding that forage for our horses was getting scarce, called for a volunteer detail to go out and procure such forage as they could find. The volunteers from the Battery numbered fourteen men.

Sergt. Wilbur J. Wilcox, Sergt. Ed. Clark, John Steele, Clarence Church, Ed. Hughes, John Clark, Samuel Fandish, Wm. Fitch, A. P. Maddock, Walter Phillips, Pitt Follansbee, W. H. Young, Fred. Kantzler and Jerome Briggs volunteered. We were furnished with a detail of infantry from the 127th Illinois volunteers of twenty-six men, which made our force forty men. We left camp about 9 o'clock A. M., on the 22nd day of July.

Crossing the Pearl River, we traveled about six miles toward the enemy, and two miles within their lines. Nothing of note happened on our way out. After loading our wagons with such forage as we could find, the boys turned their attention to their own comforts, looking for such good things as they could find to satisfy their hunger. On our way out we noticed that a man on horseback would appear in the middle of the road about a quarter of a mile ahead of us, and wait until we got within a reasonable distance of him, then disappear. He did this several times. We did not think much of it at the time; but learned later that he was a Confederate scout, sent out to watch us. We started on our return, all feeling happy. On our way back to camp we captured the scout that had watched us while going out. He told us we would have to fight before we got through; and his words came true very soon. We had traveled about three miles toward camp, and in passing through a deep cut in the road, without warning, we were fired on by a squadron of cavalry in ambush. We saw at once that it was every man for himself. True, we made a short fight, but soon saw that they were too strong for us.

Our loss on that day was Sergeant Wilcox killed, A. P. Maddock wounded, and eight of the squad captured. I well remember the man who took me in. When he rode up to me, with sword raised over my head, I thought he was the biggest man I ever saw. He looked to me to be about fifteen feet tall. He asked me where the rest of the Yankees were. Of course, I could not tell him. After questioning me awhile, he said, "Well, get up there with the rest of the prisoners," and I immediately "got." We realized then that we were prisoners, but felt thankful that it was no worse.

How strange it sounded at that time. Little did we know or realize what was before us, and, perhaps, it was better for us that we did not. We soon learned that our captors were a part of Jackson's Tennessee cavalry, numbering about 250 men. We were soon started on our march, whither we did not know. My first experience as a prisoner was marching on a road of red clay soil shortly after a rain shower. That was a slippery time, especially in going up hill. We traveled all that afternoon, passing through the rear of Hardee's army. Our march continued until about dark. That night we were put in a building that had been used as a cotton warehouse, where we rested very comfortably. As there was still some cotton left in the building, our beds, if not first-class, were soft and comfortable.

The next morning, about daylight, we were awakened by a humorous Confederate soldier, who, having gathered an armful of green corn from a field close by, opened the door of our prison, and throwing the corn in among us called out, "Breakfast." We did not relish the bill of fare at that time, but later on that same corn would have been considered a luxury and appreciated beyond price. We were marched all the next day, and at night we reached a small station on the railroad. There we remained about two days, where our number was increased by other prisoners coming in. We were soon forwarded to Mobile, Alabama, and remained there about two days. Then we were taken up the river. Our next stopping place was Montgomery, Alabama. From there our journey to Richmond commenced. Not knowing that the exchange of prisoners had been stopped, we were led by our guards to believe that we were going right through to be exchanged. Their object was to handle us with the least possible trouble to themselves. Our next stopping place was Atlanta, Ga., and our journey so far had been a picnic. Our stay in Atlanta was short. Soon we were on the move for Richmond where we were doomed to pass many weary days. We reached Richmond about the first of August. After spending one night in the city, with many other prisoners, we were marched to Belle Island, a small island in the James river, just above the city.

Our prison on the island was a bank of earth in the form of a square, covered with old cast-off tents that the Confederates had no further use for. Then we realized that we were in for it, and the next thing to do, was to make the best of it. Now we realized what hunger was. We were formed into squads of hundreds; our rations for each squad of 100, for breakfast, (any time from daylight to noon) consisted of 12 pounds of meat, mostly bone, and 25 small loaves of bread. Just think it—$\frac{1}{2}$ an ounce of meat, with a piece of bread not much larger, for a hungry man's breakfast. Supper, (any time from noon until dark), $\frac{1}{2}$ pint of dirty soup, with a small piece of bread. Such was our rations day after day—always hungry and no relief.

Thus we existed in that prison through a severe winter, without proper shelter, or sufficient clothing to protect us from the cold. Our little squad was fortunate enough to get in a tent together. I think we managed to get two old blankets, and that was all we had to protect us. One we used for our bed, the other to cover us. Imagine seven men trying to sleep under one blanket! It reminded me of a minstrel show, where the end men furnished most of the amusement. I know that ours were kept busy trying to keep under cover. During the daytime our time was occupied in watching when our next meal would come in, for we were just as hungry when through our last meal as we were before getting it.

Thus we passed the winter, until the month of March. About that time one of our squad, Fitch, was fortunate enough to get out in the cook house, where our *meat* and *soup* was cooked, and let me say to you, and to his credit, that he did not forget his comrades in the prison. He could not do much, but what he did do for us kept us from suffering from hunger as we had done in the past. He was a noble fellow, and true comrade.

In the course of time our squads would get reduced to uneven numbers, and, in order to keep us in squads of hundreds, they would turn us out of the prison and count us off into new squads. That was what we called "counting us with a club." The rebel officer would stand with a club in his hand, and, when 100 men were told off, he would make a sign with his club for the rest to stop until that hundred was put in charge of a Yankee Sergeant and moved into the prison. Every one knows how men will act who are cold and hungry and anxious to get back under shelter. They would try to crowd out, and get unruly. Then that kind-hearted officer would walk up to the weak and starved prisoners and knock them right and left. That is what we called "counting us with a club."

Thus we passed the time until the 22nd of February. On that day we were taken to the city and kept until midnight. At that hour of the night we were marched to the railroad and put in box cars. We had no idea where we were going, some supposing it was to be exchanged. We soon learned that our destination was south, but we thought that any place would be better than the island. Each car was loaded to its utmost capacity. Our journey from Richmond to Andersonville was eight days, and in that time we were permitted to get out of the cars one half day, and we fully appreciated the kindness of our escort in allowing us even that short time to stretch. Again we were put in our "side door Pullman sleepers," continuing our journey four days longer. We arrived at Andersonville about the 1st of March. We were again formed into squads of ninety men, when we were marched into the prison and turned adrift to shift for ourselves. There was no shelter prepared for us; nothing but the open air and hard ground. Our little squad, now being reduced to five, was fortunate enough to procure some extra blankets, and, by forming a partnership with new acquaintances, we soon had a fairly good shelter.

Andersonville was an open air prison of about twenty acres, surrounded by a stockade of square timbers, in height about twenty feet above ground, forming a solid wall around the prison. At intervals of about 300 feet watch towers were placed, so the guard could look down in the prison and watch the Yankees. Within the prison, about thirty feet from the stockade, was a railing placed upon 2 x 3 scantling posts. That was *Dead Line*, and, woe to the one that ventured beyond its limits, or even placed his hand on it. It was sure death. No warning to keep away, but fired upon at once. Many men were killed by approaching too close to the dreaded "dead line." As the time passed, and other prisoners coming in, our prison soon became crowded, and our sufferings increased. Our squad was now reduced to four. Fitch, Clark and Maddock being exchanged from Richmond, and Faudish passing away in the prison, leaving Kantzler, Church, Hughes and Young to continue the struggle.

After being in the prison quite awhile, and seeing our condition growing worse each day, and no hope of relief, we noticed that Capt. Wurtz, the commander of the interior of the prison, was a German, and, we having a shrewd little German with us in the person of comrade Kantzler, we thought it would be to our interest to have our German interview the other German in the hopes of bettering our condition. We learned that they had established a hospital outside of the prison, as the sickness had increased so fast they could not care for them within the walls. The result of Kantzler's interview was that in a few days he was called out to the hospital, and his promise in parting with us was, if in his power he would have the rest of us with him soon, and I am glad to say that in a few days Church and myself were sent for, soon to be followed by Hughes. Kantzler was given a place as cook, while Church and myself were detailed as undertakers, that is, we removed the dead from the hospital to what was known as the "dead house," a house built of brush to keep off the sun and rain from the dead. True, we had plenty of business, but there was not much money in it, barely a living, and a poor one at that. Hughes was detailed as nurse in the hospital; so we were all together again, our condition was vastly improved. We were put on parole not to try to escape. We saw so many that had tried it and were brought back, that we knew our condition would be made very severe if we tried it and were recaptured; and let me say that we owe to comrade Kantzler a debt of gratitude that can never be paid for his success in getting us removed from that living death. I feel, and my comrades will bear me out in it, our condition being such from long confinement on the island, that we would have been unable to stand the hardships within the prison, and the last one of us would have filled an unkown grave.

So, my comrades of Battery "A" owe it to comrade Kantzler that we are able to be with you and tell the story of our prison experience. We began to feel like new men; our work was not much of a tax on us, and we had plenty of time to attend to our laundry and keep our persons somewhat clean. We were fortunate in keeping in good health up to that time, which was much in our favor and helped to carry us through. We were always cheerful, and I fail to recall a single instance where an unkind word passed between us, or a dishonest act by any one of us, toward each other. There seemed to be a bond of friendship that could not be broken. We were as one; no ill feeling even entered our little squad, and the bond of friendship that was formed in those dark days, has lasted through the thirty-six years that has passed, and is as strong to-day, if not stronger than it was in that trying time when no one knew what the morrow would bring forth, and it will last until the last one is called to join the silent majority.

I wish to say a few words for the Confederate soldier; of those who were in the field at the front, and stood the brunt of battle. I can say, and my comrades will agree with me, that while in their hands we were treated with kindness and civility. For the home-guard and young boys that guarded us while in the prisons, I cannot speak so well of. They seemed to have no pity or feeling for us. It was their delight to make our condition as miserable as possible.

In Andersonville the saying was, that when one kills a Yankee he was entitled to a furlough. I don't know how true it was; but it looked that way. They would kill one on the least provocation. As the summer advanced and the heat increased, our dead increased with it, reaching 100 a day during the months of July and August. It is estimated that thirteen thousand prisoners perished there in the first six months, all buried in unknown graves. Who was to blame for that awful sacrifice of human lives it is not for us to say. I always thought while the Confederates might not have been able to give us "Yankee" rations, they could have given us enough of what they did have, and prepared in proper shape. Our rations at Andersonville consisted of a small amount of meat, and corn meal of the coarsest kind, about half baked, unfit for healthy and strong men. That was the food until the prison became so crowded, and they could not bake enough to supply the prisoners. After that time they did not trouble themselves to bake it, but made it into mush. Then they would load a wagon, similar to one putting in a load of coal, drive into the prison and shovel out to each squad so much mush for a day's rations. The sanitary condition of the prison was beyond description.

During the months of July and August there were confined within the stockade about 30,000 wretched human beings, about 1,500 to the acre. So we passed the Summer of 1864. About the first of September a report reached the Confederates that Gen. Sherman was coming that way that caused them to move the greater part of the prisoners to different points further South. We were again put in our "Pullman cars" and started for the South. Our destination proved to be Savannah, Ga. Our condition was much improved while in our last prison as there were not so many of us, we had plenty of room, and our food was somewhat better. Nothing of note happened in our last prison home, only our long and weary wait for the time of our exchange. We remained in Savannah about four months, until the 16th day of November 1864. Our time with the confederates was from July 22nd, 1863 until November 16th, 1864, about one year and four months. At last we were told to get ready for exchange. I did not put much faith in it, and would not believe it until I was safely on our own transports. You can imagine how anxious I was to get away, so much in a hurry that I was the third man that passed over to our transports, and in language more expressive than polite, I called back to that Confederate guard that they could all go to the warm place—they would never get me again.

Thus, comrades of Battery "A," I have tried to give you a short history of your comrades while in the different prisons of the South, that the children and grand-children of the members of Old Battery "A" may know what the young men of 1861 underwent, that they might have one flag and one country. Yours fraternally,

WILLIAM H. YOUNG.

An exciting episode occurred during the siege of Jackson, Mississippi, in which Capt. Wood received a slight wound, and he and the entire gun squad, under gunner G. M. Brown, narrowly escaped annihilation. We were posted in the front yard or park of Col. Wirt Addams, a rebel guerilla. Pits for each gun were sunk about twelve feet square and three and a half feet deep, with boards set up in front two feet high, and the earth from the pits thrown back of the boards, making a good earth-work in front of the guns, nearly six feet high, with a narrow embrasure. We were facing a rebel battery from New Orleans, with six ten pound rifled guns, and one sixty-four pound Columbiad behind heavy earthworks. The rebel small guns were spiteful shooters. One afternoon Capt. Wood was in our pit and we were standing around a little careless, and evidently the rebels got a glimpse of the tops of our heads. John Clark was behind an oak tree nearby, watching for shots—we always kept our man on watch—when suddenly he called, "down," and a shot came direct for us and struck our little earth-work four feet to the right and ten feet in front of our embrasure, and lifted dirt all over us. Gunner, G. M. Brown, called to "load," but before we could get ready, Clark called "down" again, and another shot struck about fifteen feet nearly in our front, and before we could run our gun out, another shot came and struck the cotton bales. "Fatty" Stewart had to protect our ammunition and himself; he was No. 5, cutting fuse. That shot made havoc of *one* bale of cotton and of Stewart's shanty, and blinded him—well, with cotton. All this time Capt. Wood was standing, his back against the boards that held the dirt in front, watching the excitement. When the fourth shot came and struck four feet to the left and six feet in front of our embrasure, in a direct line for Capt. Wood, and exploded, one piece of the shell, weighing nearly four pounds, plowed its way through the earth six feet and through an inch board, and through the sleeve of Capt. Wood's blouse and stopped there, and bruised and numbed the Captain's arm a little. He caught hold of the iron in his sleeve and thought it the bones of his broken arm, and started for the surgeon's quarters in the house, saying, "My arm is off." Just then we got the ten pound Parrott loaded and run it out, and gunner Brown sent a shot square into the embrasure of the gun shooting at us, and we heard no more from them that day. We afterward weighed the piece of shell. The arm was black and blue, and lame for some time, which was Capt. Wood's only injury.

From Jackson we marched back to the Big Black, where we went into summer quarters in a magnificent grove, remaining until September 27. We were then ordered to Chattanooga, going by boat to Memphis, and horses on foot and guns on cars from there to Corinth, from which place we began our march, passing through Iuka, Tuscumbia, Eastport, Elkton, Winchester, Deckherd and the Narrows, between Bridgeport and Chattanooga. We crossed the Tennessee river twice and brought up on its north bank near the mouth of Chickamauga Creek.

On the 24th of November our corps was formed for an advance in the afternoon, and occupied a spur of Missionary Ridge, without firing a shot. We entrenched for the night, and were settling ourselves nicely, when a rebel brigade came marching back to their camp, which we were occupying without their knowledge or consent.

Lieut. Rumsey, with our right section, had gone out on picket with the infantry, and met them ; and, of course, there was a fight. Here John Steele was wounded in the shin.

The next day our corps attacked the enemy's right flank and pressed it vigorously all day. At about 4 o'clock the Army of the Cumberland made a charge in the center and swept everything before them. Hooker had taken Lookout Mountain, driving Bragg from his fortifications. We followed him until he took refuge at Dalton, Georgia.

Then we came back and went into camp near Chattanooga, leaving which we took the back track through the Narrows again, which was literally paved with dead mules. We went over the mountains, some days not making more than three miles. We would hitch twenty horses to a gun, and drag it over the mountain, and then go back and get the caisson. This was because our horses were so nearly starved they could scarcely stand up.

In the assault that ended in the defeat and retreat of Bragg, our boys occupied a position from which they had the best view of a battle of any they were ever engaged in. From the eminence on which they were posted, they could see away off to the right across the Tennessee river, Gen. Thomas' assaulting columns moving upon the ridge. Following this battle of Missionary Ridge and Lookout Mountain, we were moved to Bellfont, Ala., which place we reached about Christmas (1863) where we remained about a week. Here we experienced some of the coldest weather we had in our whole army service. Pools of water froze over hard enough to hold up our mule team and wagon. On the 1st of January 1864 we went into camp near Larkinsville, Ala., reaching there at 12:30 A. M. It was bitterly cold and none of the boys were out to roll call in the morning. Here John Connell and the blacksmith made a couple of pairs of skates on the 3d and utilized them two or three days, on a small pond near the camp, which was a revelation to the natives in that locality. We settled down to spend the winter in Larkinsville, and make ourselves as comfortable as possible. Good quarters were made in log houses and warm stables built for our horses. During the winter a great mania for whittling in Laurel root broke out in camp, and many an hour was spent in that occupation. Many curious, ingenious and quite artistic articles were produced by the boys in their leisure hours. One of particular merit was a big pipe made by John Connell, which he still has. It is a real work of art, and has taken first premium at several fairs, where he has entered it for specimen of wood carving. Another interesting relic of the camp at Larkinsville, which shows how the boys occupied their leisure time and amused themselves, is in the possession of C. B. Kimbell. It is a miniature 30-lb. Parrott gun, two inches long, made of Laurel root and cut to form a watch fob. It was the work of A. V. Pitts, who was a genius and an artist in that line

Scene 1st

Starts for the Mountains

## 5

Fired on by Guerillas!!

## 6

The Escape

## 7

When he reaches camp he finds one piece of Laural which he had put in his pocket previous to the attack and he begins to whittle.

## 8

And makes the gun which is sent to Kimbell.

and was sent by him to his old chum and comrade, who was home on account of his wound. Accompanying the gun was a series of illustrated sketches made by Fred S. Church, showing the history of the gun, from the time Pitts started out from the camp in the morning in search of Laurel root, until his arrival in camp and and the successful completion of his work. The sketches indicate the strong natural artistic talent which Church then possessed and which afterwards developed, placing him in the front rank among the artists of this country.

The pleasantest winter of our whole army service was spent here. After the first cold spell the weather, was warm and dry. The boys amused themselves nearly every day, playing base ball and other games. In the latter part of the winter the famous "Larkinsville Theatre Co." was organized which furnished no end of amusement and entertainment. The talent developed, surprised themselves and all their friends in neighboring commands. "Jimmy" Milner was the playwriter and president of the combination. Fred Church who has since become as noted among the artists of the nation, as he was among his comrades during the war, was scenic artist. George Beach was the "star" and Ed. E. Williams and S. S. Kimbell impersonated the female characters well, if not to perfection, in wardrobes borrowed from all the wives of officers that were quartered for the winter, in our division. Charley Smith and Harry Long immortalized themselves in various parts, and Charley Arnold made a first-class *Satan*, and as he says "played the very Devil." The make up of *Satan* was particularly original and effective, and once seen could never be forgotten. The mask and tail he wore were of his own manufacture in camp. The tail was made by winding binding cotton around a crooked stick and covering it with a piece of rubber poncho, and the mask of another piece of a poncho, cutting holes for the eyes, nose and mouth, and surrounding them with white cloth, making a hideous enough object to answer all ordinary purposes. But Bartleson and Arnold conceived the idea of making a more hideous mask by moulding a horrible face in clay, baking it in a Dutch oven and moulding a piece of pasteboard box over that. They worked diligently all one afternoon and succeeded in producing the most devilish face ever seen. They put the mould to bake in one of the darkey cook's Dutch ovens, after he had gone out for the evening. On his return sometime in the night he noticed a fire in his oven and looked in to see what was going on, and see-

ED. E. WILLIAMS,
"Leading Lady" Larkinsville Theatre Co.
1864.

ing the horrible image within, uttering a screech like a Comanche Indian, he ran as if for his life, yelling, "its de debble sure." The fame of the Troup spread throughout the entire division.

Gen. Logan and Staff came from Huntsville to witness a performance. Gen. Sherman was a frequent spectator, and Gen. Morgan L. Smith a constant one. He invited all the performers to his headquarters one afternoon previous to a performance, where he undertook the task of "Stalling the Battery boys," as he afterward expressed it, and getting them in such a condition that they could not perform, but their heads were too level to be caught, and the best performance they ever rendered, followed, and the General acknowledged his defeat.

The following play bill will give a fair idea of the entertainments produced, and talent diplayed :

### BATTERY THEATRE, COMPANY "A," C. L. A.,
### LARKINSVILLE, ALA.

President.................................J. W. Midner.
Treasurer...........................…...C. E. Smith.
Manager......................................L. H. Beach.
Musical Director..........................S. Kennedy.
Scenic Artist..............................F. S. Church.
Stage Carpenter..............Speer, Chase and Raymond.
Properties and Costumes.............Bartleson and King.

WEDNESDAY EVENING, APRIL 27, 1864,
will be presented the celebrated drama,

### A MOMENTOUS QUESTION.

Robert Shelly (a young poacher)..................E. A. Ware.
James Greenfield (a game keeper).................G. B. Beach
Union Jack (scamp of the Village)................O. C. Foster.
Chalk (landlord of the Lucky Horse-Shoe)..........J. B. Day.
Moletrap..............   ....................T. Thompson.
Rachel Rayland................................E. E. Williams
Fanny Dossett (a servant)...  ...................A. Wilson.
Overture........by Orchestra. | Song....by.... Glee Club.

The evening's entertainment will conclude with
### COOL AS A CUCUMBER.

Plumper..................................G. B. Beach.
Old Parkins..............................O. C. Foster.
Fred Barkins.............................J. H. Long.
Jessey Honiton ..........................A. Wilson.
Mary Wiggins............................E. E. Williams.

#### SECOND NIGHT'S ENTERTAINMENT.

The performance will open with the elegant drama of
### THE YANKEE NEPHEW.

Zedekiah Hull.............................C. E. Smith.
Charles Howard............................G. B. Beach.
Dr. Hawley................................O. C. Foster.
Oldest Inhabitant.........................J. B. Day.
Servant...................................J. Maloney.
Officer...................................R. Greene.
Miss Hattie Hawley........................E. E. Williams.
Miss Delia Dayton.........................A. Wilson.

The evenings entertainment will conclude with the stunning farce of
### APOLLO D'AFRIQUE.

Old Squintum..............................O. C. Foster.
Pete......................................L. H. Beach.
Rose......................................G. B. Beach.
Jake......................................H. Roberts.
Mrs. Squintum.............................R. Greene.
Pilgarlic.................................J. H. Long.

Performance Saturday evening if weather permits.

#### THIRD NIGHT.

The evening's entertainment will open with the celebrated tragedy entitled the
### SCOURGE
OF
### SAN MARINO.

Corruvio..................................G. B. Beach.
Arrolto...................................J. H. Long.

| | |
|---|---|
| Malevolus | O. C. Foster. |
| Nobleman | C. E. Smith. |
| Satan | C. L. Arnold. |
| Demon | L. H. Beach. |
| Monk | J. B. Day. |
| Dorrugio | R. Greene. |
| Almina Dornetto | E. E. Williams. |

Robbers, &c., by gentlemen of the profession out of a job.

"SYNOPSIS."

SCENE 1ST.—Arrolto ejected from his home, retires to an old tower and sells his soul to Satan. SCENE 2ND.—Bar-room in San Marino. Arrolto collects his band. SCENE 3RD.—Ten years later—a nobleman enters the city and discloses to Corruvio and others the name of the "scourge."— SCENE 4TH.—Corruvio and Almina parting. SCENE 5TH.—Corruvio's combat with Arrolto and his defeat. Grand finale.

The evening's entertainment will conclude with the stunning farce of

## BOX AND COX.

CASTE:

| | |
|---|---|
| Box | Harry Roberts. |
| Cox | L. H. Beach. |
| Mrs. Bouncer | J. W. Milner. |

Before reaching Larkinsville we had the misfortune to lose our "mascot," which had been constantly with us since we left Paducah. No well regulated command was considered "fully up-to-date" that did not possess a "mascot," and up to this time, we had "kept up with the procession" in that respect. The article consisted of any live thing, biped or quadruped, from a chicken to a pig, or little contraband "coon." A Wisconsin regiment had an American eagle, "Old Abe," which sat proudly perched upon a frame over their banner while being carried on all their marches and through all their engagements. A company in the 51st Illinois Infantry had a kitten, but Battery "A's" mascot was a "thorough-bred" mongrel dog, a cross between a Scotch terrier and something else unknown; but he was a dog among a thousand all the same. He came to us in Paducah from some infantry regiment. He seemed to consider an artillery man a superior being, and looked with perfect disdain on any infantry man that tried to make any advances toward an acquaintance. Among his many traits he considered it his sacred duty to always carry something when on a march. Any old shoe, bootleg, bone or stick that he could pick up in the morning, would be carried all day with unfailing regularity. Charley Smith, in writing to a brother, in 1862, who was a minister in Franklinville, Ill., told the story of our "mascot," which is worthy of reproduction here:

"Our Battery dog is barking at some loose horse. That reminds me of my carelessness in not before describing so illustrious a character as that dog. He is the pet of the Battery, known as well to the horses as the men and has been associated with our interests over eighteen months. He owns no one as master, but all. On the march he will follow no one gun, but persists in leading or going beside the advance piece. He has been in four battles and twice wounded, once at Donelson and once at Shiloh. At this latter fight he learned caution, and now at the sound of firing he will hunt a tree with as much zeal as his biped friends. What is the most singular is his diet. In this respect, he is a thorough old soldier. While in camp, fresh meat, bread and potatoes, too, if we have them, are not too good for him. On the march he takes his 'hard tack' and bacon, and not a man but will give him a share. If we are on short rations he takes a meal of corn or oats with some horse. He has had as many names as the 'Old Man of the Sea.' his last has stuck to him longest, 'Tony.' In personal appearance he is not calculated to impress one with a sense of his faculties; but shaggy, black mongrel as he is, he knows more than some men, and fears no dog that lives. Although often worsted in encounters with superior-sized dogs, he never leaves the field in disgrace, but his tail is just as high over his back as ever, and one could not help thinking that the old fellow feels conscious that he has done his duty. Nights, he is invaluable at the grain pile, in driving away stray horses, and has often been my companion in standing guard. He is never absent from 'roll call,' however far he may be away, chasing a horse or otherwise, the sound of the 'assembly' has just as potent an influence on him as on us. He never loses us, and never takes any other battery for us. In fact, he is a 'wonderful dorg,' and the boys think the world of him."

During the three months service, one of our boys even entered the reptile kingdom to obtain one of these necessary articles. J. F. Stackhouse a natural scientist and naturalist, (surnamed "Snakehouse" for obvious reasons) captured a large yellow moccasin which he tamed and petted as ordinary human beings would a kitten. He devoted all his spare time to gathering snakes, lizards, toads, bugs, etc., and his collection was a source of mortal terror to all his messmates, who feared they would escape and become partners in their bunks and blankets. The Government for some reason failed to appreciate the value of any such addition to an army outfit, and neglected to appropriate anything for its support and transportation and the collection was relegated to its native jungles about Cairo.

Some very pleasant acquaintances were made by the boys at Larkensville among the native families, notably the Baker family which lived up the mountain, and included several young ladies. Parson Risley seems to have been the one most specially favored by this family, presumably so on account of his ministereal manner and bearing. He writes in his diary of Saturday, April 30th, 1864, "I went to call on our friends the Baker family, to bid them good bye. E. P. Fish went with me and Lieut. J. W. Rumsey came up afterwards. He brought my war horse 'Donelson,' and presented it to Miss Martha Baker. Mrs. Baker prepared supper for us, of spring chicken, etc. We spent a delightful afternoon and evening, with the old folks and young ladies." Sunday May 1st we regretfully broke up and took leave of our pleasant camp. Under this date the Parson writes, "Mr. Baker came in camp to see us off. He brought a bag full of nice cakes from the young ladies for their friends in the Battery. Miss Mollie sends me an extra lot of nice cookies, for which she has my sincere thanks." On this date we started off for Chattanooga, on the Atlanta campaign. We camped at night within two and half miles of Bellfont, and slept on the ground, for the first time in months. Of this night Parson Risley writes he slept well, in company with Fish and John Lord, presumably on account of the "Lord" being with them.

The next day (Monday) broke camp at 8 o'clock. Weather cool and roads splendid. Went into camp at 4 o'clock within four miles of Stevenson, Alabama. As it looked like rain, the boys pitched their V tents for the night, and crawled in for a good night's sleep, lulled to slumber by the brigade band playing "Away Down South in Dixie."

Continuing our march on the 3d, reached Bridgeport late in the afternoon, and the next day, May 4, crossed the Tennessee river on the pontoon bridge, in the morning, and reached Nickel Jack Cave in the afternoon' where we halted a half an hour, many of the boys bathing their feet in the creek during the wait, the water of which was ice cold. Passing on we came back through the Narrows and over the north end of Lookout Mountain, reaching Snake Creek Gap May 9. We passed through the Gap preceded by the Ninth Illinois Mounted Infantry and General Kilpatrick's Cavalry. The General was wounded here and taken to the rear.

We were drawn up in line of battle at its east end, looking into Resaca, where the enemy was protected by earthworks. On the 11th Johnson massed his forces on Resaca, and on the 15th we had a lively fight.

Captain Wood was taken very sick here, and Lieut. Rumsey took command of the Battery. On the 13th our position was on the slope of a hill. Two 20-pound Parrotts, belonging to the Fourth Ohio Battery, were above us, on top of the hill. These guns were firing over us into the enemy's works, which were in plain view. At 5 o'clock one of the 4th Ohio's shells burst right over us. A fragment of the shell hit Lieut. Rumsey on his right shoulder, tearing the flesh away from the bone, and effectually "killing his shoulder strap," as he expressed it. He was taken to the field hospital and Parson Risley was detailed to nurse him.

On the 20th a twenty day's furlough was granted Risley to go to Chicago with Lieut. Rumsey, who was in hospital at Resaca, which place the rebels had evacuated, burning their bridges behind them in their flight. We followed the rebel army, commanded by Johnson, and met them next at Dallas. They charged on us repeatedly, but were each time repulsed with heavy loss.

On the 30th day of May, 1864, while our Battery was in breastworks here, Generals Sherman, McPherson, Logan, Barry and Col. Taylor came to our breastwork to reconnoitre the enemy's works in our front. Sherman went over by squad one's gun by himself. McPherson came up and stood at the muzzle of No. 4 gun and raised his field glass, and Logan stood behind him, resting his left hand on the cascabel of the gun. Col. Taylor stood directly behind Logan's arm. A sharpshooter fired a bullet under McPherson's arm; it cut a gash in the top of Logan's arm, and hit Col. Taylor fairly in the left breast. Enoch Colby was one of the first to help carry the Colonel off; McPherson loosened his clothes, and the wound looked very serious. Gen. Sherman, then coming back to where we had laid the Colonel down, asked McPherson if the wound was mortal. Mc-

Pherson replied that he could not say yet. We afterward learned that the bullet had glanced a rib and went around instead of through.

It was here that comrade Stiger, of the Battery, was severely wounded by a sharpshooter, while lying on his blanket, which bullet would have probably hit Colby, but for his having changed his position around behind a large tree about one minute before, for he had been lying not two feet from Stiger and between him and the rebel sharpshooter.

An amusing incident occurred in the hospital tent at Resaca, in which Lieut. Rumsey was staying, while waiting for transportation home. He had a hard night and Parson Risley was sleeping soundly by his side. Wanting some water in the night, he called for the "Parson." He did not waken easily and John's repeated calls for the "Parson" aroused the chaplain who was sleeping in the same tent. He supposed some poor sufferer was needing spiritual consolation of a different nature from what Rumsey was calling for, and promptly came to his assistance. Rumsey was disgusted and said "I don't want you, I want this parson by the side of me." It was a surprise to the chaplain to find there was another parson in the same tent more sinful perhaps than he. The Parson managed to arouse enough to get on his feet, and forced the contents of his canteen into Rumsey's face. His manner of doing it, brought out the remark from Rumsey that he would make a better "wet nurse" than anything else. The sick and wounded received motherly care here from Mother Bickerdike and Mrs. Porter, of the Sanitary Commission. They distributed oranges and lemons, and jellies among them with their own hands, and received the warm and hearty thanks of the boys, who greatly appreciated and enjoyed the treat.

The rebels retreated from Resaca to Kenesaw Mountain, where there was fighting at close intervals from June 10th until July 3d, when the rebels were forced to retreat south of the Chattahoochee river into the stronghold of Atlanta.

While encamped near Kenesaw, Geo. Gates ("Gen. Debility") the saddler, presented Gen. Sherman with an elegant bridle, collar and martingales of his own make. They were sent with the following letter, to which Gen. Sherman sent an appreciative and characteristic acknowledgment.

NEAR KENESAW, GA., June 25, 1864.

MAJOR GENERAL W. T. SHERMAN.

*General:*—As a private of Battery "A" 1st Ill. Light Artillery, I respectfully request that you will accept this bridle and collar as a slight token of the high regard and esteem which all soldiers entertain towards you as our commander. We, as a Battery, have long served under you, as Division, Corps and Department Commander, and now as Chief in Command, and at all times have felt confident that under your leadership our final success would be achieved. Please accept this bridle and collar, General, made by me in camp at Larkinsville, Ala., simply as a slight tribute of regard and confidence reposed in you.

I have the honor to be, General, very respectfully

Your obedient servant,

GEORGE GATES,

Harness maker of Battery "A" 1st Ill. Light Artillery
1st Brigade, 2nd Division, 15th Army Corps.

To MAJOR GENERAL W. T. SHERMAN,

Commanding Military Division of the Mississippi.

HEADQUARTERS MILITARY DIVISION OF THE MISSISSIPPI,
IN THE FIELD NEAR KENESAW, GA., June 26, 1864.

GEORGE GATES,

Company "A," Chicago Light Artillery.

*Dear Sir:*—On reaching camp last evening I found your letter of June 25th with a handsome bridle with bit and bridoon and a beautifully stitched breast-strap and martingales, done by your hands, in the leisure hours of camp. I assure you such a mark of your affection and respect is more acceptable to me than many rich jeweled sword or fancy stud that are wont to be the tokens of military regard. To feel that the soldier at his post marks my constant labor to his safety and success, satisfies me that there are those witnesses close by who appreciate the truth of events far better than those in the back-ground, who judge of battles by the sound of popular clamor, rather than by witnessing the actual direction of armies and the dread missiles of war. For yourself and comrades, be assured that I have watched and noted your career with unalloyed satisfaction at Arkansas Post especially, at all the movements on Jackson and into Mississippi; at Vicksburg when you had not only your own guns, but for six weeks lay close under its walls with the 30 pd. Parrotts, which did more execution than any guns at that memorable siege.

I have always borne testimony to the peculiar intelligence, good conduct and gentlemanly deportment of the young men who compose your Battery, and when the war does close, if I survive it, I will make it my duty to give full honor and credit to the soldiers in the ranks, who, though in humble capacity, have been the working hands by which the nation's honor and manhood have been vindicated.

As Battery "A" was one of the first to fire a hostile shot in the war in the great valley of the Mississippi, I hope it will be one of the last, and that its thunder tones will in due time proclaim the peace resulting from a war we could not avoid, but which called all true men from the fancied security of a former long and deceitful peace.

With thanks to you personally, I am your friend,

W. T. SHERMAN.
Major General.

Poor Gates did not do well after the war, but led a dissipated life in Chicago, dying in that city, in 1890, a homeless wanderer on the streets.

It was about twelve miles northwest of Atlanta, on July 12, 1864, that Capt. Wood, Lieuts. McCagg and Young, with all of the three years' men, were ordered to the rear, for muster out, their term of service having expired. A number of the comrades who joined the Battery in the early part of its second year, supposing their term would expire at the same time, now found it was a mistake, and that they were obliged to remain the full three years if wanted. It was a severe disappointment to them, more on account of being obliged to separate from their old comrades, and the sad day will long be remembered, especially by those who remained behind.

The veterans were mustered out and arrived at Chicago in due time, and were given a grand reception and banquet at the Tremont House, by their friends.

A number of the members of Battery "B" had an unexpired term to serve also, so the two Batteries were consolidated, retaining the name of Battery "A," and Lieut. Smyth of Battery "I," First Artillery, was placed in command.

On the evening of the 12th, the Battery moved with its corps to the northeast of Atlanta, marching all night and all the next day. Of this march it can be said a more mournful or sad one, never was made, being separated for the first time from the comrades with whom we had been so intimately connected for two years. Having shared with them a common danger, linked together by the strongest ties of friendship, it seemed like severing the strong ties of our being to part with them. But the last pressure of the hand had been given, and each started off in the path marked out for them, one leading to freedom from war and carnage and the weary march and bivouac, to the peaceful home and dear friends whose hearts would be gladdened by their safe return, while those remaining were to take the one leading to the uncertain future of civil strife, to face again the brave and determined foe, and plod along on weary marches through storm and sunshine, with the earth for our bed and the broad canopy of heaven for our covering, yet in the distance was a bright star of hope which beckoned us on, a hope which overbalanced fatigue, hunger and exposure, which met its full fruition when one year later the white winged dove of peace again hovered over all our country, saved and reunited.

We reached the outposts of Atlanta and camped about three miles from that city. Heavy skirmishing was going on along the whole line most of the time. On the 19th, 20th, and 21st, we took part in the engagements, and lost two of our new men, Samuel Hadlock and Jacob Dielman.

On the 22nd the Battery was posted on a high ridge through which the railroad was cut, portions of the Battery being on each side. We had but a skirmish line of infantry to support us. This line became so hotly engaged when the enemy appeared in force in front, that the whole cut was enveloped in smoke, and they filed through unnoticed, and deploying in the rear of the Battery, made a bayonet attack on it, simultaneous with a similar attack in front.

The Battery being so overpowered was captured, and many of the boys were taken prisoners but very fortunately were soon afterward exchanged.

Those captured were John Thomas, John Frazier, William Senpham, William Heartt, Lewis Lake, Edward Ferry, Charles G. Siller, John F. Stranberg, Thomas Wilcox, A. C. Hall, F. Sweeney, William H. Cowlin, S. P. Coe and Lieut. Smyth. A number were killed and wounded. The killed were brave John Farl, Lieut. Raub, John P. Chalman and Alexander Biedelman. Tim Lyrch of old squad one, and Thomas Canfield, each lost an arm. Our infantry soon rallied and forced the rebels back, regaining our position, but the rebels in retreating took four of our guns with them. The two remaining guns, in command of Sergt. Ed. Clark, opened fire on the rebels with solid shot, having no other ammunition. Lieut. Smyth having been made prisoner, Lieut. Cheney was placed in command the next morning, remaining about a week, when Lieut. Echte of a Missouri battery succeeded him. We took part in the grand move to the rear of Atlanta on the 26th, which culminated in the short but severe battle of Jonesborough on the 28th, in which we were engaged without loss, and which compelled the evacuation of Atlanta. Sept. 4th a general order from Gen. Grant was read announcing its surrender. Here we were reorganized, and Capt. E. P. Wilcox, formerly of Battery "B" placed in command, and Lieut's Colby, Roberts and Dutch were selected by ballot by the members of the Battery. After about a month's encampment on the outskirts of Atlanta, we moved northward towards Hood's army, and when he countermarched by our left flank, and went south, we were ordered to Nashville where we arrived November 1, 1864, and were in the reserve line during the battle there. From here we were sent to Chattanooga, remaining till the latter part of June, 1865.

Shortly after we reached Chattanooga it was discovered that the Battery was entitled to one more lieutenant, and the comrades surprised Spencer S. Kimbell by securing a commission for him, and presenting with it a beautiful sword, sash and belt. During our stay at Chattanooga we were in the reserve and doing garrison duty. Many of our boys were detailed on detached service, among them being Ferd V. Gindele and J. W. Kimbell, in the ordinance department, and James H. Shrigley, J. H. Long, and Wm. H. Johnson which gave them the opportunity of taking part in Sherman's Grand March "from Atlanta to the sea." These comrades were mustered out in Washington, at the close of the war.

The war being virtually ended we were finally ordered home for muster out. We arrived home July 3d, and were welcomed by kind and true friends, to enjoy again the comforts and sweets of civil life. A grand banquet was given in honor of our return. Our boys took up the new struggle of life, for fame and for fortune, each in his own sphere, some in the professions others in the trades and at farming, all happy in the consciousness of having done their share towards securing a peace to the country, which it is hoped will be as lasting as the government itself.

# Record of Battery "A."

OCCUPATION OF CAIRO.
OCCUPATION OF PADUCAH.
FORT HENRY.
FORT DONELSON.
SHILOH.
CORINTH.
CHICKASAW BAYOU.
ARKANSAS POST.
CHAMPION HILL.
VICKSBURG.
JACKSON.
CHATTANOOGA.
RESACA.
DALLAS.
BIG SHANTY.
KENESAW MOUNTAIN.
ATLANTA.
NASHVILLE.

# BIOGRAPHICAL SKETCHES
## OF MEMBERS OF
# BATTERY "A," FIRST ILLINOIS LIGHT ARTILLERY VOLUNTEERS.

## *CHAPTER III.*

IN writing the history of the members of our company, it would become a monotonous repetition to ascribe to each individual member all the qualities of loyalty, patriotism and bravery which he possessed. And every member did possess them, as was fully demonstrated by their action in responding to the call of their country, with eagerness and enthusiasm, when the news of the assault upon Fort Sumter flashed over the wires, throwing the entire loyal North into a blaze of patriotism. None but brave patriots could have borne so philosophically and uncomplainingly the discomforts and privations incident to army life, adapting themselves so readily to every situation and making the best of it, often displaying an amount of versatility and inventive genius in mastering difficulties and producing comforts that surprised even themselves. Therefore, a mention on these lines in individual cases will be omitted as superfluous. Numerous difficulties have presented themselves in preparing these sketches. It has been no easy task to condense the details into such form as to make a history which all could satisfactorily peruse, both now and in later years. In some cases the data furnished has been very meager; in others, it has been so ample that it has required considerable care and judgment to discriminate as to what was best to omit or use. But what has been the most formidable difficulty to overcome has been the failure of numbers of the comrades to furnish any data for their sketches, in which cases the official records, as far as could be obtained, have had to suffice. It is hoped that the effort to make this portion of the volume a reliable record of the lives of our members has been fairly successful and will prove reasonably satisfactory to them and to all interested.

## JAMES SMITH.

The honor and credit of having founded and led into the field the first battery in the Union Army in the West belongs to Captain James Smith. He was one of the original organizers of the battery, and had been connected with, and an active worker in, it since 1847, so he was well fitted to take the lead, which he did with promptness and true Scotch vigor, and he found ready followers and supporters from among the best young men of the city, many of whom had always known him. He was born in the Parish of Old Deer, Scotland, where his childhood and youth were passed and his school education obtained. When a young man he emigrated to America and settled in Chicago. He engaged in the lumber business, and at the breaking out of the war was a member of the firm of Sheriffs & Smith, and doing a large and lucrative business. He offered the services of the battery to Governor Yates, when President Lincoln made his first call for troops. They were accepted, and he left Chicago with his battery in the first body of troops for the war April 21st, 1861. He went to Cairo, where, after a few days, he was stationed up the Mississippi River, and went into camp, which was named in his honor, "Camp Smith." It was located in a dense forest of heavy timber and undergrowth, and he at once set to work with his men and began the clearing up of ten acres, in order to have a suitable drill and parade ground and a comfortable camp. This was accomplished in due time, and under his instruction the battery soon became very proficient. He was a thorough disciplinarian, and a most careful tactician, and having had years of experience in the artillery drill and practice, was well fitted to train a body of intelligent and willing young men. During the summer his health began to fail, and in September he was obliged to resign his commission and return home. He remained in the city till the close of the war, and was very active in looking after the interests of his old battery, caring for the sick and wounded as they were sent home, and assisting in supplying those in the field with many of the comforts and even luxuries which were not furnished by the government. And the boys at the front did not forget their old commander, and appreciated what he was doing for them. While in camp before Vicksburg in 1863 they demonstrated their affection and esteem for him by presenting him with a beautiful gold watch, accompanied by the following letter:

Camp of Co. "A," Chicago Light Artillery, Before Vicksburg.
April 21, 1863.

"Sir: Two years since, in the vanguard of the sons of Illinois going to do battle in their country's cause, you headed Chicago's battery. With unyielding patience and perseverance the raw levy under your skillful guidance and care became efficient and active troops. Forced from their leadership by severe disability, you have ever been watchful of the interests of your old companions in arms. By your exertions our camp has numberless

CAPT. JAMES SMITH.

times been supplied with the delicacies and necessaries which can only be procured from home, and from those whose every care is the soldier's. Our sick and wounded have received from you a father's care, and the ashes of those brave ones gone before have been gathered to rest in peace near their own loved homes. You are, sir, in the hearts of your old command, the father as well as the founder of Company "A," Chicago Light Artillery.

Receive, sir, this watch, with the prayers of all for your future happiness and prosperity, and the assurance of the love and esteem of all of

Company A.

To Capt. James Smith, Chicago, Ill."

After the war he engaged in the mining business in the West, in which he was very successful. He died at San Jose, Cal., May 1, 1872. His remains were brought to Chicago and interred in Rose Hill Cemetery. He did not forget his old comrades, and in his will bequeathed $2,000 for the purpose of erecting a monument for them in Rose Hill Cemetery, and the beautiful and appropriate monument of a stone field piece, draped in a flag of the same material, now standing in that cemetery, was made possible by the assistance of his generous bequest.

He was married to Mary L. Stoughton in 1847. Three children were born to them, two little girls, dying in infancy, and a son, Wm. B., dying Jan. 31, 1898. A sister, Mrs. Isabella Hadley, widow of Dr. Hadley, resides in Chicago.

## FRANK S. ALLEN.

In the prime of life Frank S. Allen was called from his earthly home Jan. 25, 1894, at Los Angeles, Cal., where he had gone, hoping to regain his health which, during the last two years of his life, had become very feeble. He was born in Providence, R. I., April 4, 1836, and was therefore in his fifty-eighth year at the time of his death. He enlisted in the battery July 16, 1861, and served with credit until Dec. 31, 1863, when he was promoted to the rank of Second Lieutenant, and transferred to the Second Louisiana Colored Artillery, in which command he served till the close of the war. As a soldier he distinguished himself wherever duty called, and on many fields of battle displayed a heroism and manly courage that commanded the respect of his associates and the admiration of his superior officers. As a business man since the war he was well known for his energy, integrity and enterprise, as well as for his courteous disposition. He was one of the principals of the Chicago Scale Co., and was very successful in his business. The taste he acquired in the army for military drill and discipline remained with him to the end of his life. He was one of the most active members of the National Guard, and as an officer in Battery "D," of Chicago, did as much as any one individual to build up that splendid organization to the high position it attained. His wife had preceded him but a few years to

CHARLES L. ARNOLD.

the better world. His remains were brought to Chicago and laid to rest in Rose Hill Cemetery. His funeral was conducted by the Masonic order, of which he was a distinguished member, and was attended by a large number of his old army comrades. The remains were kept in state in Battery "D" armory, where services were held. Among the floral tributes was a large piece of artillery done in carnation pinks and roses. His comrades will ever cherish his memory for his loyalty and devotion to his friends and to principle, his love for his country, and for his fidelity to the patriotic principles of the Republican party, of which he was an honored member.

### CHARLES LEWIS ARNOLD.

It is probable that no similar organization in the Union Army had a larger proportion of very young members, ranging from sixteen to twenty years of age, than did Battery "A." And it is an undisputed fact that no soldiers in the army possessed more patriotic zeal and bravery, nor endured the hardships and privations of army life more unflinchingly and hardily than these same younger members. Chief among these was the subject of this sketch, Charles L. Arnold. He was born in Hazel Green, Wis., April 9, 1844. His father was engaged in mining at this place. When Charles was three years old his family moved to Rockford, Ill., and later on to the State of New York. When he was eight years old his family settled in Toledo, Ohio. Here Charles acquired his early school education, removing to Chicago in 1859, which city has since been his home. He was clerking for a Board of Trade commission firm on South Water street at the breaking out of the war. Throwing up his position he enlisted in the battery in Chicago July 28, 1861, as private, in which position he served until the battery reached Young's Point, when he was appointed corporal. He continued in the service with the battery during the entire three years term of enlistment, though he had one opportunity to leave it for a position in General Sherman's Adjutant General's office, when he was but nineteen years of age, but he preferred to remain with the battery. While the battery was in camp on Walnut Hills, Vicksburg, President Lincoln notified General Grant that there were six vacancies existing at West Point, from the State of Mississippi. That State being in rebellion, he was desirous of filling these with six worthy young soldiers from his victorious armies. This work of selection was turned over to General Sherman. After a competitive examination at his headquarters, Charles L. Arnold was honored with the selection to represent the artillery branch of the service. These six selections were communicated to the entire army, in a general order, and they were instructed to get ready to go on a certain day. Meanwhile the names had been sent to President Lincoln, but it was discovered that only three vacancies existed instead of six, and the names were returned to Grant to select three from. He made the selection by shaking the names in his hat and taking the first three drawn. In the drawing poor Charley was left. General Sherman deprecated General Grant's method of selection, saying he would have chosen one from each branch of the service, infantry, cavalry and artillery, in which case Arnold would have been one. General Sherman was much interested in his case, and wrote Governor Yates asking for his appointment at West Point or some "kindred institution," which letter was probably lost, as it was never heard from. He served with the battery till the end of his term of enlistment, and was mustered out at Springfield in July, 1864, and returned to his home in Chicago. His business career since the war up to 1892 has been confined entirely to mercantile pursuits. Since the latter period he has dealt in real estate, mostly in his own property. Up to the great Chicago fire, Oct. 9, 1871, he had been employed by others as bookkeeper or cashier, except for a few months, when he was in partnership with his brother, in the commission business. Since the fire he has been in business, in various lines, both mercantile and manufacturing, on his own account, or associated with others in partnership or corporation, always in an active capacity as officer and director. The firm of Charles L. Arnold & Co., dealing in cheese and provisions on South Water street, existed for nine years, beginning Oct. 23, 1871, when he sold out and went West to take up a promising mining enterprise, becoming general manager. Associated with him in this were many prominent citizens of Chicago. Although he made money, the enterprise in the end did not meet expectations. He then organized a company to utilize an invention of his own (then new) of refining cotton seed oil and compounding lard. It required the formation of three separate companies to get into successful operation, the first two failing to carry out the contract, from no fault of his or his process. The product of the third company found a market in all parts of the civilized world to the extent of $1,500,000 in value per year for six years. This business, with a number of others, was in 1891 merged into the Columbia Oil Co., with a capitalization of $1,000,000, of which Charles L. Arnold was elected Vice President and Manager. Later the Illinois Trust and Savings Bank was made trustee of $400,000 of the company's bonds. Failure to float them, the strenuous opposition of the American Cotton Oil trust, and the financial storm then setting in all over the country forced the company into the hands of a receiver. He then turned his attention to real estate, considerable of which he had acquired in the meantime. His first efforts were very successful, but later, as the panic broke and money fought shy of real estate, it became a very serious proposition and, like many others, he is carrying a load that he wishes was not quite so heavy. He was happily married to Miss Eliza A. Rowan in 1865. They have had three children, one son and two daughters; one daughter died in 1873. He resides at his own home at 1227 Michigan avenue.

## ABBOTT L. ADAMS.

Abbott L. Adams is a native of Keene, N. H., where he was born April 20, 1842, and lived till ten years of age, when his parents came to Chicago, which has been his home since. He was a clerk when the war broke out, and with his brother George E. enlisted in the battery April 19, 1861, and served with the battery at Cairo, Ill., and in Northern Missouri till August 4, 1861, when he was mustered out, his term of enlistment having expired. He re-enlisted as private in Chicago Board of Trade Battery July 22, 1862, and served until the close of the war, in Kentucky, Tennessee, Georgia, Alabama and Mississippi in the Army of the Cumberland. Was wounded at the battle of Stone river December 31, 1862. Commissioned Second Lieutenant on June 22, 1865, and mustered out of the service July 3, 1865.

He has been in the mercantile business since the war, and has never been married.

## GEORGE EVERETT ADAMS.

Hon. Geo. E. Adams, of Chicago, was one of the original three months soldiers, and served that term with the battery. He was born in Keene, N. H., June 18, 1840, and lived there till 1853, when he came to Chicago, which has since been his home. He went East in 1854 to school and finished at Phillips Exeter Academy, entering Harvard in 1856, and graduated from there in 1860. He returned to Chicago and in 1861 was a law student with the well-known firm of Scammon, McCagg & Fuller. He enlisted as private in the battery with his brother, Abbott L., April 19, 1861. He was with the section of the battery that was sent from Cairo to St. Louis and Mexico, Mo., and was mustered out by reason of expiration of his term of enlistment Aug. 4, 1861. He taught school a year, then took a term in the Law School at Cambridge, after which he began the practice of law in Chicago, and has since successfully followed that profession. He is a public-spirited citizen, and has always taken an active interest in politics, and always has been a consistent and stanch Republican. He was elected to the State Senate in 1880, and to Congress in 1882, serving faithfully and creditably until 1891. He married Miss Adele Foster and has two daughters, Isabel and Margaret.

## OLOF BENSON.

In far away north of Europe, in the Kingdom of Sweden, where the long nights of winter linger, Olof Benson was born July 14, 1836. He came to America when fifteen years of age, and acquired the English language and a fair knowledge of our institutions, etc., in a printing office at Defiance, Ohio, where he remained until eighteen. While circulator of the weekly paper, the Defiance Democrat, he astonished the Democratic editor

GEORGE E. ADAMS.

one New Year's morning by distributing to the subscribers a New Year's address, in blank verse, composed and printed by himself, and brim full of "black Republican" sentiments, being inspired thereto by reading the story of "Uncle Tom's Cabin," then being published in the Washington National New Era. When nineteen he taught a public school in English in the backwoods near Defiance, Ohio. Here he demonstrated his fighting qualities by whipping a pupil nearly twice his size, for disobedience. This same boy, some ten years later, then a volunteer in the Sixty-eighth Ohio Infantry, visited our battery one day down in Alabama, inquired for Mr. Benson, thanked him for the whipping, and said it did him good, and helped to make a man of him. Comrade Benson thinks the reason so many great men came from Ohio is because they had the right kind of training at school. He came to Chicago when twenty, in the fall of 1856. His first work, prophetic of his future usefulness, was to assist in planting a large evergreen at the residence of the late S. S. Hayes, opposite Union Park, which was then a bare prairie. In 1857, the year of the money panic, being unable to obtain work in the printing business, he improved the opportunity to acquire a better education, and, entering the old Chicago High School, took a three years' course, graduating in 1860, in the same class with Albert G. Lane and other old-time Chicagoans. When the firing on Fort Sumter sounded the tocsin of civil war, none felt a keener interest in the issues at stake. Learning Sunday, April 21, 1861, that Battery "A" was at the armory, under orders to go to the front, without consultation with friends or previous preparation, he enlisted and went as he was, dressed in his Sunday clothes, with the boys, not one of whom he then knew. By his quiet, gentlemanly demeanor, and his earnest, patriotic zeal he was not long without friends, and soon acquired the friendship and esteem of the entire battery. He served with the battery three years and three months, participating in all its hardships, privations, battles, and glories, with the greatest interest and enthusiasm. Without personal ambition for distinction, he is proud of having had the privilege of serving his adopted country by being, as he terms it, a "high private in the rear rank." He was mustered out at the end of his term of enlistment, July 23, 1864, and, returning to Chicago, immediately took up the profession of landscape gardener, and has been identified with that business ever since. Many of the gardenesque improvements of the city and State are the production of his skill. He personally designed and superintended most of the improvements of Lincoln Park, of which he was superintendent and landscape gardener for seventeen years, from 1865 to 1882, working out the wonderful and artistic transformations of barren sand dunes and stretches of frog ponds as if by magic into wide-spreading grassy glades—broad floral terraces, and large, beautiful lakes, forming landscapes that have made Lincoln Park and Chicago fa-

OLOF BENSON.

mous all over the world. The improvements of the grounds at the Soldier's Home, Quincy, Ill., were also designed by Comrade Benson. He lives on the North Side, in Chicago, is married and has six grown-up children, two sons and four daughters, all born in Lincoln Park, of which he is justly proud, as he lived in the park during his connection with it.

## EDWARD BAGGOT.

Although serving but a short time in the battery, owing to poor health, the battery has always had a stanch and true friend, both during the war and ever since, in Edward Baggot. He enlisted and went to the front with the battery April 19, 1861. He was in the gun squad that fired the first shot in the war, that brought the steamer "Baltic" to land at Cairo. He was appointed gunner of squad 5, when he was taken sick and placed in the hospital. The surgeon in charge advised and ordered his discharge for disability, and he was sent home in June. He was born in Ireland Nov. 29, 1836, and lived on a farm near Limerick during his early childhood. He attended school at Ballangarry, and emigrated to the United States in 1853, and settled in Chicago. Here he learned the trade of plumbing and gasfitting with R. D. McFarland, who was one of the leading men in that business in Chicago at that time. After his discharge he returned to Chicago, and when he had recovered his health he engaged in the plumbing and gasfitting business and established a small business, and by untiring industry, push and enterprise laid the foundation for a large and prosperous institution, of which he is still the general manager. His son, James E. Baggot, is the able President of the company. They are the leading plumbers and gasfitters in Chicago, and have one of the largest and best-appointed establishments in the West, at 171 Adams street. Although he has been a workman and employer ever since he arrived at man's estate, he boasts that he never took part in a strike but once in his life, and that was during his short term of service with the battery. On our arrival at Cairo, while the Commissary Department was getting in working order, the battery boys were boarded at the St. Charles Hotel, where they lived high for two or three days. It was too good a thing to last long, so, when one day the tables were set in the back yard for the boys they all "struck." The rations, which were principally baked beans in large tin pans, were thrown up against the walls of the hotel and at one another. As is usually the case with strikers, they regretted their action later, as they went without rations for the next twenty-four hours. He was elected President and Treasurer of the Battery Veteran Association for several years, and has always taken an active interest in his old comrades. He is a prominent member of the Sheridan Club, has been twice married, and has four sons and four grandchildren.

EDWARD BAGGOT.

## HENRY E. BREWSTER.

Henry E. Brewster is a native of the "Nutmeg" State, having been born in Rockville, Conn., March 4, 1839. He came West to Illinois when thirteen years old and settled in Chicago at twenty-one. He was employed as a clerk in 1861 and left his position to enlist in the battery as private April 16. He with a number of others were mustered out at the end of the three months' term, on account of malaria, contracted during the service. He, with others of the boys, volunteered to man a gun for a short time at Camp Douglas, Chicago, standing guard over the rebel prisoners taken at Fort Donelson. He re-enlisted in January, 1864, in Company E, Waterhouse's Battery, and served until July 15, 1865, when he was mustered out by general order of the War Department. He has followed the occupations of bookkeeper, mechanic and artisan.

He was married in 1867 to Lucretia F. Oaks, of Bellows Falls, Vt., who died in June, 1897. He married Mrs. Sarah A. Nason for his second wife July 28, 1898, and now resides at Marlboro, N. H.

## JOHN PEMBER BROWN.

Among the survivors of the battery who located in the Golden State is John P. Brown, now of Florin, California. He was born April 13, 1839, in Sodus, N. Y. His family moved to Milan, Ohio, where his mother died. After the death of his mother he went on a sailing vessel. In 1850 he went to Chicago and was apprenticed as a sailmaker to Gilbert Hubbard & Co. He served his time with that firm and was working for them when he enlisted, April 19, 1861. He re-enlisted in the United States service July 28, 1861, enlisting as private, but after the battle of Fort Donelson was made artificer for the company. He served with the battery till the battle of Vicksburg, and was discharged March 10, 1863, for disability, which consisted of a fracture of the left humerus, and three ribs and both legs broken at the knee. He returned to Chicago and, after recovering sufficiently, followed expressing for ten years, when he moved to his present home and engaged in farming and fruit growing on a farm of thirty acres, which he owns. He was united in marriage to Miss Katherine Gerhart in 1869. They have had four children, only two of whom survive.

## WILLIAM H. BAILEY.

The city of "Brotherly Love" is claimed by Comrade Wm. H. Bailey as his place of nativity. He was born in the city of Philadelphia, December 19, 1840, but removed to Baltimore at an early age. Here his childhood and youth were spent in the way usual to city children and obtaining a common school education. At the age of fifteen he removed with his parents to

HENRY E. BREWSTER.

Chicago, where in due time he was apprenticed to the trade of painter, which he was following at the time of his enlistment as private in Battery "A," in Chicago, April 19, 1861. Near the close of his three months' service at Cairo he was severely injured by being run over by a gun carriage while on drill. He was discharged with that portion of the company not re-enlisting for three years. Having fully recovered from his injury in August, 1862, he re-enlisted in the same company, serving with it and participating in all its engagements until the close of the war, in July, 1865. Joining the Chicago Fire Department on his return home, he served two years in that organization. He then obtained a position in the Chicago Post Office, and continued there until 1886, when he was taken with the Western fever and went to the Black Hills, in Dakota. Not realizing his expectations in this move, he returned to Chicago and again secured a position in the Post Office, where he is still engaged. He married Miss Kate Smith, daughter of one of the early settlers of Chicago, in 1867. His family consists of seven children and one grandchild.

## CHARLES CALVIN BRIGGS.

The city of Auburn, on the Androscoggin, in the far east State of Maine, is the native place of Charles C. Briggs. He was born Sept. 24, 1840. His childhood and youth were spent at home and at school until sixteen years of age, when he went to sea. He afterwards drifted to the West, and located in Chicago. In the spring of 1861 he was salesman for the extensive iron firm of Hale & Ayer. He enlisted in the battery in Chicago April 19, 1861, and was appointed first sergeant. He served with the battery until January, 1862, when he was mustered out for promotion in the navy, which he received as Master's Mate. Subsequently he was promoted to Acting Ensign, with battery at Fort Henry, Fort Donelson, Shiloh and Chickasaw Bayou. He resigned from the navy on account of disability, and received his final discharge March 31, 1865. Since the war he has been engaged continuously in the iron and steel trade, and for the past twenty-six years has been with "The Jones & Laughlins, Limited," and located at Pittsburg, Pa., where he resides. He married Miss Mary Gerry, by whom he has had six children.

## GEORGE M. BROWN.

At least one prominent citizen and native of the "Buckeye" State can plead "not guilty" to the charge of having assisted that State to gain the reputation with which she is credited by all the newspaper paragraphers of scrambling for the Presidential nomination at every Republican convention since Lincoln's time. Not that Ohio need to be ashamed of her Presidential

JOHN P. BROWN.

sons in the persons of Grant, Hayes, Garfield and McKinley, but this statement is made to prove that all her influential citizens are not grasping for the highest political honors, as they are so generally accused of doing. George M. Brown was born on a farm in Conneaut, Ohio, Feb. 24, 1830, and, except at short intervals, that city has been and still is his home. He was clerking in the commission house of Allen Howes, on South Water street, Chicago, in the spring of 1861, and left his position to enlist as "high private" and corporal in Battery "A," April 17, 1861. He served three years and three months with the battery, was in every front line and every fight or skirmish in which the battery was engaged. He has successfully followed the hotel, mail service and mining business, and is now engaged in banking, being President of the Conneaut Mutual Loan Association. It is sad to say Comrade Brown has never married, nor applied for a pension. He has never regretted his army experience. He is proud of his service and record, as well he may be. He made many a telling shot with a 10-pound Parrott gun, also with a 30-pounder. His squad, with himself and Capt. Wood, had a miraculous escape from utter annihilation at the siege of Jackson, Miss., as noted elsewhere in this history. He had the honor and credit of stopping the steamer Vicksburg from escaping down the river from Vicksburg one night, which he did with his 30-pound Parrot. He also made a shot at Jackson, Miss., with a 10-pounder which knocked the trunnions off a 64-pound columbiad of the enemy. He is in the enjoyment of good health and a comfortable competence, and has the best wishes of all his old comrades for their continuance.

## MARTIN A. BARTLESON.

That the so-called "wild and woolly West" allured many of the veterans of the war at its close is a well-known fact. Battery "A" furnished its full share of citizens for the far West, prominent among whom is the subject of this sketch. Martin A. Bartleson. He was born in Macomb, Ill., July 16, 1842, and lived at home, attending to the ordinary vocations of youth, until the spring of 1860, when he went to the Pike's Peak gold regions, where he remained till late in the autumn of the same year, when he returned, and shortly after went to Chicago, where he was living when the war broke out, attending Commercial College. He enlisted in the battery as private "in the front rank" April 19, 1861, and served with the battery continuously and faithfully till mustered out at the end of his three years' enlistment, at Springfield, Ill., July 23, 1864. He was appointed corporal by Captain Wood April 1, 1864. He returned to Chicago soon after his discharge from the army, and was engaged in railroading for several years. He then took a course at the Medical and Dental College of St. Louis, and after graduating went to Denver, Colo., and Santa Fe, New Mexico. From

WILLIAM H. BAILEY.

1881 to 1888 he spent most of the time in San Francisco, New York, London and Paris, and then returned to Denver, where he remained until 1895, practicing his profession. He then went to Chicago and engaged in a manufacturing business. In 1896 he met with a severe accident in his factory, which very nearly resulted fatally, and from the effects of which he is still a sufferer to a greater or less extent. His mishap was a fall of several stories through an open elevator shaft, landing on top of the cage, breaking his left arm and shoulder and dislocating his hip and knee. He will never fully recover from the injuries sustained. He was elected President of the Battery Veteran Association at its annual reunion in September, 1896. His injury occurred soon after and he has not been able to attend any of its meetings since. He is now engaged in mining, and has interests in mines in Arizona and Sonora, Mexico, with fair prospects ahead, which all his old comrades hope will materialize. He was married March 6, 1866, at Utica, N. Y., to Miss Abbie N. Ray, a niece of Hon. W. H. Ray, Congressman from Illinois. They have no children.

### JEROME PATTERSON BRIGGS.

Jerome P. Briggs, a popular member of the battery, now deceased, was born in Ogdensburg, New York, Aug. 15, 1841. He lived there, attending school, till thirteen years old. He then came to Chicago with his parents. He learned the trade of painter and glazier, and was so engaged when he enlisted in the battery on the first call for troops April 19, 1861. He served as postillion till mustered out at the end of his term of enlistment, July 23, 1864, and returned to Chicago. He had a beautiful gray team of horses, of which he was very proud, and which received his most careful attention. He had a narrow escape from being killed at one time, when he received a kick from his favorite horse, between the eyes and on the forehead. This was the only injury he received during his service. After the war he entered the employment of Mr. Hathaway, an old resident and prominent citizen of Chicago, and went with him to Texas to buy cattle. He died of yellow fever at Galveston in April, 1872. His mother and sister, and brothers, Harvey D. Briggs and Wm. C. Briggs, reside in Chicago.

### SAMUEL WILLIAM BUTTERFIELD.

A bright and honored light went out from the ranks of Battery "A" survivors when Samuel W. Butterfield passed away at his pleasant home, 296 Elm street, Chicago, April 7, 1887. He was born in Cleveland, Ohio, July 7, 1838. His parents both died in that city, where he lived and attended school until he grew to a young man. He worked for a while in his native city in a drug store. He came to Chicago and changed his business, engaging with the Putnam clothing store, where he was employed at the

CHARLES C. BRIGGS.

breaking out of the war. He enlisted as private in the battery in Chicago, July 28, 1861. He was not naturally of strong physique, and the rigors of camp life proved too severe for his slender constitution, and, though the spirit was more than willing, he was reluctantly obliged to accept a discharge for disability in the spring of 1862. Returning to Chicago he again took up the clothing business as soon as he was sufficiently recovered, and was in the employ of Browning, King & Co., one of the largest retail clothing houses in the city, up to the time of his last sickness. For many years he was one of their most reliable and trustworthy employes. He did not forget his comrades in the field, and while the war lasted was ever active in looking after the sick and wounded who were sent home to recover. He was one of the principal movers in the work of erecting our battery monument in Rose Hill Cemetery. He married Miss Alice M. Eames, of South Farmingham, Mass. She was a devoted and faithful wife, caring tenderly for her delicate husband, but no care or nursing could prolong his life. He died beloved and respected by all who had the good fortune to know him. He never had any children. His widow still lives in the comfortable home which, by his industry and frugality, with the help of his faithful wife, he had acquired a few years before his death. His remains were laid to rest in Graceland Cemetery.

## HENRY BURDICK.

One of the youngest members of the battery was Henry Burdick. He was born on a farm in Richmond, McHenry County, Illinois, in 1845, where he lived, attending the district schools and working on the farm, till his enlistment in the battery July 11, 1862. His father had enlisted in the battery several months before, and had left the farm in charge of Henry, but he was young and full of patriotism, and his restlessness could only be quieted by joining the ranks of the army, so he naturally came to the battery with his father, who felt that it would be useless to oppose his enlistment when he was determined to enlist, and felt that it was better to have him with him than to be among strangers in some other command. Although among the youngest he was also among the best and bravest, if there could be any distinction, and served with credit until mustered out with the company at the close of the war in July, 1865, with rank of private. He returned home after the war and followed the trade of brick-making for sixteen years. He then took up carriage painting, and is still working at that business in Woodstock, Ill. He married Mrs. Anna G. Hughes in 1894 and has four children by a former marriage and seven grandchildren. Those who have not seen him since the war will find it hard to recognize the beardless boy in the bewhiskered veteran seen in his picture, but a strong resemblance to the father is apparent.

GEORGE M. BROWN.

## JACOB CLINGMAN.

Jacob Clingman was born in Centre County, Pennsylvania, in April, 1838. His early years were spent in the place of his birth, but for the greater portion of his life Chicago was his home. When the war broke out he was engaged in the clothing business with his brother William. They were one of the leading firms in that line at that time. He threw up a good position to answer his country's first call for men, and enlisted in the battery, April 19, 1861, re-enlisted July 16, 1861, and served the full term of his enlistment, three years and three months, with rank of first sergeant, and was mustered out July 23, 1864. He was in every engagement and skirmish, and took part in every march with the battery during his service. He was always ready for any duty, and never flinched or faltered in performing it. He was never wounded, but his hearing was very much impaired by the frequent concussions of his gun during some of the heavy engagements. After the war he returned home and engaged in the grocery business, which he followed up to the time of his death, which took place Dec. 3, 1888. He was buried in Rose Hill Cemetery, many of his old comrades assisting in the last sad rites. He was married to Miss Mary Whitney, who survives him, and now lives at Wilmette, Ill. They had a daughter and one grandson.

## EDWIN D. CLARK.

Another comrade is missing; he will answer no more at roll call. Edwin D. Clark, who went to the front as one of the first to aid in defense of his country's flag, and to put down an uncalled for and unholy rebellion, departed this life at his late home in Chicago, on Feb. 15, 1895, after an illness of several weeks. He was born in Greenfield, Mass., Nov. 16, 1833, and was an only son. He came West in 1854, and settled at Richmond, Ill., a year or two previous to the breaking out of the war. In December, 1860, he married Miss Henrietta L. Boutelle, of Richmond, Ill. His occupation in 1861 was that of sailor on the lakes, with headquarters at Chicago. On the 12th of October, 1861, he bade good-by to his young wife and joined Battery "A," First Illinois Light Artillery, then in the field. When he reached his command at Paducah, Ky., he found it preparing for active service, so that from the time of his first entrance into the army his life as a soldier was one of exposure, hardship and peril. He took an active part in all the work of the battery during his connection with it. On the 22d of July, 1863, while in the line of duty near Jackson, Miss., he, with ten of his comrades, was taken prisoner, but succeeded in making his escape, and was the first to return from the expedition to report the capture of nine of his comrades. Again, the 22d of July, 1863, in the battle of Atlanta, Ga., he, with several others

MARTIN A. BARTLESON.

of the battery, was surrounded by the enemy, and again fortunately made his escape. In this battle he had command of a section of the battery, which he handled with great courage and skill. He was one of the coolest and bravest men in action, and was always to be found where duty called him. He participated in eighteen battles and numerous skirmishes, marching thousands of miles, never complaining or wavering, but nobly performing his duties as a private, and later as a sergeant in charge of a gun and caisson. His comrades knew and appreciated his true worth, whether in battle, on the march, in camp or bivouac. Of those who went with him from McHenry County but one, Wm. H. Cowlin, survives. He was mustered out Oct. 12, 1864, at the expiration of his term of enlistment. Though he passed all through the war uninjured, he lost an arm July 4, 1871, while assisting to fire a national salute, by the premature discharge of a gun. He was employed at Lincoln Park for many years as clerk and bookkeeper. His widow survives him and lives in Chicago. He left two children, a son, Walter R., and daughter, Cora E. Clark. Walter served a short term as assistant engineer on board the United States steamer "Bennington" during the late Spanish war. Comrade Clark was an honored member of the Masonic order, A. O. U. W., G. A. R., and the Chicago Union Veteran Club. Members of the orders to which he belonged escorted his remains to Richmond, Ill., where they were laid to rest.

## JOHN HENRY CLARKE.

One of the survivors of six months' rebel imprisonment, along with a term of hard, active service in the battery, was John H. Clarke. He was among the foraging party that was captured at Jackson, Miss., and endured with the others the suffering and hardships of six months of captivity, so vividly portrayed in another chapter, by Comrade W. H. Young, one of the number. He was born at Mt. Jackson, Pa., July 8, 1844. His childhood and youth were mostly spent in the town of New Castle, Pa., and his early education was acquired in the public schools there. When the war broke out he was living on a farm with his uncle, Dr. Frank Henry, near Areola, Ill., from which place he enlisted in the battery in the fall of 1861, as private. He was mustered out at the end of his term of enlistment, Oct. 11, 1864. At the siege of Atlanta, some five days after his term of enlistment had expired, he lost his left arm near the shoulder. After the close of the war he remained in the South, and filled the responsible position of superintendent of the Glen Mary coal mines in Tennessee. On Jan. 5, 1890, he met with an accidental death at Glen Mary, being killed by a runaway team. He was married to Miss M. E. Logan, who survives him, and lives at Poland, Ohio, to which place his remains were brought and buried. They had no children.

JEROME P. BRIGGS.

## CHARLES EDWIN CLARK.

The first eleven years of the life of C. E. Clark were spent in Boston, the city of his birth. He was born Jan. 13, 1843. He came to Chicago in his twelfth year, and that city has since been his home. He was working at his trade, that of painter, when the war broke out. He enlisted in the battery, as private, in Chicago, in July, 1861, and served till the expiration of his term of service, being mustered out in July, 1864. He worked in various public offices in Chicago until nine years ago, when his health gave out, and he has been in poor health since, and is now at the Hospital for Consumptives, at Dunning, Ill. He has never married. The long years of his sickness exhausted his accumulated earnings, and his only income now is that received from the government in his pension, with which Uncle Sam remembers his disabled defenders to a greater or less degree.

## NATHAN THOMAS COX.

One of the three members of the battery, who for many years was reported on the Veteran Association records as "dead," but afterwards turned up as "a very lively corpse," as the boys used to say in the army, was Comrade Nathan T. Cox, who is now living in Denver, Colo., which has been his home for the last eight years. He was born Jan. 6, 1840, on a farm in Adams County, Illinois, ten miles from Quincy. His childhood and youth were spent on the farm working from early spring till late fall, and going to the primitive country schools during the winter. His father died when he was about twelve years old, and his mother died about four years later. They were poor, the farm was sold, and the family scattered. He worked among the neighboring farmers for a while, and finally attended a Methodist seminary at Quincy a couple of terms. In the fall of 1860 he went to Chicago and found work in a restaurant, and became acquainted with Frank Greene, a photographer, a brother of Comrade W. C. Greene, and went with him to learn the trade, and consequently was enlisted as an "artist" by occupation. While working for Greene, the Presidential election occurred, and he cast his first vote for Abraham Lincoln, when he lacked two months of being of age. He enlisted as private in the battery April 16, 1861, and served three months at Cairo, "drilling, log-rolling, cleaning drill ground, fighting mosquitoes and malaria." When he enlisted he thought it was for the war, but when three months were up he discovered his time was also up, and on July 16 he re-enlisted with the company for three years. He was one of the expedition that went to Mexico, Mo., returning to Cairo shortly before our departure from that place to occupy Paducah, Ky. At Paducah he was taken sick with typhoid pneumonia, and was in the hospital there until discharged for disability Jan. 28, 1862. After his discharge he returned to Adams and Pike Counties, where his relatives lived. After regaining suffi-

SAMUEL W. BUTTERFIELD.

cient strength to work, he again went to farming, which he followed until he moved to Denver, having lived in Illinois, Missouri and Colorado. He was married to Miss Mary A. Keel Feb. 15, 1863, and she has been his faithful partner and helpmeet ever since. Her guiding star has been duty to home and friends, and she has been an active and earnest worker in the Woman's Relief Corps ranks. They have three sons and one married daughter, living on a homestead in Northern Nebraska. They have two grandchildren. When he went to Denver he lived in Barnum, one of the suburbs, and was Town Clerk of that suburb nearly two years, when it became a part of the city of Denver. Then he took up shoemaking and cobbling until June, 1898, when he was appointed Assistant Adjutant General of the G. A. R., Department of Colorado and Wyoming. His time will expire this spring. He does not expect a reappointment. He is "poor but honest," and has no income except a $6 per month pension and what he earns, but coming of righteous parents, and profiting by their precepts and example, he believes in a sure promise for the future.

## HORACE W. CHASE.

No member of Battery "A" enjoyed to a greater extent the confidence and esteem of his comrades in arms than Horace W. Chase. He was born July 1, 1835, in Hunter, Green County, N. Y., and was there reared and educated, receiving during youth a fair knowledge of the lumber business in the yards and mills of his father, Charles Chase. His ancestors were from Massachusetts, of an old colonial family. He came to Chicago and was tendered the position of foreman in the lumber yards of Larned & Chase, the junior member of the firm being the elder brother of Horace W. He accepted the responsible position and at once entered upon his duties and thus continued until 1861, faithfully discharging his duties and acquiring much practical knowledge of the lumber trade in the bustling and enterprising market of Chicago. In fact, the foundation of his knowledge of the lumber business was gained during this period, though the ripening and fruiting seasons of his energetic life were yet to come. When the government was plunged into war and all patriotic men were urged to come forward and maintain the Union of the States, the stirring call met with a quick, responsive answer from Horace, and April 19, 1861, he promptly tendered his services as a private, and enlisted in Company "A," Chicago Light Artillery, served three months, then he re-enlisted for three years and served with his command until July 16, 1864, when he was mustered out at Springfield, Ill., and honorably discharged from the service. He served in all the engagements of the battery and filled the important position of Commissary of the company all through the service, in a highly creditable and satisfactory manner. He at once returned to Chicago after receiving

HENRY BURDICK

his discharge, and purchased a small interest in the lumber firm of Howard & Chase, at the same time assuming the duties of a responsible position with the firm, for which he drew a salary until 1867, when he became the junior member of the firm of D. F. Chase & Brother, with yards at Halsted street bridge. A strong, yet safe and conservative business was conducted by the brothers from 1867 to 1872, when D. F. Chase withdrew from the firm and D. S. Pate was admitted as a partner, and the style of the company became Chase & Pate. May 1, 1892, Mr. Chase withdrew from the firm and retired from active business. He was one of Chicago's most public-spirited citizens, and heartily co-operated in all undertakings that were for the good of the city, and especially of his old comrades of the Battery Association. Mr. Chase was a man of simple tastes and domestic habits, warm-hearted and generous, enjoying his family and home. His life was full of earnest and valuable exertion, and it seems to all who knew him to be a strange dispensation of Providence that he should have endured three years and three months of the dangers, privations and exposure of army life unscathed, and passed through thirty-two years of active and successful business life, with the brightest prospects for a comfortable and pleasant old age, to be stricken down suddenly, as he was, from a malignant carbuncle on the neck, attacking the brain. Death claimed him Sept. 6, 1896, after an illness of but a week. He resided in a pleasant and commodious home at 3226 South Park avenue, and attended Rev. Dr. Thomas' People's Church. He was a Master Mason, was a staunch Republican, a member of Geo. H. Thomas Post, No. 5, G. A. R., and belonged to Battery "A" Veteran Association, of which he was and had been Treasurer for many years. He was also President of the "Cairo Expedition Survivors' Association." He was first married in 1872 to Mrs. Elizabeth Tebbetts, by whom he had two children, Volney H. and Eleanor E. His wife died Oct. 23, 1883. In March, 1885, he wedded Miss Anna L. Odlin, a native of Dayton, Ohio, who, with the two children, survive him. His funeral was largely attended by his business associates, friends and old army comrades. In his death the city lost one of her most valuable citizens, his family a kind protector, husband and father, and his memory will always be cherished by those who knew him well.

## MORRIS A. CHITTENDEN.

Morris A. Chittenden was born Feb. 8, 1841, at Carthage, N. Y., where he lived till 1855, when he moved with his parents to Park Ridge, Ill., a suburb of Chicago. After his school days were over he served his time with his father at the cooper's trade. He was working as a carpenter and builder at the breaking out of the war. He enlisted as private in the battery at Chicago the latter part of June, 1861, and was mustered into the three years' service the 16th of July following. He served his full time, first as can-

JACOB CLINGMAN.

nonier, then as postillion, and was mustered out at Springfield, Ill., July 25, 1864. He, with Harry Spaulding, was one of the boys that helped to save squad two's gun and get it off the field at Shiloh, amidst a hot fire of musketry at close range. After his discharge from the army he followed the trade of carpenter and builder till April, 1889, when, losing the sight of his right eye from the effects of an accidental shot in the forehead at Memphis, when Wm. Kirk discharged the gun loaded with canister in the camp by mistake. He was in danger of losing the other eye, and was obliged to give up work requiring its steady, close use. He moved to Kansas and located on a small fruit and vegetable farm three miles southwest of Atchison, where he still lives. He married Miss Emma J. Dunphey, of Chicago, June 16, 1867, and has four children; two boys and two girls, and they are living a life of quiet and contentment in their comfortable Western home.

## WILLIAM H. COWLIN.

The city of Tiverton, Devonshire, England, is the native place of William H. Cowlin, one of the youngest and most esteemed members of the battery. He was born Nov. 19, 1844, and lived in his native city until ten years of age. He then came with his parents to America, who settled in Chicago, where they resided for three years. He attended the public schools a portion of this time. From Chicago the family moved to Franklinville, Ill., where William H. partly learned the shoemaker's trade with his father. When he was fifteen years of age he started out for himself and began clerking in a boot and shoe store in Woodstock, at which he was engaged at the breaking out of the war. Though but a little over seventeen years old, he enlisted in the battery at Woodstock, Feb. 3, 1862. He was with the battery from the time of his enlistment until taken prisoner at Atlanta, Ga., in July, 1864. Until that time he was never absent a day, nor in hospital a moment, and was in every engagement and skirmish, as cannonier, being No. 3 in squad 6, with the exception of during the battle of Shiloh, when he was put into squad 4 and given the position of No. 2, which he filled till the close of that battle, having never drilled with the battery but twice before. When captured at Atlanta he, with seventeen other comrades, was taken to Andersonville prison. He was reported as badly wounded. While fourteen of those taken prisoner with him were exchanged in less than six weeks, he, with Thomas Wilcox, of the battery, was held a prisoner in Andersonville and other rebel prisons till the close of the war. He was discharged to date from June 12, 1865, by order of the War Department mustering out all who had been prisoners of war, but he was not furnished with his discharge, and was still in the service till August 5, 1865. For about six months after his discharge he was an invalid from the effects of his prison

ED. D. CLARK.

life. He then engaged in the grocery business with a partner, and was doing well, but on account of continued ill health he was obliged to give it up and sell out his interest. He was confined to his home for three months, and, when able, engaged in the photograph business with a practical photographer for a partner, at Jefferson, Wis. His poor health continued, and in less than a year he was forced to give it up. Returning to Woodstock in 1869, he established himself in the boot and shoe business in that city, and, with partners, continued it for twelve years, doing an extensive and prosperous business. During the last three years he was in the firm he sold goods on the road for the extensive boot and shoe firm of Selz, Schwab & Co., of Chicago, his territory embracing Northern Illinois and several counties in Southern Wisconsin. He had never recovered his health and was compelled to quit traveling and close out his interest in the store. For nearly two years he was confined to his home, much of the time bedridden. While still an invalid his wife, whom he married in October, 1869, died, after an illness of several months. She was Miss Susan M. Whitson, a sister of Comrade Oscar Whitson, of our battery. Three sons were left him by this marriage, two of whom are married. He has four grandchildren. His youngest son, Oscar, served in Company "G," Third Illinois Infantry, all through the late war with Spain. That he is a "chip of the old block," or, more elegantly speaking, a "worthy son of a noble sire," will be seen when it can be said of him he was never absent from his command nor sick a day during his more than eight months' service, several months of which were spent in Porto Rico.

The condition of Comrade Cowlin's health convinced him that he could never again take up active work or business requiring any physical exertion, and, being determined to do something to occupy his time, and help support his family, he began studying the pension laws, and those pertaining to other government business, and in less than two years was admitted to practice in all the government bureaus in Washington. He has been very successful in this profession, and has worked up an extensive business, reaching into nearly every State in the Union, although his old disability, contracted at Andersonville, still clings to him, and at different times has nearly cost him his life. His office is at his residence, and has been since engaging in the pension business, and it is well known, far and near, as "Wm. H. Cowlin's War Claim Agency." Sept. 30, 1888, he married a second time to Eliza Boutelle, of Kensett, Iowa, a cousin of his first wife. They have one daughter, four years old.

He takes a deep interest in Grand Army matters, and has ably and vigorously conducted the "Veterans' Column" in the Woodstock Sentinel, the leading Republican newspaper of McHenry County, for fifteen years, a voluntary task, which few in his physical condition would care to assume.

NATHAN T. COX.

## JOHN T. CONNELL.

The light of day first shone upon the eyes of John T. Connell, at Watertown, N. Y., Dec. 1, 1832. After obtaining a school education he began clerking in a store, and continued until 1854, when he went to Chicago and worked as shipping clerk for A. T. Spencer & Co. (Western Transportation Co.). He was working for I. J. Rice in the spring of 1861, and was down town after goods when the news came of the assault on the Massachusetts troops in Baltimore, and was one of the first to enlist in old Battery "A" when the roll was opened. He served three months, then re-enlisted July 16, 1861, for three years. He was with the battery in every engagement while he was in the service, including the famous "Calloway March," mentioned in the history. He, with Church, Hoffman and Young, while in camp at Paducah, built a comfortable brick house for their squad, Connell acting as boss bricklayer, while the others mixed the mortar and carried the hod. They had no more than settled themselves in their new quarters, prepared to take comfort, when camp was broken up and we took the field for Forts Henry, Heiman, Donelson, etc. During the engagement at Fort Donelson, Moses Hawks, who was thumbing on the same gun with Connell, was hit on the arm with a spent ball and disabled. Connell took his place during the remainder of the engagement. They were using double charges of canister with telling effect. Connell suggested to Captain Wood that their canister would not last much longer, and he ordered a shrapnel and canister for each load, with fuse of shrapnel cut close. Toward the last of the fight they ceased firing for a moment. When orders were given for action, Fred Church sang out, "Load!" John Steele, No. 1, replied, "There is a charge in." Church thought he said, "They are charging us," and answered "Let them charge and be d——; load." So down went another charge, and the result of firing this triple charge was a graceful somersault by most of the gun squad, and Comrade Connell has been totally deaf in his right ear ever since, and he is quite hard of hearing with his left. When the battery reached Memphis, General J. D. Webster was appointed commander of the post. He sent an order for Comrade Connell to come to his headquarters, and appointed him his private secretary, which position he held until General Webster was superseded by General Hovey. He continued with General Hovey until Colonel D. C. Anthony was appointed Provost Marshal, and he was his deputy until the battery had orders to move, first on the Coldwater expedition, and down the Mississippi later. Connell left the office without orders, and with a good horse rode after, caught up with and joined the battery. On the return of the battery to Memphis from the expedition he returned to the office, but made frequent visits to the battery camp. The battery boys had all doors of the Provost Marshal's office open to them while Comrade Connell was in charge, and none of them abused the privi-

HORACE W. CHASE.

lege. When the battery went up to Arkansas Post Comrade Connell was in no condition for hard service, and Captain Wood ordered him to remain on the boat, but when the last caisson went off the boat he was on it and took part in the fight the next day. At Vicksburg he had charge of the detail that was sent to the landing to get the guns of a new battery that were assigned to our company by General Sherman, and bring them into camp. After being mustered out as corporal at Springfield, Ill., his three years' enlistment having expired, he visited a short time in Chicago, then went to his old home in New York, intending to return to Chicago, but was persuaded by his parents, brothers and sisters to remain, which he did, until 1884. During this time he was engaged in a store, in insurance business, and on the road six years selling dry goods, etc. In 1884 he came West, and has resided at Grand Island, Neb., since, and has been engaged in the grocery and real estate business. He married Miss Gertrude Horr, in Carthage, N. Y., Jan. 9, 1866. They have no children. Mrs. Connell is an active worker in the Woman's Relief Corps in the State of Nebraska. She has served as Department Treasurer four years, Department Secretary one year, and Department President one year. Deputy Counselor one year and member of National Executive Board one year, a worthy helpmeet to a noble, patriotic husband.

## THADDEUS STEVENS CLARKSON.

One of the most esteemed members of Battery "A" is Thaddeus S. Clarkson. He was born at Gettysburg, Pa., April 26, 1840. When eight years old he moved to near Antietam, Md. He was educated at College of St. James, Washington County, Md., near Antietam, graduating in 1857, when he moved to Chicago, and became a resident of the future great city of the United States. He was clerking in a commission house at the breaking out of the war, but threw up his position and enlisted in Battery "A," April 16, 1861, in which battery he served as private, corporal and sergeant, re-enlisting July 16, 1861, for three years. Dec. 1, 1861, he was honorably discharged to accept a commission as First Lieutenant and Adjutant in the Thirteenth Illinois Cavalry. He was promoted in November, 1863, to Major of the Third Arkansas Cavalry, and resigned in December, 1864. Since the close of the war he has been in active business in Nebraska. He was appointed postmaster at Omaha by President Harrison, and served very acceptably from 1890 to 1895. Genial, warm-hearted and brave, he naturally takes a great interest in his old comrades, and the Grand Army of the the Republic. He was Department Commander of Nebraska in 1890, Junior Vice Commander-in-chief in 1891, and was elected Commander-in-chief at the St. Paul, Minn., National Encampment, in September, 1896, serving until September, 1897. In all these positions he showed remarkable

MORRIS A. CHITTENDEN.

executive ability, and when the Trans-Mississippi and International Exposition was organized in 1898 he was chosen as General Manager, the exposition continuing from June to November. He was married Nov. 11, 1862, at Chicago, Ill., to Mary B. Matteson, and they live with one son in Omaha, Neb. They have three daughters and five grandchildren. He is in the enjoyment of perfect health, and a long life of happiness and prosperity is wished for him by all his old comrades and associates.

## JAMES F. CROCKER.

One of the "older boys" of the battery is James F. Crocker, a native of Massachusetts, and who is now an inmate of the new Soldier's Home at Danville, Ill. He was born in Nantucket, Oct. 1, 1829, where he lived until eleven years old, when he moved with his father to Cayuga County, New York, where he had purchased a farm. He lived at home, working summers and attending the district school winters, until eighteen years of age. He was then apprenticed to learn the carpenter trade, at which he was working when the war broke out. He enlisted in the battery as private, in August, 1861, at Cairo, having first served three months in the Twelfth Illinois Infantry, and remained with it until the expiration of his term of enlistment in August, 1864. He worked at his trade after the war, when, losing his wife and becoming broken down in health, he went to the Soldier's Home in Milwaukee, where he remained until the opening of the new home at Danville. He has a grown son and daughter living. Through a similarity in names, Comrade Crocker was reported by the authorities of the Soldiers' Home at Quincy, Ill., as dead, and suitable memorial resolutions were passed by our Veteran Association, but he turned up alive and well.

## GEORGE COOPER.

George Cooper was born at Olcott, near Lockport, N. Y., in 1834. He lived in his native town till nine years of age. His father was then elected Sheriff of Niagara County, and moved to Lockport. After his father's term of office expired, he purchased and moved onto a farm, and George worked on the farm summers and attended school winters. After a few years of farming his father sold the farm and again moved to Lockport and engaged in the grocery business. George clerked for his father till he came West, settling in Chicago, entering the service of Long John Wentworth, with whom he was engaged at the breaking out of the war. He enlisted in Battery "A" April 21, 1861, and served three months, when he was mustered out. He was a popular bailiff in the Cook County courts for many years. He died in Chicago, Dec. 17, 1887. He married Miss Romelia Sanders, June 28, 1866, who survives him.

WILLIAM H. COWLIN.

## ENOCH COLBY, JR.

The subject of this sketch is one of the most reliable and well-known members of the battery. He was born in Camptonville, N. H., Dec. 6, 1840, where he lived till May, 1854, when his father moved with his family to Port Hope, Canada West, remaining there one year, during which time Enoch worked with his father building railroad bridges. In May, 1855, the family came to Illinois, where they have since lived. He was working on a farm at Arcola when the war broke out, and enlisted as private in the battery at Cairo, Aug. 1, 1861. He re-enlisted as veteran volunteer at Bellfont, Ala., Jan. 1, 1864, was appointed quartermaster sergeant in July following. In September he was promoted to Second Lieutenant in the battery, and in May, 1865, was made First Lieutenant. He has a record of service of which any old soldier might well be proud. He never missed a march, skirmish or battle in which the battery took part from his enlistment to the close of the war, was never wounded or sick, nor an hour in hospital, during his entire service. He was mustered out in Chicago at the close of the war, July 10, 1865. He married Miss Amelia A. Hawley April 2, 1865, while home on veteran furlough, and they now live in a snug, comfortable home at 64 37th street, Chicago. They have no children, and, as he says, "never had any, therefore have no grandchildren." He has been principally engaged in the grain business since the war, as foreman of elevators, buying grain, etc., and for ten years prior to 1893 was State Grain Inspector in Chicago.

## JOHN D. DYER.

Very few of the members were born south of Mason and Dixon's line. Prominent among those that were is John D. Dyer. He was born in Springfield, Ky., April 25, 1838, and lived there till thirteen years old, when he went to Newport, R. I., where he remained at school four years, and came to Chicago in 1855, which city has since been his home, excepting a few years spent in DeKalb County. He enlisted April 19, 1861, in Chicago, and re-enlisted July 16, 1861, for three years. He had the lead team on the caisson of squad one for the entire latter term, and he is justly proud of his service, which was always promptly and fearlessly performed. He was mustered out at the end of his term of enlistment July 23, 1864. He was married to Miss Abbie E. Wood, of DeKalb County, in November, 1867. They have two sons, George W. and William H., worthy and industrious young men, who are now engaged in the market and grocery business with their father at 1267 East Ravenswood Park, Chicago. At the close of the war John was check clerk for six months in the city, for the American Express Company, then was messenger on the road for the same company five years, was salesman for A. M. Thomson, Western Coffee Mills, about four years, and on a farm

JOHN T. CONNELL.

in DeKalb County, and in a market at Sycamore ten years. He is hale and hearty, and enjoys the companionship of his old comrades as well as he did in the old war days, and is an active member in the Battery Veteran Association.

## JAMES M. DUSENBERRY.

James M. Dusenberry is a native of of Michigan, and was born in 1840. He came West when a child, and lived on a farm at Waukegan, Ill., and attended the academy there until about fourteen years of age, when he went into the grocery business, and continued in it until 1861. The war fever growing strong, and having an opportunity to dispose of his store, he sold out and enlisted in the three months' service in Captain Ennis' Infantry Company, at Waukegan. The company was sent to Springfield, Ill., where he was appointed orderly sergeant, and was sergeant of the guard at the arsenal during the three months' service. He then enlisted in the battery, serving three years, holding every position on the gun, and was mustered out after the fight at Atlanta, at the expiration of his term of enlistment. At the close of the war he came to Chicago, where he worked in the building of the postoffice for four years, in the capacity of mechanical engineer. He went to New York in 1874, and went into the electric lighting business with the Fuller Electric Co., and was with them ten years. At the expiration of that time, he went to Buffalo, N. Y., and bought the Richelieu Hotel, which he refitted and furnished, and was its proprietor for fourteen years. He has a wife, but no children, and is now located in San Francisco, Cal., where he is doing well. His address is 525 Front street, San Francisco, Cal.

## ALBERT DIXSON.

The Empire State can claim Albert Dixson as her native son. He was born in East Rush, Monroe County, New York, August 22, 1830. A portion of his childhood was spent in Rush and with an uncle in Flint, Mich. He came to Chicago in 1853, remaining till 1856, when he went to California. The bustle and activity of Chicago being more to his liking, he returned there in 1859, and followed his trade, which was the painting business. He enlisted as private in the battery in Chicago Aug. 22, 1861, and served faithfully with the company, participating in all its battles, until Dec. 23, 1863, when he was discharged for disability at Memphis, Tenn. Recovering his health, he re-enlisted as private in the Twenty-fourth New York Cavalry in 1864, and was afterwards appointed quartermaster sergeant, and served with that command till the close of the war. He has been engaged in the painting business since the war. He was married to Miss Mary A. Young Sept. 21, 1865. She died at Palmyra, N. Y., Jan. 12, 1897. They had no children. He is now living a widower at 321 North Clinton street, Rochester, N. Y.

MRS. JOHN T. CONNELL.

## JAMES B. DUTCH.

During the last year of the war Battery "A" was composed of members of Batteries "A" and "B," who, at the time of the mustering out of the three-year men, had only served about two years, thus forming what was known as the "consolidated," or new, Battery "A." Among those who joined from Battery "B" was James B. Dutch. He enlisted in Taylor's Battery "B" in Chicago, Aug. 5, 1862, as private, was promoted to sergeant, and after consolidation was elected Lieutenant, and served about one year, or till the close of the war, being mustered out July 10, 1865. The consolidated battery did some hard fighting, and had its first severe engagement at Atlanta only ten days after it was organized. They went into the fight with only two officers. One was killed, and the other, with twenty-five men, was captured and sent to Andersonville. Four of their guns were captured, but were afterwards retaken. They immediately drew a new battery and had another sharp engagement with the rebels on July 28, only six days after. James was born in New York City June 1, 1839. He lived in his native city until eight years old, when he came to Chicago, which city has since been his home. In 1861 he was captain of a tug boat in the harbor of Chicago. After the war he returned home and began business on the Board of Trade, at which he is still engaged. He married Miss Mary H. Stout and has two children. His home is at 6637 Parnell avenue, Chicago.

## JOHN BATTERSBY DAY.

The United States Volunteer Army, during the civil war, contained no more patriotic and loyal a native son than John B. Day, a native of Dublin, Ireland, but a full-blooded, ardent American citizen by adoption. He was born Dec. 25, 1842. His days of boyhood and youth were spent in New York City and Gambier, Ohio, attending school. He came to Chicago and was clerking in the postoffice at the time of his enlistment as private in the battery, July 16, 1861. He served three years, faithfully and creditably, and was mustered out July 24, 1864. He was a clerk for some time after the war, but latterly has cultivated a farm in Bedford, N. Y., where he lives in comfort and contentment with his mother and sisters, and is an "old bachelor," as he expresses it, but his old comrades cannot think of him in any other light than the young, genial, warm-hearted, and brave John B. Day.

## JAMES G. EASTWOOD.

James G. Eastwood was born in Cattaraugus County, New York, Aug. 4, 1844, which date places him among the youngest members of the battery. He lived in the State of New York till about ten years of age, and from that time until he entered the United States service he lived in Woodstock,

THADDEUS STEVENS CLARKSON.

Ill. He was a student at Todd's Seminary at Woodstock when the war broke out. Leaving his studies he enlisted as private in Battery "A," at Woodstock, Feb. 3, 1862, and immediately joined the battery in the field. He served his full term of enlistment faithfully and honorably, and was not in the hospital or unfit for duty more than a day or two at a time during his entire service. He was promoted to corporal in the winter of 1864, and was mustered out at the end of his term of enlistment. Returning to his home after his discharge he engaged as clerk in a grocery store, and later went into business for himself in Chicago, dealing in cigars and tobacco for about three years. He then went to Indianapolis and had charge of a news and cigar stand in a large hotel. About 1877 he returned to Woodstock and again resumed the cigar, tobacco and news business, where he remained till the spring of 1880, when he secured an appointment in the Census Bureau then being organized, remaining till the census was completed, when he received an appointment in the Adjutant General's office in the War Department at Washington, where he remained till 1889, when, on account of failing health, he was compelled to resign. He was married to Marie C. Schuyler, June 16, 1886. A daughter was born to them Oct. 16, 1888, who was named Katherine, both surviving him. He died in Washington, Aug. 8, 1890, having been entirely helpless for about a year previous. The disease which caused his death was easily traced to his army service, it having troubled him when discharged, gradually growing worse till death relieved him of his sufferings. As a soldier, citizen, husband and father, Comrade Eastwood was brave, faithful, loving, steadfast and true. He served his country long and well, as became a brave man, dying while yet comparatively young, from causes resulting from his service.

### FREDERICK A. EMORY.

Sixty-nine years ago, in the quiet Quaker City on the Delaware, Frederick A. Emory was born. When he was but two years old he lost his father and was sent to live with an uncle in New Jersey, with whom he lived till ten years old, when he returned to Philadelphia. He started to learn the carpenter trade, at which he worked three weeks. This work not being to his liking he went to sea and grew to become a sailor. At the age of twenty-one he was second mate of a ship. When the war broke out he was master of the schooner "Echo," running between Buffalo and Chicago, and earning a salary of $95 a month. He resigned this position and enlisted in the battery at $13 a month in Chicago, Aug. 1, 1862, serving until July 10, 1865, when he was mustered out at Chicago, the war having closed. He was made corporal when the batteries were consolidated, which was his rank when discharged. He was in every battle and skirmish in which the battery was engaged during his service. He resumed his calling as sailor after the war, and was master of

ENOCH COLBY, JR.

sail and steam vessels all over the great chain of lakes until 1895, when he left the lakes and is now master of a tug on the Nancemund River. He holds a government license as master and pilot on all the lakes and bays, and rivers connected with them; also Albemarle and Pamlico sounds and all tributaries of North Carolina and Hampton Roads and Nancemond River. He owns a farm of fifty acres at Magnolia, Va., on which he lives, and runs with his tug on the river. He was twice married. His first wife was Miss Kate Caswell. His present wife was Miss Mira Marquett. He has five children. He still has in his possession a book presented to him by Fred Church, containing the plays performed in the Larkinsville Theater, illustrated by Comrade Church.

## DANIEL R. FARNHAM.

The second victim to offer up his life as a sacrifice to his country on the bloody field of Shiloh was brave, noble, Christian Daniel R. Farnham. No member was more universally loved and honored by his comrades than he. He was filling a lucrative and pleasant position as bookkeeper in Chicago when the war broke out. Throwing this up and taking a hasty leave of his widowed mother and sisters, he enlisted as private in Battery "A," April 19, 1861, and served through the three months' term, re-enlisting for three years July 16 following, and served faithfully and creditably until his untimely end. He was born in Warsaw, N. Y., Jan. 31, 1834. His childhood and youth days were spent in Silver Creek, N. Y., and in the city of Buffalo, where his early school education was acquired. He came West when a young man, and located in Chicago. He was fitted by education, talents and habits for the highest walks of business and social life, yet when his country called he promptly exchanged the comforts of home and the bright prospects of the future for the hardships of a private soldier's lot. He fell nobly in defense of the old flag, and his memory will be held in sweet remembrance by all his old comrades and friends. His remains were brought to Chicago and laid to rest in Graceland Cemetery. His name is among those engraved on the battery monument in Rose Hill Cemetery. He has three sisters, Louisa M. Farnham, Mrs. T. R. Albee and Mrs. J. I. Stowell, all residing in Chicago.

## WILLIAM PITT FOLLANSBEE.

The subject of this sketch was a native of Chicago, having been born in that city Oct. 29, 1841. His parents were Mr. and Mrs. Charles Follansbee, who were among Chicago's most prominent, old and wealthy families. He always lived in the city of his birth, attending her schools during his boyhood days. After leaving school he was engaged as salesman for C. H. Beckwith, wholesale grocer, and was so occupied when the war began. He left his situation and enlisted as private in Battery "A," July 28, 1861. He

JOHN D. DYER.

was with the battery continuously, taking a conspicuous part in all its engagements until mustered out at the expiration of his term of enlistment, July 23, 1864. He then returned to Chicago and engaged in the grocery business with Lewis F. Jacobs, also a member of the battery, both having been messmates in the same squad throughout the war. He quit this business and went to Larkspur, Colo., where he purchased a large ranch and embarked in the cattle business, in which he was engaged at the time of his death, which occurred Feb. 23, 1876. His remains were brought home and buried in Graceland. He had never married. His mother and brothers still live in Chicago.

## ORRINGTON C. FOSTER.

Like many other members of Battery "A," O. C. Foster was a native-born Chicagoan. From six to twelve years of age he attended the public schools of the city. He afterwards entered the Northwestern University at Evanston, which institution he left to enlist in the battery as private April 19, 1861. He was made gunner of squad five at the attack on Jackson, Miss. While the company was in camp at Memphis he, with others of his squad, had a very narrow escape from an accidental death, through an oversight of one of the officers. They were sitting at the squad table one day when clever, honest Blacksmith William Kirk innocently fired a gun loaded with canister, pointing directly toward the table. The battery forge and a big mule intervening received the charge and prevented anything more serious than a good-sized scare. The gun had been used on the river below Memphis, and a charge that was not fired had carelessly been left in the gun. Kirk was entertaining visitors at the camp at the time, doing the honors as an old soldier. Wishing to show them how firing was done, he inserted a friction primer in this particular gun and pulled away. Kirk, who was of a decidedly dark complexion, was fairly pale for several days, as a result of his demonstration. Comrade Foster was battery bugler in the early part of the war. He was appointed corporal after the battle of Shiloh. He served creditably in the battery, taking part in all its engagements until July, 1864, when he was mustered out, his term of enlistment having expired. He was an active worker socially in helping to relieve the monotony of camp life, notably as one of the members of the Larkinsville Theater Company, improvised by the members of the battery; also as one of the Kennedy Glee Club, and at the challenge concert at Jackson, Miss., given by the Jackson citizens, by request of several Union officers, responding alternately to songs of Southern sentiment. He has been engaged principally since the war in the railroad business, and is now with the Northern Milling Co. He is married and has three children, two boys and one girl, and lives with his family in their pleasant home at 527 La Salle avenue, Chicago.

ALBERT DIXSON.

## WILLIAM FURNESS.

As loyal to the State of his nativity in his maturer years as he was to the Union in the days of his younger manhood, is William Furness, now residing in Ogdensburg, N. Y., in which city he was born Jan. 1, 1831. Here he spent his childhood days, and when of suitable age he entered Union College, in Schenectady, N. Y., from which he graduated as civil engineer in 1852. He went West and worked one year at his profession, in Peoria, Ill., then returned home and engaged in the insurance business. In 1861 he was clerking in the banking and insurance office of B. W. Phillips & Co. in Chicago, and left his position to enlist as private in Battery "A," April 19, 1861, re-enlisting July 16, 1861, for three years, serving with the battery at Cairo and Paducah, Ky. On the 28th of January, 1862, at Paducah, he was discharged from the service on surgeon's certificate of disability, from sickness contracted in the line of duty. After his recovery he worked at different occupations. For four years he was in the government employ under the alien contract labor law and United States customs. He married Miss Margaret G. Bird, of Peterboro, Ont., in 1871. They have two grown-up sons and one grandson, A. Wm. Furness, residing at Montpelier, Vt., and Gilbert B. Furness, residing at Mandan, North Dakota. He is Past Commander of Ransom Post, No. 354, Department of New York, G. A. R. At present he is speculating in grain and stocks.

## EDWARD P. FISH.

The Empire State can have the credit of furnishing more native sons for members of Battery "A" than any other State in the Union, excepting, of course, Illinois. Prominent among these is Edward P. Fish. He was born at Clarkson, N. Y., Sept. 14, 1831, and lived there until he was eleven years old, then moved with his parents to Lewiston, N. Y., where they lived four years. He attended school two years at Albion and Madison, N. Y. He then learned the tinsmith trade, at which he worked a number of years. In September, 1852, he went to Princeton, Ill., remaining there till 1858. He then went South, where he remained till Jan. 26, 1861, when political matters, partaking too much of the nature of the climate, became too hot for any honest Northern man, and he returned to Princeton in February following. He had not taken up with anything permanent when the war broke out, and soon after President Lincoln's first call for 75,000 men he recruited a company of rifle sharpshooters and offered his services with his company to Governor Yates, but at that time he had no authority to accept and commission them, and they disbanded, scattering about in other organizations. Not at all discouraged, he came to Chicago and enlisted as private in the battery July 16, 1861. He participated in all the battles and engagements of the battery during his term of service, but was not engaged at Shiloh,

JAMES B. DUTCH.

which has always been a source of regret to him, as he came of true fighting stock, and never shirked a duty while a soldier. Out of six brothers in the family five of them were in the Union army before October, 1861. No draft by Uncle Sam was necessary to secure the services of such defenders as the Fish boys. The older brother enlisted in the Illinois Cavalry under General Steele, the next was in a company of Wisconsin cavalry, under General Dodge, Sixteenth Army Corps; Edward enlisted in the battery; the next younger brother, Lucien J. Fish, enlisted in the ordnance department and went through with Sherman to the sea and on to Washington in 1865, was color guard from Chattanooga to Washington, and never received a scratch; the youngest brother, Charles H. Fish, was signal officer on General Logan's staff from Chattanooga to the capture of Atlanta, and had charge of the famous work of signaling to General Corse at Altoona when the rebels were trying to capture that place. The three younger brothers are still living. Comrade Fish was mustered out of the service July 22, 1864, his term of enlistment having expired. He was never wounded nor has never applied for a pension. He celebrated Lincoln's second inauguration by getting married on that day, March 4, 1865, and started housekeeping the day he was assassinated. The happy bride was Miss Althea D. Trask, of Buda, Ill. They have one daughter living and two granddaughters. He moved to Missouri in 1869 and from there to Pueblo, Colo., in July, 1874, where he has since resided. He has followed the business of plumbing and gasfitting, and by untiring energy, strict integrity and upright dealing has established a large and lucrative business, and ranks among the solid and reliable citizens of Pueblo. He has a comfortable, pleasant home, and the latch-string is always out to any of his old comrades visiting that far Western town.

## FERDINAND V. GINDELE.

Ferdinand V. Gindele was born in the city of Schweinfurth, Bavaria, Germany, July 12, 1842, and came to the United States with his parents Oct. 10, 1850, living in Wisconsin till 1852, when they came to Chicago, which city has since been his home. He attended the old No. 3 district school on Madison, near Halsted street, and took a course at Bryant & Stratton's Commercial College. For nearly a lifetime he has been engaged in the cut stone business in Chicago, in which he served a full apprenticeship as a boy, assisting during that time to cut the stone in the old original high school building and the Douglas University. He was working at his trade when the war broke out, and enlisted April 19, 1861, at Chicago, in Battery "A." He served three months and returned home, but re-enlisted August 5, 1862, and served with the battery, participating in all its engagements until July 12, 1864, before Atlanta, when he was detailed on detached service as clerk

JAMES G. EASTWOOD.

in the Assistant Adjutant General's office of the Second Division, Fifteenth Army Corps. He went through with Sherman on the march to the sea, and the campaign through the Carolinas, and was mustered out of the service at the close of the war in Washington, D. C., May 26, 1865, and returned home. With the exception of two years when he was engaged as assistant in the engineer corps in the original deepening of the old canal, which is now being changed into the largest drainage canal in the United States, he has followed the cut stone business, in different positions, and is now, and has been for a number of years, conducting the business for himself. He was married to Caroline Haverlund March 3, 1870. They have surviving one son and two daughters and one grandson.

## MERIC GOULD.

Meric Gould was born in East Pembroke, N. Y., Feb. 28, 1835. His childhood and youth were spent in his native town and in Medina County, Ohio, attending school, helping on the farm, and doing his share of the "neighborhood deviltry," as he humbly confesses it, until old enough to go sailing on the Great Lakes, in which occupation he was engaged when the civil war broke out. He enlisted in the battery as "high private" in Chicago, July 28, 1861, and served with the company till Jan. 28, 1862, when he was discharged at Paducah, Ky., for disability contracted in line of duty. Discharge states disease was malaria cachexia, which was the same with many of the sick and discharged soldiers from that place. Being restored to comparatively good health he afterwards re-enlisted in the Nineteenth Ohio Light Artillery Independent, on Aug. 7, 1862, and served with that command till the close of the war. Since the war he has engaged in farming, lumber business and manufacturing hardwood lumber. He is now living at Brest, Mich., where he is justice of the peace and postmaster. He is in poor health and unable to perform any manual labor. Comrades will remember him as the "old sailor," as he was familiarly called during his term of service with the battery. He was married to Lydia Dewey Nov. 16, 1865, who died in March, 1866, and has four children living, one dead and five grandchildren.

## ALLEN W. GRAY.

The subject of this sketch is a native of Chicago, and one of her most prominent and successful physicians. He was born Dec. 16, 1839, and lived in the city till twelve years of age, when his parents moved to Niles, Cook County, where they lived four years, moving from there to their farm in the Town of Jefferson, which is now within the city limits, and where they lived the remainder of their lives, both dying a few years ago. His father, John Gray, was a prominent citizen of Chicago and Cook County, and served as Sheriff of Cook County during the years 1859 and 1860. He at-

WILLIAM PITT FOLLANSBEE.

tended the district schools in the neighborhood where his parents lived until 1858, when he went to Evanston to attend the Northwestern University. He was the first student to enlist from that institution in the civil war, having enlisted in Battery "A," April 19, 1861. He served through the three months' service as private in the battery and re-enlisted for three years in the same company July 16, 1861, at Cairo, Ill. During the three months' service he was on the expedition to Mexico, Mo. He was sick in hospital at Cairo from July 18 to Aug. 21, 1861, with camp fever, which was the extent of his sickness and disability during the entire war. He was one of the battery who served on a cavalry expedition to Mayfield, Ky., Oct. 21 and 22, 1861. On Dec. 13, 1861, by special order of the War Department, he was transferred to the Fity-first Regiment, Illinois Infantry. He was appointed regimental commissary sergeant Jan. 1, 1862; reinstated a veteran volunteer in same regiment Feb. 8, 1864; was promoted to First Lieutenant, Company G, same regiment, April 1, 1864, and appointed First Lieutenant and regimental Adjutant June 27, 1864. He resigned and was mustered out of service Jan. 31, 1865, having served three years, nine months and fourteen days, participating in the battles of New Madrid, Island No. 10, Farmington, Iuka, Corinth, Chickamauga, Mission Ridge, march to relief of Knoxville, Rocky Face Ridge, Resaca, New Hope Church, Kenesaw Mountain, Peach Tree Creek, Siege of Atlanta, Jonesboro, Spring Hill, Franklin and Nashville, besides numerous skirmishes. He married Miss Sarah H. Adams, of Northfield, Ill., Oct. 13, 1862, and they now reside in a substantial and beautiful home at 1410 Washington boulevard. They have three sons, two daughters and one grandson. He kept a country store one and a half years, after leaving the army, then studied medicine at Chicago Medical College, graduating in 1868, since which time he has been in active practice of medicine in Chicago. He was United States Examining Surgeon for Pensions at Chicago from June, 1889, to June, 1893, and was reappointed in June, 1897, and is still serving in that position. He takes an active interest in the Grand Army of the Republic and is a Past Commander of U. S. Grant Post, No. 28, Department of Illinois. He is also an active member of the Ancient Order of United Workmen and of the Royal League.

## ADAM CLARK HALL.

There are many members of old Battery "A" who, if asked regarding their memory of Adam C. Hall, would hesitate a moment before replying, but if asked in regard to "Garibaldi" there would be no faltering for an affirmative reply. "Garrie," as he was familiarly called by all the boys, was one of the prominent members from the very starting of the battery for the front, April 21, 1861. When the battery was moved up the river from Cairo to Camp Smith, and the work of cleaning up the heavy timber and undergrowth

EDWARD P. FISH.

was begun, Capt. Smith placed Hall in charge of it, and he proved to be an expert in the business. Many a tenderly reared boy took his first lessons at hard work in wood-chopping, grubbing and log-rolling from him, and he was always a good-natured, cheerful instructor. The huge bonfires which burned nightly while the work of cleaning up continued, were always surrounded by a jolly group of boys, who whiled away the time in singing sentimental and patriotic songs and listening to stories told by one another. "Garrie" was a capital story-teller, and always enjoyed a good joke, even when he was the victim. He was a native of the Green Mountain State, having first seen the light of day in Pittsford, Vermont, Feb. 28, 1834. His early years were spent on a farm in his native place. He learned the trade of railroad engineer when a young man, and, coming to the West, was engaged in that occupation when the war broke out. He enlisted in the battery April 15, 1861, re-enlisted at Cairo July 16 following, and again at Bellfont, Ala., Jan. 2, 1864. His rank was corporal. He was severely wounded at the battle of Shiloh, and narrowly missed being captured by the enemy, but escaped and assisted several of his wounded comrades from the field and prevented their capture. He was not so fortunate at the battle of Atlanta, July 22, 1864, but was taken prisoner there with a number of others of the battery, and held until April 19, 1865, when he was paroled at Camp Fisk, Miss. He was mustered out at Chicago July 27, 1865, by general order of the War Department discharging paroled prisoners. While a prisoner he was confined the whole time at Andersonville, and endured with so many others the horrors of that accursed prison pen, coming out a perfect skeleton, and but a mere shadow of his former self. When he was captured he weighed 218 pounds and when paroled but 128 pounds. After his discharge, as near a physical wreck as it was possible for a man to be and live, he, at the urgent request of his dear aged mother, quit railroading, took up the trade of carpenter and builder in Chicago, and followed that until July, 1868, when he removed to Des Moines, Iowa, and resumed work at his carpenter trade. This he was obliged to give up on account of his health, and he returned to his work as stationary engineer. He secured a position as engineer in the Des Moines water works, which he filled for nearly eight years, but at last was forced to give up steady work at his trade in 1893, on account of poor health. He then secured a few acres of land in the suburbs of Des Moines, and after partially regaining his health, fitted up a snug, comfortable home, and, by cultivating his little tract of land, raising fruit, vegetables and small grains, manages to live in comparative comfort. How long he can hold on to life he can not and does not pretend to say, as, according to records and reports, he is destined to be a very old man. The Illinois Adjutant General's report from 1861 to 1865 has him dead since Nov. 16, 1861, grave 12060, and he was reported as lost on the steamer "Sultana," but he still lives and

FERDINAND V. GINDELE.

feels much more like continuing to do so than he did thirty-six years ago, and, like the Irishman, he has concluded that he will stay on earth and "live as long as he can see anyone else do so." He suggests, in recording the history of the boys, "to give each one their full share of the honor, as there is enough to go around," and he will be content to take his chance with the rest. He was married Jan. 23, 1866, to Miss Sophia B. Morrow, in Chicago. They have had but one child, David Perry Hall, who died in July, 1872, when only five years of age.

## EDWARD S. HILLS.

Among the few battery members who located in the South after the war is Edward S. Hills. He was born in Manchester, Conn., in 1840, but his boyhood and youth were spent in Buffalo, N. Y. In the spring of 1861 he was working at his trade, blacksmithing, in Chicago, where he enlisted as private in Battery "A," April 19. He served through the three months' service, re-enlisted with a majority of the battery July 16, 1861, and served with the company till Jan. 9, 1863, when, on account of severe sickness and weakness, he was discharged on surgeon's certificate for physical disability. He has been in the United States postal service since December, 1869, was married in October, 1875, and has one son thirteen years old. He lives at Atlanta, Ga., where he is located in his own home.

## HOXIE LEE HOFFMAN.

One by one the survivors of our battery are fast joining the silent majority. The last one to answer the final summons was genial, brave Hoxie L. Hoffman, who passed away at the Soldiers' Home, Los Angeles County, California, Feb. 12, 1899. On Jan. 19 previous he wrote that he was comfortably situated in the Home, which, as he expressed it, was the "Garden Spot of the Earth," where his every want was supplied, and where, in the natural order of things, he would soon be called upon to respond to the last roll call, as he was in his sixty-eighth year. He was born in Warsaw, N. Y., Feb. 20, 1831. From the time he was four years of age until twenty he lived with his father on a farm in Half Day, Lake County, Ill., where they had many years of hard work and poor returns. When twenty-one he was offered and accepted a position with his brother-in-law, William Clingman, a leading clothier of Chicago, receiving the munificent salary at that time of $50 per month. He was so engaged when the war broke out, and on April 17, 1861, left his position and enlisted as private in the battery. He served with the battery until Jan. 17, 1863, when, on account of severe sickness, he was obliged to resign his commission as Second Lieutenant, to which he had been promoted, having been advanced to that position from previous promotions of corporal and sergeant. After his resignation, as soon as he had re-

MERIC GOULD.

covered sufficiently, he went into the sewing machine business, in which he continued for fifteen years, most of the time being located in St. Louis. He then changed to the Board of Trade business in Chicago, which proved a disastrous venture. He remained single until August, 1893, when he married and went to California, settling at Los Angeles. This also proved an unfortunate move, and, as he says, the "last move on the chess board," was to make application and be admitted to the Soldiers' Home, where he was so soon to end his days. In writing his last letter he extends his kind regards and remembrances to all his old comrades, and says when he shall have passed away he will have a marble slab to mark his last resting place," inscribed with all necessary statements." He says in his lonely condition he would give $1.10 to hear Fred S. Church call out, "Dinner, Squad 3," but it was his present belief that he would "never hear his gentle voice again," seeming to have a premonition of his near approaching dissolution. The news of his sudden taking off was received by all his old comrades with surprise and sorrow.

## MOSES HAWKS.

The oldest member and survivor of the battery is Moses Hawks. He was born at Hannibal, N. Y., Dec. 14, 1821, on a farm, where he lived and grew to manhood. He came West, and, when the war began, was general agent for an agricultural implement manufacturing company. He enlisted in the battery in Chicago in July, 1861, as private, and served the full term of his enlistment, enduring the hardships and privations of army life as ruggedly as any of the younger members. He received slight wounds both at the battles of Donelson and Shiloh. His first vote was cast in 1841 for James G. Birney, the Abolition candidate for President. At that time he was serving as conductor on the Underground Railroad from his native town to Oswego, N. Y. Since the war he has dealt in farm stock and been a manufacturer of butter and cheese. He lives in Phoenix, N. Y., and has never married.

## EDWARD HUGHES.

Edward Hughes is a native son of Chicago, where he was born Feb. 9, 1838, and which place has ever since been his home. His school education was obtained in the old Kinzie School, on the North Side, where he attended until fourteen years old, when he commenced work for A. Clybourn, Chicago's oldest butcher, in the old North Market, and continued working for him till he enlisted in the battery in July, 1862. He served as private, taking part in all its engagements until July 22, 1863, when he was taken prisoner at Jackson, Miss., and held until Oct. 19, 1864. A graphic account of the experience of those captured on that day is given by Wm. H. Young

ALLEN W. GRAY.

in the chapter on the Siege of Jackson. Comrade Hughes lost an eye while in prison at Andersonville. He returned to Chicago and engaged in the market and provision business, which he has since followed. He married and had two children. His wife and both children are dead. He has two grandchildren.

## EDWARD JOHNSON.

Edward Johnson was born in Richmond, Richmond County, New York, Oct. 8, 1837, where he lived and attended the village school until fourteen years of age. During the following two years he assisted his father, clerking in his general store. From 1853 until 1860 he was clerking in various mercantile lines in New York City. He went to Chicago in 1860, reaching there during the session of the national convention that nominated Abraham Lincoln for President. He engaged as clerk in a wholesale grocery house, which position he resigned to enlist as private in the battery July 28, 1861. Being proficient in clerical work, and ability of that nature being needed, he was detailed for extra duty in the Subsistence Department at Paducah, Ky., shortly after the occupation of that city in September, 1861, and continued in such employ until mustered out for disability June 21, 1862. He continued in the service of the United States government, however, and for sixteen years was in the departments in Washington, D. C. He is now clerk in the Quartermaster's Department at the National Military Home, Leavenworth, Kan. He married Mary E. Gunsaloes at Washington, D. C., Sept. 30, 1867, and has two married daughters and three grandchildren.

## LEWIS F. JACOBS.

In the western part of far-off Norway, Europe, Lewis F. Jacobs was born, in 1835. When eleven years old he came with his parents to America, settling in Kendall County, Illinois. He had one brother and two sisters. His parents were poor, and immediately on their arrival in this country Lewis began to work to support himself and assist his parents, working on a farm. When in the country but three years the entire family was stricken with the cholera, and all were carried away with it except Lewis and his two sisters. He soon after went to work as a brakeman on the railroad, and finally became a baggagemaster, at which work he was engaged when the war broke out. He was in the first body of troops to leave Chicago for the front, having enlisted in the defense of his adopted country, in Battery "A," April 19, 1861. He re-enlisted the following July 16, and served till mustered out, July 23, 1864. A more faithful, zealous and brave soldier than Lewis could not be found. He was a universal favorite with all the com-

ADAM C. HALL.

rades of the battery, and he was very much attached to them. His friendship continued until his dying day, when he remembered them by donating a lot he owned in the southern outskirts of the city, to the Battery Veteran Association, for the purpose of caring for the battery monument and lot in the cemetery at Rose Hill, and providing for the care and comfort of any deserving and needy members, and for keeping up the association while any of the members lived. The publishing of this history, to perpetuate the achievements of our gallant battery, and the memory of its living and noble dead, was made possible by Comrade Jacobs' donation. He was engaged in the mercantile business in Chicago for a few years after the war. He then secured a position in the United States Government Gauger's office, which place he filled for many years, till failing health compelled him to resign. Two of his battery comrades, having such implicit confidence in his honesty and integrity, were on his official bond during the entire time he was connected with this office, and their trust was never betrayed. Honest, brave and true, generous to a fault, were his natural qualities, and he died sincerely mourned by all his comrades and friends. His death occurred after a lingering illness in hospital, Oct. 21, 1889, and he was laid to rest by his comrades in the battery lot in Rose Hill Cemetery. His grave is the only one on which an individual headstone was allowed to be placed. It is a beautiful granite stone, and is inscribed with his name, date of death and the very appropriate inscription of, "Noble Patriot, Brave Soldier, and True Friend." He has a sister, Mrs. Sarah Erickson, living at Stony City, Iowa. He was never married.

## WILLIAM H. JOHNSON.

A few of the battery members can claim the honor of having gone with General Sherman on the memorable march "from Atlanta to the sea." Among these is the subject of this sketch, Wm. H. Johnson, now living at Alpena. Mich. He was born at Kishwaukee, Ill., Feb. 10, 1840. He moved to Milwaukee when a child, and lived there till 1857, when he went to Chicago and engaged with the American Express Co., where he was employed at the time of his enlistment as private in the battery, Aug. 6, 1862. He was No. 3 in squad one until June 16, 1864, when, at Big Shanty, Ga., he was detailed to report to Lieutenant Mitchell, Ordnance Officer of the Fifteenth Army Corps, for whom he acted as clerk until his term of enlistment expired. He was with the corps on the "grand march," and was mustered out at Washington, D. C., May 25, 1865. He married Miss Mary G. Nason, formerly of Chicago, and has three children. He is a prominent and successful business man, is engaged in the lumber business and a bank in the city of Alpena, Mich.

HENRY H. HANDY.

## FREDERICK M. KANTZLER.

Among the worthy, patriotic citizens of Chicago that Germany has furnished, is Fred. M. Kantzler. He was born in that empire Sept. 3. 1840. In 1852 with his parents he crossed the Atlantic. Making their way to Chicago, they located at Blue Island, a southern suburb. He secured a position as clerk in a country store, and was so engaged at the breaking out of the war. A number of Blue Island boys, friends and acquaintances being members of Battery "A," he came to Paducah, Ky., and joined the battery Dec. 1, 1861, enlisting as private. He served with the battery, taking part in all its engagements, until July 22, 1863, when he was taken prisoner with a number of others of the battery, at Jackson, Miss. He was taken to Belle Island, Va., where he was held for six months, then removed to that rebel hell-hole of Andersonville, where he remained seven months, and, surviving all this, he was taken to Savannah, Ga., and kept for two months longer, when he was exchanged Nov. 18, 1864. He was mustered out Jan. 12, 1865, his term of enlistment having expired. After the war he was in active business in Chicago until May, 1897, when, having acquired a comfortable competency, he retired from active business. He married Miss Elizabeth Forrest, of Canton, Mo. They have five children and live in their pleasant home at 3030 Vernon avenue, Chicago.

## HARRISON KELLEY.

Harrison Kelley was one of the popular and prominent members of the battery during the three months' service, enlisting as private April 21, 1861, in Chicago. But the three months with the battery was by no means the extent of his military service in the civil war. He was appointed First Lieutenant in the Forty-fourth New York Infantry Volunteers, July 4, 1861, and served in that position till July 3, 1862. He was then promoted to Adjutant in the same regiment and served in that capacity till Feb. 9, 1863. He was commissioned as captain in the same command Feb. 25, 1863. During all his military career he says the first day's service with the battery, when he rode as cannonier on the limber of a gun through the streets of Chicago, behind four green and fractious horses and equally as green and awkward postillions, the cheers and surging of the thousands of spectators that lined the streets frightening both animals and men nearly out of their senses, impressed itself more vividly on his mind than anything in his later experience. He was with his regiment in the battles of Gaines Mill, Antietam, Fredericksburg, and others, but at no time was so "nearly scared to death" as upon that memorable march through the city of Chicago, when, as an ex-bookkeeper and cashier, he was required to jump off the limber and down among the heels of the fractious horses, about once every five minutes, and to try to quiet and dissuade them from their efforts to straddle everything in sight,

EDWARD S. HILLS.

including the pole, traces and himself, and to plunge about generally. To his mind and memory no more dangerous duty was devolved upon him during the war. He was born in New York City Aug. 14, 1840. The first four years of his life were spent in his native city. Thereafter until 1853 he alternated between different places in the State of New York and Chicago, settling in that year in the future great city of the West. He was employed as bookkeeper and cashier with the extensive hardware firm of Larrabee & North, and left his position with that firm to join the army. When he left school at eight years of age, he began work as a cash boy, and was advanced to bookkeeper and cashier, in which capacities he has been employed ever since, except while in the army, and a few years in the hardware business for himself. Since 1876 he has been the efficient secretary of the well-known and popular People's Building and Loan Association of Chicago, which position he still fills. He is married and has two children living and one grandchild.

## CORNELIUS KENDALL.

Cornelius Kendall, one of the prominent three months' members of the battery, was born in Quincy, Ill., May 22, 1839, and lived there until 1853, when he came to Chicago, which was his home till 1870. He was working in his father's well-known bakery, on the corner of Washington and Dearborn streets, when the war began, and enlisted as private in the battery April 19, 1861, and served three months at Cairo. He went to Toledo, Ohio, in 1870, where he still lives, being established in the steam-fitting business, in which he has been successful and prosperous. He married Miss Ida L. Knapp in 1873, and has no children.

## THEODORE WYLIE KENNEDY.

A loyal, brave and true citizen and soldier was Theodore W. Kennedy. He was born in Green County, Alabama, July 28, 1843, which placed him among the youngest members of the battery. His parents moved to Chicago in 1846. Here Theodore was raised to manhood, and with the exception of a few months that city was his home until his death, which occurred Nov. 10, 1881. He enlisted in the battery with the first members, April 19, 1861, served three months and re-enlisted for three years, serving his full term faithfully and creditably, taking part in all the work of the battery. He was mustered out in July, 1864, and returned to Chicago. He was employed as mail carrier, at which he served for many years. He resigned but a short time before his death, for the purpose of going into business. He married Miss Eliza Stewart in Chicago in 1865. His widow, in fair circumstances, and four children survive him.

HOXIE L. HOFFMAN.

## SAMPSON KENNEDY.

A native-born Southerner, but loyal to the core to the Union, can be said of Sampson Kennedy. He was born in Green County, Alabama, Feb. 23, 1839, and came north to Chicago in 1846, which city was his home until 1867. He learned the printer's trade and was working at it when he enlisted in the battery in Chicago, July 12, 1861. His brother, Theodore W., was already serving in the battery, having been with it during the three months' service. He served his full term of enlistment, without a furlough, and, being quite sociable and musical, contributed in no small degree to the pleasures and enjoyments of camp and army life, especially in the part he took in the Glee Club at Paducah, Vicksburg and Larkinsville. In 1871 he engaged in the business of printer and publisher at Moline, Ill., continuing it till 1887. He is still living at Moline.

He married Miss Adeline Whiting in Monmouth, Ill., Nov. 6, 1866, and six children have blessed the union, Mate, who died at birth; Robert B., Adeline, Philip S., Alice, and Sampson W. His second son, Philip, served in the First Nat. Infantry, Company M, in the late war, and participated in the capture of Manila.

## ARTHUR MAGILL KINZIE.

The subject of this sketch is a lineal descendant of the first white family that settled in Chicago, when it was but a mere Indian trading post. Arthur M. Kinzie was born in Chicago, March 24, 1841, which city has always been his home. He attended his first school there, then continued at Racine College, and later on entered Kenyon College, Ohio, where he was studying when the war broke out. He enlisted in the battery in Chicago, April 19, 1861, and served three months as private and corporal. After the three months' service he was appointed a Second Lieutenant in the Ninth Illinois Cavalry, and was immediately detailed as aid-de-camp to Major General Hunter, commanding the Department of Missouri. He was afterwards promoted to Captain and A. D. C. to the Major General commanding the Tenth Army Corps. To Comrade Kinzie belongs the credit of having organized and equipped the first regiment of colored troops raised in the Union service, which he did by command of Major General Hunter, in May, 1862. It was called the First South Carolina Union Volunteers, but was not recognized by the Secretary of War, and was ordered to be discharged. Six months afterwards, however, the government ordered the enlistment of colored troops, and this regiment formed the neucleus of the colored troops of South Carolina, which proved such valuable auxiliaries in suppressing the rebellion. He was in the rebel prison at Cahaba, Ala., three months, having been captured by the rebel General Forest's cavalry. He served till the

MOSES HAWKS.

close of the war, and was mustered out in November, 1865. He returned to Chicago, and has been paymaster of the Wells & French Car Co.

He married Miss Carolina G. Wilson. They have five children, John H., married to Nellie Reed, of Savannah, Ga.; Eleanor G., married to Geo. W. Gould, of Chicago; Adele L., married to John S. Driver, of Riverside; Sarah M. and Julian Magill Kinzie. They have three grandchildren.

## GEORGE KING.

Genial, jovial, happy and good-natured George King was a general favorite with the whole battery. Always as ready for work as for play, he never shirked a duty or missed a skirmish or battle. He enlisted with a majority of the earliest members on the 19th of April, 1861, re-enlisting July 16 following, and served faithfully and well three years and three months, without receiving a serious wound or injury, and was mustered out July 23, 1864. He was born Feb. 28, 1836, in Amherst, N. Y., and lived there on a farm until seventeen years old, when, acting on the advice of Horace Greeley to "go West, young man," he came to Chicago and located, working as machinist and engineer. Since the war he worked at the same trade, principally, fourteen years of the time being in that employ with the Elgin National Watch Co., at Elgin, Ill. He died in that city July 14, 1898, leaving a widow, Mrs. Mary King, to whom he was married in Elgin. He left no children, but one son and two daughters by a former marriage with Miss Martha Williams, who died in 1885, survive him. He also had one grandchild.

## MR. AND MRS. MARTIN N. KIMBELL, SR.

Mr. and Mrs. Martin N. Kimbell, Sr., were the parents of the three Kimbell brothers that served in the battery during the civil war. They were both natives of the State of New York, and came West to Chicago in 1836. They became acquainted after their arrival, and were married in 1837 and at once settled on a wild prairie farm of 160 acres, which Mr. Kimbell had bought of the government, five miles northwest of the site of the present courthouse. Here they lived for the remainder of their lives, over sixty years, rearing a family of six sons and two daughters to maturity, enduring and overcoming all the hardships and privations of early pioneer life, and enjoying a comfortable home and competency in their declining years, surrounded by their numerous descendants. They had witnessed the marvelous growth and development of Chicago, growing from a frontier Indian trading post to be the second city of the nation. They always took an active interest in educational matters. The first school in their district, organized in the early '40s, was taught in their own humble home, which consisted of but two rooms, and the first two seasons they boarded the teacher gratui-

EDWARD HUGHES.

tously. Scholars came from a distance of one to three miles across the open prairie, and when the weather was severe, they frequently remained with the Kimbells all night. As they prospered and their home was improved and enlarged, it was a much frequented resort for a multitude of friends, and old and young came there always sure of a warm welcome and a visit of good cheer. Mr. Kimbell was a public-spirited citizen, always ready to aid in forwarding every good endeavor and to extend general education and good government. He was one of the original founders of the Republican party, and remained a stanch and consistent member of that party till his death. He was a Universalist in religious belief, and contributed liberally toward the building up of three churches of that faith in Chicago. He never aspired to political honors, though often urged to do so. He served in minor public offices for many years, especially as school officer for thirty years. He was a member of the first Board of Supervisors of Cook County, and served as Deputy Sheriff for a short time under his lifelong friend, Sheriff John Gray. When the war broke out he took a firm and unflinching stand in support of the government, and when war was declared he gave his tearful consent to the enlistment of his oldest son, Charles B., in Battery "A," and a year later his second and third sons, Julius W. and Spencer S., followed with like consent. The interest that Mr. Kimbell always took in the battery, from the beginning till the close of the war, justly gained for him the title of "Father of the Battery." He devoted months of his time in visiting them in the field, and after every severe battle would go immediately to the front and assist in caring for the wounded and sick. He served gratuitously as hospital steward on the Mississippi River hospital boats the greater part of two winters. He, with Mrs. Mary A. Livermore and Thomas B. Bryan, organized the Sanitary Commission in Chicago, which did such valuable and efficient work all through the war. Mrs. Kimbell was not behind her noble husband in doing her share to cheer and sustain the boys in doing their patriotic duty. During the early part of the war, when the battery was accessible for home supplies, scarcely a week passed that a box of dainties, jelly, jam and a nice jar of golden butter, all made by her own hands, did not find its way to the boys in camp, and many a sick boy, tired of army supplies, remembers the appetizing things sent by her, which were always generously divided. A barrel of currant wine, made from fruit in her own garden by herself, was sent to the Sanitary Commission for the hospitals. When the battery was in camp at Vicksburg, in April, 1863, the boys, wishing to show their appreciation and esteem for Mr. Kimbell, procured a beautiful gold-headed cane, and had it suitably inscribed and sent to him, accompanied by the following letter. The cane is now in the possession of his son, Spencer S., and will always be prized as a precious heirloom by his descendants:

EDWARD JOHNSON.

"Camp of Company 'A,' Chicago Light Artillery,
"Before Vicksburg, April 12, 1863.

"Dear Sir—During the long and weary months we have been absent from our homes, battling for our country's honor, the evidences of your kindness and regard have never been absent from us.

"We realize how you have watched over our interests and cared for us, sick and wounded, with a tender care and a never-wearying zeal.

"We appreciate your noble efforts in our behalf, and can never repay them—the reward of such deeds is in the Almighty's hands.

"Permit us, however, to offer you this cane, a slight testimonial of our regard, hoping that you may carry it many years, and that it may support the declining steps of an honored old age.   Co. 'A,' C. L. A.
"To M. N. Kimbell."

Mrs. Kimbell was in poor health for many years in the latter part of her life, and passed away in her old home, in her 81st year, Nov. 24, 1896, nearly two years after the death of her husband. Mr. Kimbell, being of a strong and vigorous constitution, enjoyed good health until about the year 1890, when he began to have trouble with his feet, which gradually developed into gangrene. This continued to increase steadily until, in January, 1895, it was decided by a council of physicians, that, in order to save, or even prolong his life and relieve the intense suffering he was enduring, it would be necessary to amputate his left leg above the knee. This was accordingly done, with his full consent, and with the hope on the part of his family that his otherwise robust constitution would enable him to rally from the operation. But his advanced age of 83 years was against him, and he sank gradually until the end, which came Feb. 13, 1895. The last years of the lives of this worthy couple were spent in quiet retirement, surrounded by their numerous family, enjoying the fruits of an early life of hard and honest labor, combined with temperance, benevolence and frugality, useful and exemplary lives, well worthy of emulation by rising generations.

## CHARLES BILL KIMBELL.

The eldest of the three Kimbell brothers serving in Battery "A" was Charles B. He was born Dec. 6, 1839, on the farm which was the Kimbell homestead for over sixty years, now in the city of Chicago. His school education was obtained in the primitive district schools in the neighborhood, working on the farm during the summer seasons and doing his share in assisting his parents in maintaining a home and caring for the younger children of the family. He finished up his studies with a course at Bryant & Stratton's Commercial College, from which he graduated in the spring of 1858. When but 16 years of age he engaged to teach a small country school at "Whisky Point," which he taught one summer, receiving the princely salary of $8 per month and board. His services were appreciated suffi-

LEWIS F. JACOBS.

ciently to command a re-engagement the following summer at the surprisingly munificent salary of $18 per month. The third summer school was offered him at the same rate, but his inclinations were more for active business, and in the spring of 1857 he secured a place with the stone firm of Singer & Talcott, in Chicago, as weigh-boy in their yard. Here he found his life work, as he remained with this company and its successors for thirty-three years, filling every position in the business, from weigh-boy to president and general manager. He also became interested with his brothers in the brick business, the Purington & Kimbell Brick Co., and the Chicago Hydraulic Press Brick Co., all leading firms in their lines. In 1889 his health began to fail, his ailment being stomach trouble, with which he is still afflicted, though not to the extent that he was a few years ago. In 1892 he was obliged to retire from active business on account of his health, though still retaining all his business interests, and being retained in the directory of the Western Stone Co., which succeeded his old company. He enlisted in the battery April 19, 1861, served three months and re-enlisted July 16, 1861. He returned on a ten-day furlough at that time, the first few days of which he did not enjoy to the fullest extent, on account of not being able to sleep on a soft bed at night. At his father's suggestion he tried sleeping on the floor, with only a blanket over the carpet, and he found immediate relief from restlessness and wakefulness. He remained with the battery till the battle of Shiloh, where he was severely wounded in the afternoon of the first day by being shot with a one-ounce minie ball in the left leg. Six other members of his squad were wounded at the same time in saving their gun from being captured. Mr. Kimbell and one other comrade, C. C. Nelson, are the only survivors of the seven wounded, all the others, sooner or later, passing on to their reward. He lay in a tent pitched in a corn stubble, on the banks of the Tennessee River, all the first night, along with many others, some of whom died during the night. His comrade and chum, A. V. Pitts, attended to him as best he could until the next afternoon, when he was placed on a hospital steamer and taken with a large number of other wounded to Mound City Hospital. He had telegraphed his father from Paducah, and he at once started and met his son at the hospital, where he remained with him, assisting to care for him and other wounded boys of the battery for two weeks, and helped save Charles' leg from being amputated, which operation had been decided upon by the surgeons as necessary to save his life. The high water of the Ohio and Mississippi rivers forced the abandonment of the Mound City Hospital, and Mr. Kimbell secured a special car of the I. C. R. R. Co., and, with a flat boat, took his son and four other wounded battery boys from the second story of the hospital and poled the boat to Villa Ridge, which was as far as the cars could run on account of the high water. The cots were shoved through the car windows with the

WILLIAM H. JOHNSON.

boys on them, and placed on top of the backs of the seats, and in this manner brought to Chicago, a distance of 365 miles, where they were received by kind and loving friends, who did all in their power to assist in their recovery. By September Charles had recovered sufficiently to be able to get about quite comfortably with a cane, and in this condition rejoined the battery at Memphis, taking his two younger brothers and seven others along with him as recruits. His wound did not improve as favorably as he had hoped in camp, and when he went with the battery on the Cold Water expedition, he found he could not endure the privations of field service, and when the expedition returned to Memphis he was discharged for disability, Nov. 10, 1862, and returned to his home. He married Miss Almira H. Bartholomew Oct. 10, 1863. They have two sons, Sherman T. and Horace M., both married, and one daughter, Sarah M., living at home. They lived in Chicago until 1893, when his failing health compelled his removal, and he removed to Hinsdale, a beautiful suburb of Chicago, seventeen miles from the city, where he has built and fitted up a beautiful and comfortable home, with large grounds and gardens, set out with fruit and shade trees and shrubbery. Here, surrounded by his children and grandchildren, he finds his greatest comfort, and with partially restored health he hopes to continue the struggle of life till called home. He has always kept up an active interest in his old army comrades, and has been the Secretary of the Battery Veteran Association since its organization. He is a member of U. S. Grant Post, No. 28, G. A. R., Chicago, and of the Union Veteran Club, of which he was once Vice President. He is a life member of Cleveland Lodge, No. 211, A., F. & A. M. He joined the Second Universalist Church Society of Chicago in 1859, and still retains his membership in that society. He is serving his third term as President of the Board of Trustees of Unity Church (Unitarian) of Hinsdale, and since living in Hinsdale was elected and served a term of two years in the Village Board of Trustees. His last work has been the writing of the history of his old battery, which, although a great undertaking in his condition of health, has been such a labor of love that he has really improved under it, and feels amply repaid for his labors by the many flattering and grateful expressions of thankfulness for his efforts from all his comrades and many of their friends.

## JULIUS WADSWORTH KIMBELL.

The first break in a band of six brothers, all grown to manhood and past the middle age, maintaining the closest brotherly relations, was made by the sudden taking off of the second brother, Julius W. Kimbell, at his home in Chicago, July 17, 1897. He died suddenly of heart disease, the bereavement to his family and friends falling all the heavier from the absence of knowledge of the sad fact that there were reasons for anticipating

HARRISON KELLEY.

a sudden approaching departure. He was a quiet and unassuming man; such hours as were not given to business were spent in the dearly enjoyed companionship of his family and intimate friends. He belonged to no clubs or secret societies, preferring the happiness of the delights of domestic life. He was born on the old Kimbell homestead in Chicago, Feb. 6, 1841, and lived and died within a few rods of the spot where he was born. He enlisted in the battery in August, 1862, and served with it until after the battle of Arkansas Post, where he was severely injured by the windage of a cannon shot, and was discharged on account of the injury, and returned home. In January, 1864, he had sufficiently recovered to rejoin the battery, which he did at Larkinsville, Ala., and served till the close of the war. He was detailed on detached service in the Ordnance Department, and went through with Sherman on his march from "Atlanta to the Sea." He was sent via New York to Washington, where he was mustered out at the close of the war and returned home. For the first few years he remained on the farm, then associated with his brothers in the brick business, continuing his connection and being actively engaged up to the very day of his death. He was married to Miss Libbie A. Cummings, March 14, 1889. Two sweet little daughters blessed the union, and, with their widowed mother, live in the pleasant little home he had prepared for them. He had won an enviable record, not only as a gallant soldier, but as a reliable, honorable and upright business man and citizen. He had always kept himself closely in touch with his old army comrades, many of whom showed their respect to his memory by attending his funeral services, at which Comrade Rexford was present and sounded "taps" in a very feeling manner, that added greatly to the impressiveness of the services. At the annual reunion in September following his death, the association adopted the following beautiful and touching memoriam:

"In memoriam of Julius W. Kimbell. Again has the grim conqueror invaded our ranks. Since we last met he has called our loved friend and comrade, Julius W. Kimbell, from the midst of loving friends, suddenly, after his last good-night to his little ones.

"Surely it was a bright and shining mark that was selected to sadden our reunion, for in this gentle, kind and brave comrade, one ever ready with sympathy, with words of cheer for friends, and with a smile and a welcome for every duty, however hard or dangerous, we will miss him sadly.

"It was said at the battle of Shiloh the instructions to the enemy were to shoot to wound, as it would require two men to help the wounded man from the field. Our Secretary, Charles B. Kimbell, was wounded there, and was carried from the field, not by two comrades, but on the limber of his gun, drawn by the one surviving horse, and the response to the shot that disabled the elder brother was two more Kimbells to take his place, one of them the friend we mourn to-day, and better, braver soldiers never followed the flag.

"It was a custom in the battery, when on a march, for the dismounted men to walk ahead of the command and await its coming, resting.

CORNELIUS KENDALL.

"These comrades, who have left us are not lost to us, but have gone on before and are resting, waiting for the battery to come up. Let us look forward to the meeting, the greatest reunion, and the last of old Battery 'A.'"

### SPENCER SMALLEY KIMBELL.

The youngest of the three Kimbell brothers serving in the battery was Spencer S. Kimbell. He was born Oct. 8, 1842, on the Kimbell homestead farm, in the city of Chicago, and the home in which he now lives is within a few hundred feet of where he was born. His school education was acquired in the district school, with a course at Bryant & Stratton's Commercial College. His first work away from home was with the stone firm of Singer & Talcott, with whom he began when seventeen years of age, and with his brother, Charles B., was connected with the same firm for twenty-one years. He then bought an interest in the Excelsior Stone Co., which he managed for five years, when he formed a partnership with D. V. Purington in the brick manufacturing business, which has been his line of work ever since. He is now and has been for nine years the general manager of the Chicago Hydraulic Press Brick Co., one of the largest firms in the West. As a business man he has been eminently successful, and by strictly honest, legitimate and honorable methods, has amassed a comfortable fortune of earthly treasures, and established for himself a character for honesty, integrity, sound judgment and punctuality among his business associates, and throughout the great city of his birth, and his word is regarded as good as his bond. As a true citizen of this great Republic he recognizes fully his responsibilities and duties as such, and has taken an active and intelligent interest in public affairs, and has sought to wield a worthy influence in behalf of honest government and honorable and legitimate methods. He has held several political offices, though never of his own seeking. He was School Director for four years, Village Trustee two years, Township Treasurer seven years, County Commissioner two terms, and member of the City Council two years. He has always given the same careful attention to public business entrusted to his hands that he has to his own. He enlisted in Battery "A," Aug. 6, 1862, and joined the battery at Memphis, Tenn., remaining with it continuously till the close of the war, never missing an hour's duty, or a march or engagement, and never having a moment's sickness, and returned home stronger and healthier than when he enlisted. He joined the battery as private, was promoted to first sergeant and to Second Lieutenant, with which rank he was mustered out July 10, 1865. He was married Sept. 6, 1864, to Miss Isabella P. Millard. They have four children living, Mrs. Lucy Kimbell Heafield and Mrs. Fanny Kimbell Binyon, and Florence and Mary Kimbell. The married daughters live close by their father's home, and

T. W. KENNEDY.

three lively little grandchildren brighten their homes and gladden their hearts. He is a thirty-second degree Mason, is a member of Ben Butler Post, G. A. R., and of the Chicago Union Veteran Club. It is needless to say that he is and always has been a stanch and uncompromising Republican in national politics. He is a Universalist in religious belief, and has been connected with the Third Universalist Church of Chicago for over ten years. He has served continuously on its Board of Trustees.

### FREDERICK B. LEAVITT.

No member of Battery "A" will ever forget genial, clever "Old Morpheus," as Fred. B. Leavitt was affectionately christened by his comrades, from his ability to put in more sleep when off duty, with less effort, than any other member of the battery. This happy trait would not apply to him in any respect when on duty, however, as a more ready and willing worker did not belong to the company. Fred. was born at St. Charles, Ill., Oct. 6, 1840. After he was old enough to attend school he moved to Chicago, where he went to the public school, and one year at college till 1861. He left college to learn the brick-making trade with his uncle at Park Ridge, Ill. He left this employment to enlist as private in the battery July 16, 1861, at Chicago. He was with the battery in every engagement during his three years of service, which was continuous, excepting a thirty-day furlough after the siege of Jackson, and was mustered out July 23, 1864, at Springfield, Ill. He married Miss Jessie F. Dannells Feb. 6, 1883, and has one daughter. The first two years after the war he was in business in Chicago, since which time he has followed railroading, at which he is still employed. He lives in Austin, a suburb of Chicago.

### JAMES HENRY LONG.

One of Chicago's most substantial and reliable citizens is J. H. Long. He is well known in railroad circles, and has established a large and prosperous business as dealer in railroad supplies. He is enjoying success and the esteem and confidence of all with whom he has social or business relations. He was born in Chicago March 5, 1844, and was one of the youngest members of the battery, in which he was enlisted as private in February, 1862, at Chicago, by Major Willard. He attended the public and high schools of the city, and at the time of his enlistment was working as teller in a bank. He participated with the battery in all its battles from April, 1862, to March, 1865. He was ordnance sergeant of the Fifteenth Army Corps from August, 1862, to 1865, when he was mustered out at the expiration of his term of enlistment. He was married to Miss Belle Johnson, of Galena, in 1867, and resides in a pleasant home at 4735 Kimbark avenue.

SAMPSON KENNEDY.

## WILLIAM LOWE.

William Lowe was born in New York City, Dec. 21, 1838. He came to Chicago when a youth, where he attended school till sixteen years old, when he went as rodman for James Potter, a civil engineer. After two years' service with him, he worked as assistant engineer with the same gentleman. He was so engaged when he enlisted as private in the battery, April 16, 1861. He served with it for three full years, from "start to finish," and was mustered out July 28, 1864. After his return from the army he engaged with the city of Chicago in the sewerage department, as assistant engineer, up to June 1, 1895, when he was appointed principal engineer. In October, 1896, he was made expert engineer, and in 1897 was appointed to the responsible position of Engineer in charge of the division of intercepting sewers of the city, which position he holds at the present time. He married Miss Kate E. Fish, in September, 1865. They have one daughter. His picture shows him as he looked when forty-five years old. He is now in his sixty-first year, though much younger appearing.

## CHARLES A. LAMB.

The veteran of the battery in years, as well as in wisdom, experience and goodness, which were commensurate with his age, was Charles A. Lamb. He passed away at his home in Albion, Mich., Sept. 23, 1893, in his seventy-ninth year. He had attended an annual reunion of the battery in Chicago exactly two weeks before, at which time his feeble condition made it painfully apparent to his comrades that he would undoubtedly soon be called to answer the last roll call. So, while his taking off was sudden, it was not entirely unexpected, and it was a great satisfaction to his comrades, as it was a pleasure to him, to have met so many of them so short a time before his departure. To all the members of the battery he seemed like a father, or an older brother. While he made no loud professions of piety or morality, his daily life was a constant example worthy of emulation. His patriotism, zeal and energy were not excelled by any of the younger members, and his words of counsel and advice were ever ready for and and heeded by them.

He was born in Salisbury, Conn., Aug. 21, 1815, where he lived till early manhood, when he went to Albany, N. Y., and learned the cabinetmaker's trade. He afterwards moved to Maumee, Ohio, where for several years he carried on the furniture business on his own account. Here he built up a good business, and had a cosy home, and had a number of men in his employ. As this place (now South Toledo), was only ten miles from Toledo, he, with numbers of others, moved their establishments to Toledo, where he opened a store, on Summit street. The sinking of a cargo of furniture he had purchased from Buffalo, uninsured, ruined him financially, and

GEORGE KING.

he was ever after a salesman or manager for others in that line, which was his life business. After closing up his affairs in Toledo he came to Chicago. On the 19th of April, 1861, he enlisted in Battery "A," in Chicago, served three months as artificer, and re-enlisted for three years, July 16, 1861. He served continuously and faithfully the full term of his enlistment, and was mustered out July 23, 1864. On his return to Chicago he was met at the depot by his former employer, who had always been a warm friend of Mr. Lamb. He informed him his place was ready and waiting for him, and he began work the next day, without loss of time. In October, 1865, he began work in the employ of Charles Tobey, a large furniture dealer. In May, 1870, he went to Omaha to take charge of a branch establishment in that city for the Thayer & Tobey Furniture Co., where he remained nearly two years. Returning to Chicago early in 1872, he took a position with the furniture concern of A. L. Hale & Bro., which he filled for nearly two years. From Chicago he removed to Albion, Mich., where he lived in quiet retirement until his death. His wives were estimable ladies, from Sharon, Conn., adjoining his own native town. His widow, Matilda Benedict Lamb, survives him, and now resides at Sharon. He had one daughter, two sons, and two grandsons. His daughter, Anne C., resides in New York City, where she has been a teacher in private schools for nearly twenty years. One son, Fred Reed Lamb, has lived in Chicago since early youth. He was also a soldier in the Union army about a year, and since the war has been in the employ of Selz, Schwab & Co., extensive boot and shoe manufacturers. Another son is George A. Lamb, of New Haven, Conn. Mr. Lamb's remains were buried in his native town of Salisbury, Conn.

## FRANCIS MORGAN.

A great deal of the efficiency of the battery can be attributed to its early training and discipline under Lieutenant, afterward Captain, Francis Morgan. He was one of twelve children, nine sons and three daughters, born in Surrey, near London, England, July 3, 1837, and came to Chicago with his parents in 1844, and that city was his home during the remainder of his life. After coming to Chicago he was placed in Russell's Military School at New Haven, Conn., and there took a full course of an education the line of which he followed almost constantly during his life. His tastes were almost wholly confined to military lore, and when the war broke out he was particularly well fitted to do good service for his adopted country. He joined the battery in Chicago, April 19, 1861, serving the three months' term and re-enlisting July, 1861, for three years in the same command. Not being of a strong physical nature, his health succumbed to the hardships of the campaign, and while the battery was stationed at Paducah, Ky., he was forced to return home on a sick furlough. Before he had fully recovered

MR. AND MRS. M. N. KIMBELL.

he returned to the battery just before the advance on Fort Donelson. Participating in that battle he was again stricken down with sickness and was sent home just before the battle of Shiloh, and resigning his commission as Captain, and his poor health continuing, did not again enter the service. He rendered valuable service during the Chicago railroad riots in 1887, being on the Governor's staff at that time. Previous to this he had been on the staff of Governor Beveridge. He died at 193 Michigan avenue, "The Beaurivage," a building which he named, Aug. 6, 1897. The Loyal Legion, of which he was an old and active member, had charge of his funeral. As a charter member of the Chicago Club he made the club his residence for a number of years. He had never married. Among his army comrades and friends he was held in the highest esteem as a thorough gentleman and a man whose integrity of character and innate honesty had never been questioned.

## THOMAS A. McKNIGHT.

The Eleventh Indiana Infantry Regiment contributed one valuable member to the battery, in the person of Thomas A. McKnight, who was detailed from Company "B," of that regiment, at Paducah, Ky., in September, 1861, by order of General U. S. Grant, to serve as blacksmith in the battery. He had only enlisted the month before, but, being a first-class blacksmith, he preferred working at his trade when he could do so and be serving his country at the same time. He remained with the battery, doing faithful duty, until the expiration of his term of enlistment, and was then mustered out at Atlanta, Ga. After his discharge he went to Covington, Ind., where he resumed work at his trade, also dealing in horses. He married Miss Helen A. Gish in 1867. They have four children, all girls. He was born in Middletown, Ohio, April 7, 1838.

## GEORGE McCAGG.

Less than two years after the close of the war one of the most honored and beloved members of the battery, George McCagg, passed away at his home in Chicago. His health and constitution had been undermined by his three years and three months' hard and faithful service in the battery, and the hope of his friends that a change to his home climate, and proper care and treatment might work a cure, was not realized, and he passed to the higher life April 8, 1867. George McCagg was a true, natural-born gentleman, and a brave and faithful soldier, a noble example of the two qualities being combined in the same individual, without ostentation, or the giving of offense to his associates. He was born in Hudson, Columbia County, New York, July 22, 1831. He lived the early years of his life with his father on a farm

CHARLES B. KIMBELL.

in Stockport, in the same county, and later on came to Chicago and engaged in the lumber business, and was so occupied when the war broke out. He enlisted in the battery in Chicago, April 19, 1861, was appointed corporal, and served through the three months' service. He re-enlisted for three years July 16, 1861, and served the full term of his enlistment, being mustered out in July, 1864, as Lieutenant. He had, previous to his promotion as Lieutenant, served as quartermaster sergeant, succeeding E. P. Tobey, who was promoted to Lieutenant. He passed through the entire service without any serious injuries, though he had some very narrow escapes. His horse was shot from under him and killed at the battle of Arkansas Post. He was as cool and brave a soldier as the army contained. Captain Wood, in his official reports of the battles of Shiloh and Arkansas Post, made especial mention of him and the part he bore in those engagements. He was offered a position by General Sherman on his staff, and, while appreciating the honor, respectfully declined, preferring, as he expressed it, to remain with the "boys," to whom he was greatly attached, and which attachment was fully reciprocated. He died unmarried, and his remains were taken to Stockport, N. Y., and buried with those of his parents.

## JAMES W. MILNER.

No member of the battery was better known or more universally well liked by all his comrades than James W. Milner. Those who have never stood side by side, elbow to elbow together, behind or beside our country's flag, while following it amid the scenes of battle and strife, can little understand the emotions that fill the heart and cause the eyes to dim of one who is left to write of a comrade's worth, patriotism and valor, while serving during those terrible years of civil war. He was born at Kingston, Ontario, Canada, Jan. 11, 1841, and came to Chicago with his parents at an early age. While a youth he traveled and studied for a while with the Rev. Dr. Goodfellow. He then entered the Northwestern University at Evanston, and was a student in that institution in 1862 when he enlisted as private in the battery in Chicago, serving the entire three-year term of his enlistment, and was mustered out Aug. 24, 1864.

He was always at his post, ever ready and willing. As a friend and brother soldier, in camp or field, he was "true blue," ever kind and obliging, honorable to a fault, and always a gentleman. It can be truly said he was beloved by every officer and private in our battery. At the terrible battle of Atlanta, on July 22, 1864, when almost a hand to hand encounter was being enacted, and so many of our brave boys were captured, he miraculously escaped, although the last man to leave the gun. He had always said he would as soon be killed as to be captured and perhaps starve to death in

JULIUS W. KIMBELL.

some rebel slaughter pen. This resolve possibly led him to take some desperate chances to escape, which others would not have taken.

While the battery was in camp at Larkinsville, during the winter of 1864, he contributed more than any other member, in dispelling the blues and rendering camp-life endurable, if not enjoyable, by writing and placing upon the boards a play for the theatrical combination of which he was President and Fred S. Church scenic artist. It proved a great attraction and success. After being mustered out he returned home, and later on was appointed Department United States Commissioner of Fish and Fisheries, in which position he rendered very efficient service until his death, which occurred at Waukegan, Ill., Jan. 6, 1880. Prof. Baird, of the Smithsonian Institution, in writing to his widow at the time of his death, said: "He was the best posted man in fish culture in the United States, and the eyes of the fish world were upon him." He and his family were always proud, and justly so, of the fact that after the publication of the first Government Report, the Northwestern University recognized his literary accomplishments by conferring upon him a degree, the only instance in which an undergraduate had been so honored. He was married to Miss Sarah Fay, at Waukegan, Ill., Jan. 1, 1872, by whom he had two daughters, who, with their widowed mother, survive him, and now reside in Chicago.

## EDWARD MENDSEN.

One of the oldest and most prominent lumber men of Chicago is Edward Mendsen, of Evanston, Ill. He was a member of the battery when the war broke out, having joined in 1856 and continued his membership. He served during the three months' service as orderly sergeant, and was in charge of the gun squad and was stationed at Big Muddy Bridge in the beginning of the war. The boys had no tents while there, and Mendsen's shelter was an old hollow tree. He was mustered out at the end of the three months' service, his term of enlistment having expired. He was born in Cherryville, Pa., Dec. 31, 1834, and lived on a farm there until fifteen years old, when he came to Chicago in August, 1849. He served an apprenticeship of three years with Welch & Launder, carriage manufacturers, receiving the princely salary of $25 per year and board. In 1861 he was in partnership with his brother, J. F. Mendsen, in a carriage manufactory, at the corner of Ann and Randolph streets. They closed out their business in 1863, and Edward entered the lumber business, which he is still successfully engaged in. He married Mary E. Boggs Oct. 17, 1861, and has three children and eight grandchildren. Mrs. Mendsen died in 1874, and he married Mrs. James D. Kline for a second wife, in May, 1884, and resides in Evanston, Ill.

SPENCER S. KIMBELL.

## LEWIS B. MITCHELL.

A war record of which any comrade may well be proud is the one made by Lewis B. Mitchell, now residing at No. 50 Astor street, Chicago. He was born at Akron, Ohio, May 6, 1841, where he lived until 1852, when he went to Chicago and remained there until the war broke out, and has resided there since the war. He was clerk in the general freight office of the Illinois Central Railroad at the time of his enlistment as private in the battery, April 17, 1861. He served in squad six through the three months' service, and re-enlisted July 16, 1861, for three years. Soon after his re-enlistment he received a Lieutenant's commission (Junior First), in Campbell's Battery, and later was appointed Senior First Lieutenant in Battery "H," First Illinois Artillery. He was Captain and A. D. C. to General Logan, and was breveted Major U. S. V. He was mustered out by general order from the War Department Sept. 6, 1865, the war having ended. He married Miss Nettie Bodman, of Fort Atkinson, Wis., has had two daughters, one living. He has been engaged in the commission business on the Board of Trade, and enjoys the confidence and esteem of a large number of comrades and business associates.

## CONANT CONRAD NELSON.

Of the seven members of squad two wounded in the first day's fight at Shiloh in saving their gun, two only survive, the subject of this brief sketch, and C. B. Kimbell. They have not seen each other since the fateful day, and for many years the comrades of the battery lost all trace of Comrade Nelson, but of late years correspondence has brought them near each other, and he is living in hopes of meeting with them in person in the near future. He was born in Lewis, Essex County, New York, May 24, 1831, on his father's farm. Here he grew up from childhood, attending the district school and working on the farm, until 1845, when he went to Burlington, Vt., and went to work as an errand boy, and subsequently as clerk, until 1847. He then went into a law office in Syracuse, but that work not being to his taste, he again went to work in a dry goods and general grocery store. After a few years he came West and went on the road as a traveling salesman for the large dry goods firm of Bowen Bros., having the Northern and Western States for his territory. He had just come in from a trip about the middle of April, 1861, and was invoicing preparatory to starting out again when the war fever broke out and took hold of him strong, and he enlisted in the battery April 19 and left the city with it on the 21st for Cairo. He re-enlisted July 16, 1861, for three years, and was in the service as private up to and including the first days' fight at Shiloh. Here he was severely wounded late in the afternoon, a ball entering his left arm near the elbow, and passing down

FRED. B. LEAVITT.

into the wrist, where it was extracted two weeks after by Dr. Taylor, of Chicago, who was boat surgeon on the boat that carried a large number of the wounded to the hospitals at Evansville and Paducah. His wound was probed in a log cabin hospital on the battlefield the night he was wounded, but the bullet was not found, and he was put on a steamer and taken down to Savannah. He was placed in a building on a brick floor, with no blanket, and did not sleep for two nights, and suffered excruciating pain from his wound. He was taken to the hospital at Evansville, Ind., from which he was discharged on account of his wound June 16, 1862. He then went to Chicago for a short time. Since the war, except about ten years when conducting a small business for himself, he has been a government clerk, and at present is a clerk in the Pension Office. He was married to Miss Jane Chute, of Indiana, who died Oct. 1, 1898, leaving him a widower with two girls and a boy, the eldest seventeen years of age. He lives in Maryland, six miles from Washington, and finds his time fully occupied at work and going back and forth.

## ALFRED W. PENDLETON.

The State of "wooden nutmegs" furnished a goodly number of native sons for Battery "A," among them being Alfred W. Pendleton. He was born in Norwich, Conn., July 1, 1837, and passed his early years in Connecticut on a farm. He came to Chicago, and at the breaking out of the war was a member of the fire department. He quit the service of the city in fighting fire to undertake the more perilous service of fighting for his country, and enlisted in Battery "A," Aug. 6, 1862, in Chicago. He served as private, postillion and sergeant, in which rank he was serving when mustered out in July, 1865, at the close of the war. He was severely wounded in the breast by fragments of a shell before Vicksburg, July 3, 1863, which was the only injury he received in the service. Returning to Chicago at the close of the war he re-entered the service of the fire department, and served his time till pensioned and retired. He married and has two children and one grandchild.

## JAMES PHILLIPS.

To be the hero and a veteran of two wars is a distinction which but a few of the members of Battery "A" could claim. Among those who could was James Phillips. He enlisted in the Mexican war in 1848 and served nine months, the closing of the war terminating his service. He was born in Michigan Nov. 17, 1825, and his childhood and youth were spent in his native State and New York. He came to Chicago in 1851, and at the breaking out of the war was truckman for the large foundry concern of P. W.

JAMES HENRY LONG.

Gates. He enlisted in the battery in Chicago, July 28, 1861, as private, and served as postillion till mustered out at the end of his term of enlistment, July 23, 1864. He was married to Miss Mary Barns before the war. They had four children, one of whom died during his lifetime. He was driver in the city fire department for eleven years after the war, then with the Michigan Southern road till his death. He died in Chicago, March 27, 1893, and was buried in Oakwoods Cemetery. At the time of his death he had three children, four living grandchildren and one great-grandchild. His widow still lives in Chicago.

### AURELIUS VERNON PITTS.

On the 1st of March, 1895, there passed from the ranks of the survivors of "Battery 'A'" one of its most esteemed and popular members, A. V. Pitts. He died at his home in Chicago on that day, after having been a sufferer from poor health for many months. He left a devoted wife and a fifteen-year old son surviving him. He was born in Winthrop, Maine, Oct. 3, 1836. In 1849, with his father's family, he came to Illinois, and located at Alton, where they remained two years. They came to Chicago in 1851 and established a plant for the manufacturing of the celebrated Pitts threshing machines, of which his father, Hiram A. Pitts, was the inventor. They also manufactured horse powers and other farm implements. His father died in 1860, after which the sons, A. V. Pitts and three brothers, took charge of the works. After the great Chicago fire the works were removed to Marseilles, Ill. Aurelius was fifteen years old when he came to Chicago. He received his primary education in his native city, and afterwards attended the public schools of Chicago. He learned the trade of machinist in his father's works, and became a practical operator in them. He enlisted in Battery "A" in Chicago, April 19, 1861, re-enlisted in same company July 28, 1861, and served continuously and faithfully, as private, until the end of his term of enlistment, and was mustered out and returned to Chicago in July, 1864. A. V. Pitts was a naturally inventive genius, and many of the obstacles and difficulties of army life were overcome by means suggested by his thoughtful attention. Whenever any difficulty presented itself he would at once set his mind at work to solve it, and his suggestions were usually heeded and commended by the officers and his comrades of the battery. A notable instance of his tact was illustrated at the battle of Shiloh. In the first day's fight, toward its close, five of the members of his squad, himself among them, were shot, four of them seriously. He being less severely wounded was detailed to take charge of them the first night, and all were placed in a V tent on the bare ground, pitched in a corn stubble near the bank of the river, under the shelter of the guns of the gunboats. C. B. Kimbell, who had been his messmate from the beginning, was among the most danger-

WILLIAM LOWE.

ously wounded. When Pitts succeeded in getting the hurried attendance of a surgeon for a few moments, some five hours after his being shot, the surgeon prescribed a poultice of flax meal and pulverized charcoal the full length of Kimbell's leg, which was now as black as a stovepipe and swollen as full as the skin would hold. In the demoralized condition of everything after a hard day's fighting, commissary and medical stores were not easily obtained, and where to get the material to carry out the surgeon's directions would have discouraged many a less thoughtful man. Not so with A. V. Pitts. He went into the woods a distance until he found the remnants of a burnt log heap, and digging into it secured a quantity of very passable charcoal. This he put into a gunny sack and, pounding it between two stones, soon had quite a quantity of a very good article of charcoal. Flaxseed could not be had but he thought wheat bran would be a very good substitute, and, going to the river bank, he secured a sack from the quartermaster's stores, and getting a pail mixed it full of coal and bran, well wet, and ripping up a fine gunny sack he spread the improvised poultice on it, and before midnight had the leg of his suffering comrade wrapped in it and made as comfortable as possible under the difficult circumstances. The surgeons afterward said that, only for the prompt and thoughtful action taken by Pitts, Kimbell would have undoubtedly lost his leg and perhaps his life. Kimbell and Pitts enjoyed each other's firm and lasting friendship until the day of his death, and Kimbell, with other comrades of the battery, assisted in the sad duty of laying his remains in their final resting place in Rose Hill Cemetery. He married Miss Mary Bentley, of Chicago, in Rockford, Ill., May 25, 1865, who, as before stated, survives him. The marriage ceremony was performed by the Rev. Robt. Bentley, a brother of Mrs. Pitts.

## WILLIAM R. PAGE.

One of the prominent and successful lawyers of Chicago is the subject of this brief review.

He was born at Jefferson Barracks, Missouri, Oct. 9, 1843, his father, Captain John Page, of the Fourth United States Infantry, being at that time in command of the post. In the Mexican war, at the battle of Palo Alto, Captain Page was mortally wounded. From that time and for many years Wm. R. Page was without a permanent home, until, in his later and mature life, he came to Chicago. In 1852 he accompanied his mother to Rome, Italy, where he remained a year, then entered a preparatory school in Florence, which he attended for three years. He then went to Paris and was admitted to the "Lycee Bonaparte," one of the colleges of the Napoleonic empire, in which he prosecuted his studies until 1858. Returning to the United States he became a student of the Northwestern University at Evanston, Ill., where he continued his studies until 1861. On the call for troops

CHARLES A. LAMB.

he immediately abandoned his studies and, with his brother, now General John H. Page, of the Third United States Infantry, enlisted in Battery A, Chicago Light Artillery. He served as a private in this battery at Cairo, and at Paducah, and in the fall of 1861 was commissioned a Second Lieutenant in a detached company of Ohio troops, known then at the Benton Cadets, which was to be consolidated with other companies into a regiment. He immediately reported to St. Louis, and was ordered to the front at Jefferson City, where the main army under General J. C. Fremont had been concentrated. From this point commenced the chase of General Price's army, which was unremittently continued as far as Springfield, Mo., when General Fremont was relieved by General Hunter, and the Army of the Missouri was ordered back to Rolla. Lieutenant Page on arrival at Rolla was informed that nearly the entire family was then in service, and that sickness and family interests demanded the return of some one of them. Lieutenant Page was the one selected, and against his desire and under protest acceded to the request. He took immediate charge of the business interests of the family, and at once, after examination, was admitted in the class of 1864 at Harvard University. He was graduated from that class, and subsequently took his degree of LL. B. at the Law School of Cambridge in 1866. Returning to Chicago he began his career as a lawyer, which he has followed to the present time. In 1871 he was married to Florence N. Talcott, daughter of the late Colonel E. B. Talcott. He has two children living. Lieutenant Page has always been a Republican, and has, without any desire for office, taken an active part in political affairs, insisting at all times upon the selection of reputable men for office. He was, against his will, elected Supervisor of the South Town of Chicago, which office he filled with credit to the State and City. Since then he has absolutely refused to accept public office. Lieutenant Page has always taken an active interest in charitable institutions. He has been a director of the Chicago Athenaeum for twenty years, director of the Glenwood Industrial Institution, and is one of the Trustees of the Illinois Soldiers' Orphans' Home at Normal. He is now 56 years old, and it is hoped that his busy life may be prolonged for many years of activity and usefulness.

## JOHN H. PAGE.

If any member of Battery "A" was a soldier from infancy, General John H. Page, of the Third United States Infantry, can rightfully claim that distinction. He was born in the army at New Castle, Delaware, March 26, 1842, his father being at that time a captain in the Fourth United States Infantry. He moved from post to post with his father, who was mortally wounded at the battle of Palo Alto, the first battle in the Mexican war. In 1851 he went to Italy and France, where he remained at school until 1857.

CAPT. FRANCIS MORGAN.

Returning to the United States he attended the Northwestern University at Evanston, Illinois, where, in 1861, when the civil war broke out, leaving his studies, he enlisted in Battery "A," as did also his only brother, Wm. R. Page. He served with the battery at Cairo and Paducah, Ky., where he was discharged to accept a commission as Second Lieutenant in the Third United States Infantry. He joined his regiment at once and remained with it until the close of the war, having participated in nearly every battle with the Army of the Potomac, from the battle of Bull Run to the close of the war. He was brevetted Captain for gallant services at the battle of Chancellorsville, and Major for gallant and meritorious services at the battle of Gettysburg. After the civil war he served for many years in the West, and was engaged in numerous campaigns against the various tribes of Indians. He was promoted to Major in the Eleventh United States Infantry, then to Lieutenant Colonel in the Twenty-second Infantry, and to Colonel of the Third United States Infantry, which regiment he still commands. He commanded the regiment at El Caney and San Juan, Cuba, and during the siege of Santiago commanded the brigade consisting of his own regiment and the Twentieth Regular Infantry. For his services in the Cuban campaign he was promoted to the rank of Brigadier General of Volunteers. After the Cuban war he returned to Fort Snelling, Minn., and a part of his regiment was immediately sent to quell the outbreak of the Pillager Indians in Northern Minnesota. General Page will sail about Feb. 1, 1899, for the Philippine Islands. He was married to Mrs. Eliza T. Shaw in 1871, and has six children, all of whom will accompany him to his new field of service.

## JEREMIAH D. POWELL.

The first victim of rebel lead in the battery was brave, handsome "Jerry" Powell. He was killed during the early part of the first day's engagement at Shiloh. His right arm was taken off at the shoulder by a cannon shot, and he survived but a short time. His body was taken to Savannah, Tenn., and buried by some Missouri infantry. His brother, Moses W. Powell, came from Chicago for the purpose of getting the remains and taking them home for interment, but they could never be found, and he rests among the unknown dead. Jerry was a universal favorite with the whole battery, and his death being the first in that line cast a gloom of sadness over the entire company, which was only dispelled by the bloody and desperate fighting later on. He was born in Ebensburgh, Pa., in 1836, and lived on a farm near that place during his childhood and youth. Coming to the West he located in Chicago, engaging in the roofing business, which he was following at the breaking out of the war. He enlisted as private in Battery "A," April 19, 1861, and served three months, re-enlisting July 16 following, for three years. At the time of his death he was sergeant of his squad.

GEORGE McCAGG.

## JOHN MILTON PETERS.

A plant or shrub of Northern growth will not always flourish and thrive when transplanted in Southern soil, and the same can be said of the human species. But John M. Peters is an exception to this rule, and is a good example of a hardy Northerner settling on Southern soil, and flourishing and thriving with the best of the native-born Southerners. He was born in Poughkeepsie, N. Y., Feb. 5, 1841, and lived there until the spring of 1857, when he left school and went to Chicago. He was educated in the public schools of Poughkeepsie and at McGeorg's Academy in that city. After coming to Chicago he was engaged as bookkeeper by Clough & King, wholesale hide dealers, and left their employ to enlist as private in the battery, April 16, 1861, and re-enlisted for three years July 16, 1861. He served with the battery, being in all its engagements until the siege of Vicksburg. At Young's Point he was taken with typhoid fever and was sent to Memphis, where he lay in Overton Hospital several months. Recovering, he was placed on detached service as chief clerk in the Adjutant General's office, Department of the Army of Tennessee, and remained there until mustered out at the expiration of his term of enlistment with rank of corporal, at Chattanooga, Tenn., in July, 1864. He returned to Memphis after visiting his family in Chicago, where he has since lived, engaging extensively and successfully in manufacturing and steam-boating, as owner, and was cashier of the German Bank six years. He ranks among the most prominent and respected citizens of Memphis. He married Miss Eliza J. Andrews, of Tuscumbia, Ala., in November, 1865, by whom he has had one son, Joseph A. Peters, now living in Chicago.

## GEORGE A. PRATT.

George A. Pratt is a native of the Green Mountain State. He was born in Woodstock, Vt., Feb. 25, 1838. He lived there and attended school until fourteen years old, then he learned the bookbinder's trade, and for a time was clerk in a hotel. Coming to the West he took a position as messenger for the American Express Co., on the C. & N.-W. R. R., which place he left to enlist as private in the battery at Chicago, Aug. 6, 1862. He served with the battery till March 10, 1863, when he was discharged at St. Louis for disability from sickness contracted in the line of duty. He participated with the battery in the battles of Chickasaw Bayou and Arkansas Post, was opposite Vicksburg guarding the canal, and saw the "Queen of the West" run the blockade. When he enlisted at Chicago he and a number of other recruits, among them being Wm. Johnson, Al. Pendleton, Harry Roberts, Ed Hughes and others, were formed into a squad and sent to join the battery at Memphis, going via St. Louis. Here they found they were likely to

JAMES W. MILNER.

be detained for some time, waiting for transportation. They were asked in the meantime to assist in guarding the rebel prisoners being held there. Not relishing the idea of serving as home guards, which was not what they enlisted for, they consulted together and decided to do a little "skirmishing" on their own account. They found a small steamer about ready to start down the river, and made a bargain with the captain, paying him $1 apiece for deck passage, which left only money enough in the squad to buy a barrel of bread. Thus equipped they started on their way rejoicing. All would have gone fairly well if the boat had not run aground on a sandbar, where it stuck for three days. Their provisions ran low, but a friendly sergeant on board in charge of supplies agreed to be busy in other quarters while the boys took bread from his stock to fill their barrel, and, after a five days' trip they reached the battery well tired out and hungry. Comrade Pratt and this squad have the credit of introducing to the battery Geo. F. Root's famous song, "The Battle-Cry of Freedom," which had just been published. They sang it on the boat going down the river to appreciative audiences, and the first night of their arrival at Memphis the soldiers came from all sides to hear the new song, which was enthusiastically received. Comrade Pratt was at one time offered a commission on board a gunboat, but preferred to remain with his friends in the battery, where he would have served his entire term if his health had permitted. He married Miss Sarah P. Hall June 22, 1864. They have an interesting family consisting of a son, daughter and one granddaughter. Comrade Pratt is agent for the C. & N.-W. R. R. at Ft. Atkinson, Wis., and is also prominently interested in manufacturing interests in that city.

## PERRY POLK POWELL.

One of the youngest of the many young members of the battery was Perry P. Powell. He was born in Chicago, Jan. 11, 1845, on a farm on the corner of Milwaukee and Armitage avenues, which at that time was on the open prairie, and is now a densely populated portion of the city. His boyhood days were passed in attending school in a little country schoolhouse during the winter, one and a half miles from home, and working on the farm with his brothers during the remainder of the year. He enlisted as private in the battery, Aug. 6, 1862, when seventeen years and seven months old, and served with it until after the siege of Vicksburg, when, on account of sickness contracted in the line of duty, he was discharged Aug. 7, 1863, at Camp Sherman, Miss. He returned home and after regaining his health, enlisted in the Chicago Light Guard (Captain Henry J. Milligan), May 14, 1864, and was mustered into the One Hundred and Thirty-fourth Illinois Volunteer Infantry as Company "E," for 100 days. They were in service in Kentucky and Missouri during Price's last raid, and were mustered out

EDWARD MENDSEN.

Oct. 25, 1864. In February, 1865, when it was apparent that the war must soon be brought to a close, and being determined if possible to "be in at the death," he again enlisted on the 21st of that month in Captain R. G. Rombauer's Company "G," First Regiment, Illinois Light Artillery, to serve one year. The battery's service was in Tennessee and the last days of his drilling with it at the close of the war was on the same ground where Battery "A" was drilling when he joined it in August, 1862. He was mustered out at the close of the war, July 24, 1865. He returned home and successfully engaged in mercantile business, farming, and real estate, in which latter business he is still engaged. He married Miss Mary E. McGregor, by whom he has had three children, one aged nine years, two grown to maturity. He owns a small fruit farm at Winfield, Kan., where he has resided a portion of the time since the war; also a stock ranch of 1,040 acres thirty miles from Winfield. He has spent several winters with his family at Melbourn, Fla., though his principal headquarters are on the ground of the old homestead where he was born.

## STEPHEN N. PEASE.

Stephen N. Pease is a native of Vermont. He was born Nov. 27, 1837, and lived in the State of his nativity till 1846, when he came to Chicago, which city has since been his home. He was engaged in teaming in the spring of 1861. He enlisted as private in the battery April 19, and re-enlisted at Cairo in July following. He was appointed stable sergeant, and served the full term of his enlistment, being with the battery in all its service during that time and was mustered out at Springfield, Ill., in July, 1864. He returned to Chicago and has worked at the carpenter's trade since. He married, but has lost his wife. He has five children and seven grandchildren, and lives quietly and comfortably on the West Side of the city, with some of his children.

## HENRY HARRISON POND.

One of the busy, hustling business men that help to make up the busy city of Chicago is Henry H. Pond, who, since the close of the war in 1865, has been engaged continuously in the general commission business on the noted thoroughfare of South Water street. His firm is one of the leading ones in the business, and success has crowned his industry and close attention to business. He was born in Catskill, N. Y., July 15, 1840. From the age of two years until thirteen he lived in Montgomery, Ala., and attended the common schools of that city. Owing to the death of his father at that time he journeyed north to Whigville, Conn., where he worked until the spring of 1857, when he left in April and came to Chicago, which city has since been his home. He obtained a position as retail grocery clerk in the store of

LEWIS B. MITCHELL.

John H. Bowers, which was located on the southeast corner of State and Madison streets, where Schlesinger & Mayer's dry goods house now stands. He enlisted in the battery as private in Chicago, July 16, 1861, and served the full three years' term of his enlistment, taking an active and creditable part in all the battery's service, without an injury, and was mustered out at Springfield, Ill., in August, 1864. He married Miss Mary Murphy, of Chicago, May 18, 1865. They have no children. Comrade Pond has always been an active member of the Masonic fraternity, and stands high in those circles. He is a life member of Cleveland Lodge, No. 211, A., F. & A. M.

## WILLIAM B. PHILLIPS.

William B. Phillips was born at Jersey Shore, Lycoming County, Pennsylvania, June 28, 1829, where he grew to be a young man, attending school three months in the year when a boy, assisting with the work about home the remainder of the time. When a little over sixteen years old he began to learn the carpenter trade, at which he served his time, and when the war began was working in a sash and door factory in Galena, Ill. He enlisted in that city in the beginning of the war, in a three months' infantry company. He was transferred to Battery "A." and joined the company as private, together with his brother Walter S., on July 16, 1861, and served continuously with the battery the full term of his enlistment, being mustered out Aug. 16, 1864. He celebrated a birthday while in the army thumbing a gun at Kenesaw Mountain. He was married and had two children when he enlisted. Seven children have been born to him since the war. His wife is dead and he is a widower and lives in quiet retirement at Marion, Iowa. He worked at his trade for many years after the war, and had charge of a bridge-building gang on the C., M. & St. P. R. R. for twenty years.

## JAMES OSCAR PADDOCK.

James Oscar Paddock was born in Wyoming, Wyoming County, New York, Oct. 14, 1841.

He was the son of Robert Paddock and Josephine Wilder his wife, and came of a direct Puritan and fighting ancestry, his forefathers being prominently identified with every war, colonial and otherwise, that our country was engaged in. At the breaking out of the civil war he served with the ninety days' men, and re-enlisted in Battery "A," Chicago Light Artillery, July 28, 1861.

He left a lucrative position of honorable trust in the office of Mears & Bates, lumbermen, because, to use his own words, "My country needs her loyal sons." He was mortally wounded at the battle of Shiloh while doing his duty, on the 6th of April, 1862, and died April 14, at Paducah, Ky.

HARRY MORGAN.

He was a young man of sterling worth and unblemished character, and, to quote words of his early friend, Wm. M. Hoyt: "If James Paddock had lived he would have been one of the foremost men of Chicago. I never knew a young man of better business sagacity or greater ambition."

So, while this great city, in which he would in all probability have played his part well, has grown in greatness and power, he, who gave his young life to his country, has been sleeping the years of his manhood away in beautiful Rose Hill.

## CHARLES WIGHT POOLE.

One of the "older boys" of the battery is Charles W. Poole. He was born in Williamstown, Vt., Dec. 26, 1831, where he lived till 1848, when his family started for Illinois, coming through New York by the Erie Canal to Buffalo and around the lakes to Chicago, then by the Illinois and Michigan Canal to La Salle, from which place they went by team to Dover in Bureau County. Here he lived and worked on a farm till 1853, when, in September, he came to Chicago, which place has since been his home, working in a machine shop at the time of his enlistment as private in the battery, April 19, 1861. He was appointed sergeant in September, 1861, and quartermaster sergeant the following December, in which position he served until mustered out, July 23, 1864, by expiration of his term of enlistment. He returned to the South and entered the Quartermaster's office, with Major T. H. Capron, of the old division, and remained there until August, 1865, when he left Little Rock, Ark., for home, and resumed work at his trade. In the fall of 1869 he went into the internal revenue service and remained there nearly five years. He was afterwards engaged for nearly fifteen years as gauger at the city distilleries. For the last eight years he has been in the employ of the C., B. & Q. R. R. He was married in 1869 to Mary E. Breese, and has had three sons, the oldest dying in 1877. He lives with his family in their home at Western Springs, Ill. He was elected President of the Battery Veteran Association at its annual reunion Sept. 10, 1898, and has served as Vice President for one year in the same organization.

## HARVEY B. RISLEY.

The "parson" of the company was Harvey B. Risley. He says, if the old family Bible is correct, he was born Dec. 15, 1835, in a log house in the woods, near the Desplaines River, a few miles south of the city of Joliet, Illinois. While in his infancy his father moved on a farm west of Joliet. He attended the public schools of that city. His first school, and where he received his first punishment, was held in a room in his father's farm-house. He does not remember what his misdemeanor was, but his punishment consisted in being placed under his mother's bed in an adjoining room. While

so confined he discovered a box of raisins, with which he proceeded to fill himself to pass away the time. When the teacher called him out and asked him if he had taken any raisins, he remorsefully says he did not imitate George Washington. In 1844 his father was elected Sheriff of Will County, on the Whig ticket. As farming was so unprofitable, pork selling at $1 per hundred and everything else in proportion, they left the farm and moved into Joliet. His strong religious nature was not developed in his younger school days, as he received the usual amount of punishment from all his teachers, which consisted principally of sitting between the girls and standing on the dunce block for not getting his lessons, which latter operation occupied a good portion of his time. He reformed later and developed into a steady, thoroughgoing youth and student. At the age of fourteen he began dividing his time between going to school and clerking in his father's store. In the winter of 1850 he went to Chicago in a sleigh, the only means of traveling in the winter in those days, and took a position in the Chicago postoffice under Richard L. Wilson, P. M. The office was kept in a brick residence on Clark street, near the Sherman House, where the "parson" often went up in the cupola with a spyglass to see if the steamer was in sight that brought the Eastern mail. At that time the entire postoffice force, including the assistant postmaster, consisted of eight men, all of whom, excepting Comrade Risley, have passed over the dark river. President Taylor died, and Postmaster Wilson was soon after removed for political reasons, and the "parson" went with him. He then returned to Joliet, traveling by canal, on the packet New Orleans, which important event made a lasting impression on his mind, and gave him an exalted idea of his ability to get through the world. The following winter he returned to Chicago and attended a select school, where he was a schoolmate with Edward Russel, of the battery, who was killed at Shiloh. During the latter part of his school days he joined the Volunteer Fire Brigade, and was attached to "Red Jacket" No. 4, famous in Chicago's early history for getting to fires first and throwing the highest stream of water. He fluctuated between Chicago and Joliet till 1858, in the meantime taking a course at Bell's Commercial College, studying bookkeeping and attending lectures on commercial law, and working in a bank in Joliet with his father. In 1858 he engaged for a year in the commission business in Chicago, and in 1859 went into the grocery business in the same city, in which he continued until March, 1861. On the 14th of April following he signed the muster roll of Battery "A," and went to the front as a private. He served with credit three years and three months, and was mustered out with the company at Springfield, in July, 1864. He obtained the appellation of "parson," which clung to him through the service, and will through life with the boys, during the three months' service at Camp Smith. An old couple of natives, "Uncle Jimmy" and "Auntie," lived in a shanty near the camp.

ALFRED W. PENDLETON.

"Auntie" endeared herself to the boys by making for them dried apple pies with sole leather crusts, while old "Uncle Jimmy" occupied his time in hunting, fishing and smoking, principally the latter occupation, as forlorn a specimen of humanity as was often seen. "Uncle Jimmy" up and died one warm day in June, and old "Auntie" was disconsolate and perfectly at a loss to know what to do, so she naturally came to her friends in the battery, and we decided to do the honors to the dead citizen. Risley was chosen as "parson," singers were selected, and Will Vernon, the only sincere and sober one in the whole lot, was selected to offer prayers, and all acted their part to perfection, especially the "parson" in his brief remarks of consolation to the weeping widow, and his excellent choice in selecting the Scripture lesson. When the hearse came up from Cairo with the pine coffin, the driver, acting under instructions from his boss, would not unload it until the bill was paid, which amounted to $12.50. Twelve dollars was all that old "Auntie" could scrape together in five and ten cent pieces, her savings from the boys' pie money. She was discouraged for a moment, but thinking of the two quarters which Hod Foote had recklessly placed upon the eyes of the deceased, to prevent him from seeing where he was going, as he explained his act of apparent extravagance, she went in to get them, and found the eagles had mysteriously flown. The boys then jerked the coffin out of the hearse and sent the driver back to the city with only $12, which was about double what the box could possibly have cost. The boys, with crepe around their arms, a big Bible in an old carpet bag, the army wagon for a hearse, with the mules' tails done up in crepe, wended along the wooded road to the silent city of the dead. "The Star Spangled Banner" was sung, and the coffin was tenderly lowered into its final resting place during the sobbing of the heart-broken old "Auntie" and the assumed solemnity of her sympathetic friends. Old "Auntie" continued to dispense her dyspepsia-producing pies to the boys while we remained at Camp Smith, and when we broke up the camp and left she was utterly disconsolate. In the fall of 1864 Comrade Risley married Miss Mary Easton. Five children were born unto them, four sons and one daughter. The daughter, aged 19, and Harrie, aged 21, were taken from them. Three sons are now living, Charles R., Edward E., and Harvey B. Jr., the two former being married. Charles having two children. In the spring of 1865 he was employed in the Board of Public Works of Chicago, and from 1867 till 1871 was in the Chicago postoffice. In 1876 he removed to Joliet, where he was engaged in various occupations until the spring of 1889, when he crossed the plains westward, and spent the summer on a ranch in Montana. In the fall he crossed the Rockies and Cascade Mountains and landed in what he considers the most picturesque city in this country, Seattle, Washington, where he has resided since. He spent the winter of 1894 at Port Washington with his invalid wife. In March of that year she passed

JAMES PHILLIPS.

away and left the partner she had loved and honored from girlhood, alone with his motherless children. She was a faithful wife and fond mother, was an active member of the Woman's Relief Corps, Bartleson Post, No. 140, Joliet. Her memory still brings thoughts of sacred sadness to her family and friends.

Comrade Risley is in the drug business in Seattle, and says he is the only "private" on the Sound, as Comrade J. W. Rumsey, who lives in the same city, is the only Lieutenant, all other resident soldiers having received higher promotions since the war. He is and always will be the same good-natured, genial old "Parson" Risley to all his comrades of old Battery "A."

## WILLIAM O. RICE.

Among the oldest members of the battery was William O. Rice. He was born in Berkshire County, Massachusetts, July 15, 1825, where the early years of his life were spent. As soon as he was old enough to learn a trade his father, who was a mason, took him with him, and he acquired that trade, which has since been his occupation. He enlisted in the battery in Chicago, Oct. 16, 1861, and served as postillion and gunner until the 31st of March, 1862, when he was mustered out at Pittsburg Landing, by reason of disability incurred in the line of duty, being a severe injury in the knee. Recovering sufficiently from his injury on Jan. 5, 1865, he enlisted in the Twelfth Wisconsin Light Artillery, in which he served until the close of the war, being mustered out at Madison, Wis., June 17, 1865. In late years he has been in feeble health and during the winter and spring of 1899 has been confined to his bed. While so confined his aged wife, who had been his partner in his joys and sorrows so many years, passed away. That he may be restored to health and strength is the earnest wish of all his old comrades. He has five children and sixteen grandchildren to cheer and comfort him in his old age.

## HARRISON ROBERTS.

The State of "wooden nutmegs" furnished few, if any, better native sons for the ranks of the Union army than Harrison Roberts. He was born in New Haven County, Conn., in 1840, where he lived until four years of age, when his family moved to New York State, settling, in 1848, at Seneca Falls, where his school education was acquired. At the age of fifteen he went to work to learn the trade of machinist. He went West in 1858 and located in Chicago, securing a position in the paid fire department as stoker on the old steamer "Enterprise," No. 2, on which his father, the late George Roberts, was engineer. At that time two steamers, the "Long John" and the "Enterprise," constituted the entire paid fire department of Chicago. D. J. Swenie, the present chief, was then chief engineer. "Harry" enlisted in

AURELIUS V. PITTS.

the battery as private in September, 1862, and served with that rank until the consolidation of "A" and "B," in July, 1864, when he was elected First Lieutenant, vice George McCagg, whose term expired. Before his promotion he acted as gunner in the various skirmishes and engagements at and around Atlanta, and had previously participated in all its engagements, and acquitted himself so creditably that he was selected for promotion without opposition. After the evacuation of Atlanta the battery was mostly doing camp, garrison and reserve duty at Nashville and Chattanooga. He was mustered out with the battery in Chicago at the close of the war in 1865. Since the war he has worked at his trade at Seneca Falls, N. Y., where he still resides. In 1866 he was united in marriage with Miss Sarah Frances Babcock, of that city. They have no children.

## ROSCOE EUGENE REXFORD AND EVERETT HEBER REXFORD.

Roscoe Eugene and Everett Heber Rexford were the only sons of Heber S. Rexford. They were born in West Carlisle, Ohio, in the years 1839 and 1841, Roscoe being the senior by two years, less one month. Their family moved to Blue Island, Ill., in the spring of 1845. They remained in the village until 1852, when their father purchased a farm about a mile distant, where they were living when war was declared. In April, 1861, they joined the "Yates Phalanx," the company being commanded by Captain Everst.

After drilling in the old wigwam of Chicago for two or three weeks without any prospect of being accepted by "Uncle Sam," they yielded to their father's entreaties and returned home, having his promise that as soon as they were needed they might re-enlist.

When the boys of Company "A," Chicago Light Artillery, had served three months, they re-enlisted and were granted furloughs. Meeting one of them, an old friend, Wilbur Wilcox, he informed them that there was now an opportunity to join the battery. Knowing several of its members, among them Harry Morgan, who afterwards became Everett's brother-in-law, the brothers were delighted to return with the boys to Camp Smith, Cairo, and were sworn into service in July, 1861.

After the battle of Donelson Roscoe was taken sick; at Pittsburg Landing he was placed on board the City of Memphis, a hospital boat, and removed to Cairo, where his father met him. They journeyed northward and arrived at Kensington, near Chicago, when Roscoe became too ill to travel further, and he died in a few days, at the home of a cousin. Roscoe is buried in Mt. Greenwood, Ill., and on his tombstone are the words of a song he used so sweetly to sing in camp. "Lorena" was his favorite ballad, which

JEREMIAH D. POWELL.

so many times charmed the visitors who came to us while the battery was encamped at Paducah.

While the battery was stationed at Paducah Everett was made bugler, and from this time on he became an object of censure of the boys who disliked early rising, early retirement and other military duties which interfered with their own personal comfort and happiness. The stealing of his mouthpiece caused the battery boys to be drawn up in line. Major Willard, thinking to cause the guilty party to return this necessary article, claimed he knew the offending party, and stated that if the mouthpiece was not returned before a given time, that dire punishment would be inflicted. But the bluff did not work, for "Eb" Howard knew that no living soul had seen him deposit it in the bottom of the Ohio River.

The morning performances when in camp were always a great source of amusement to Everett, and it well repaid him for his shortened allowance of sleep. Although five minutes intervened between reveille and assembly call, no movement in tent or sound was noticeable, but when assembly warned the inmates that only three minutes remained for toilet and to fall in line, the tents would sway back and forth as if struck by a hurricane, while shouts and calls issued, such as, "Rex, your watch is fast," "Rex, what in the d—— are you sounding roll-call at this time of day for?" "Blame that old bugle," etc., and, crawling out from various parts of the tents would be seen men, some in one boot dragging the other, some in one pant leg, the other dangling, some with jacket in hand, hopping, tumbling, scrambling, falling into line, any way to get there in time to answer to their names, the bugler always receiving the grimaces and threatening looks of the belated ones.

After three years of continuous service he left his faithful horse, "Japhet," with Comrade Tom Wilcox, the two being captured afterwards, the day McPherson was killed. With the other volunteers of 1861 he was mustered out in Springfield, Ill., in July, 1864.

Returning to the old farm he readily resumed old duties, and continued farming for several years. In 1872 he married Miss Sarah E. Robinson, a teacher in Chicago. They have one child, a daughter, Laura Ballard, who is now an accomplished professional violinist. In 1891 he joined his family in Europe, where his daughter was perfecting her musical studies. On his return from Europe he began dealing in real estate, and is now manufacturing the Rex Fuel Saver. He has been a member of the Board of Education for the Blue Island Public Schools. In 1893 he served as Mayor of the town, now, in 1899, is a member of the Board of Trustees. His bugle still sounds assembly, and he had the honor of being made National Bugler of the G. A. R. in 1898, under his old comrade, Thad. S. Clarkson, Commander-in-chief, and also of the Union Veteran Legion. He likewise "toots

GEORGE A. PRATT.

his horn" whenever the battery gives the command, and no gathering of his old comrades is considered complete without "old Rex," as he is affectionately called. His home is in the village of Blue Island. It is large, roomy and pleasant, and the latchstring is always out for the boys of Battery "A."

## JOHN W. RUMSEY.

"The only Lieutenant on the Sound," is what "Parson" Risley says of John W. Rumsey, who, with Risley, resides in the far-off beautiful city of Seattle, Wash. He was born on a farm near Batavia, N. Y., March 6, 1838, where he lived till 1855, when he went to Chicago. His youth was uneventful, working on the farm and attending the district school three to four months in the winter. On his arrival in Chicago he began working as clerk for the commission firm of Rumsey Bros. & Co., and was still engaged with them when the war broke out. The next morning, after a Charleston, S. C., newspaper said, "Although Lincoln is elected President, he shall never reach Washington, D. C., alive," P. P. Wood came into the Rumsey office and said, "Jack, you read the morning paper; if we are ordered out will you go with us?" John replied, "Yes." "Then come to the armory to-night," said Wood. He was there. This was the last of January or early in February, 1861, but his enlistment proper in the battery dates April 19, 1861. He served three years and three months with the battery as private, sergeant, Junior and Senior Second and Junior and Senior First Lieutenant, being mustered out with the latter rank. In December, 1861, he was offered and declined a Captaincy in the Commissary Department. Again, while in Memphis, in 1862, he was offered a commission as Captain of a battery, but refused, being determined to remain with his first choice. Late in 1862, much to his disgust, he was detailed as ordnance officer of the division, and returned to the battery at the earliest possible opportunity. In a fight near Resaca, Ga., he was seriously wounded in the shoulder, and was incapacitated for further active service in the battery. He was mustered out at Chicago in March, 1864, but his discharge was dated the same as the muster out of the company, as he was not able to travel to Springfield at that time. From the close of the war until November, 1888, he was engaged in the commission business on the Chicago Board of Trade. He then went West and settled in Seattle, Wash., engaging in the real estate business, which he is still following. He married happily to Miss Charlotte M. Day, in Stafford, N. Y., Nov. 7, 1866, and eight children, three boys and five girls, have been born to them. None of the children are married. They are blessed with good health, but the family circle was broken June 4, 1898, by the death of the daughter Margaret, aged 22 years. Comrade Rumsey was elected the first President of the Battery Veteran Association, which was organized in 1885.

STEPHEN N. PEASE.

## JEREMIAH NICHOLAS SHERMAN

Jeremiah N. Sherman was born in the State of New York in 1839. His father moved to the West when "Jerry" was a child and settled in Cook County on a farm through which the Des Plaines River runs. He and C. B. Kimbell were schoolmates one year when boys. His father and stepmother both died in 1848. He was enrolled as a farmer on his enlistment as private in the battery in Chicago, July 16, 1861. He served with credit in the battery till honorably discharged at the expiration of his term of enlistment, having participated in eleven battles and four skirmishes. His position was No. 1 in squad two. He was severely injured by an accident while on drill at Paducah, Ky., and received three slight wounds at the Battle of Shiloh. After his return from the war he was in poor health, and until 1868 was almost continuously under the care of a physician, his health being impaired by his army service. Partly recovering his health, he took up his trade of carpenter, but of late years he has been wholly incapacitated for manual labor, and was admitted to the Illinois Soldier's Home at Quincy, August 12, 1891, where he is still quartered. He is a bachelor.

## JOHN STEELE.

Among the younger members of the battery was John Steele. He was born in Buffalo, N. Y., in 1844, where he lived until 1852, when, with his family, he moved to Milwaukee. He attended the public schools of that city until 1858. In 1859 he came to Chicago and learned the trade of cigar-making, at which he was employed when he enlisted in Battery "A," in Chicago, April 19, 1861. He re-enlisted July 16, 1861, and served with the battery, taking a creditable part in all its engagements until the battle of Mission Ridge, where he was severely wounded and incapacitated for further active service. He was sent home on wounded furlough, but was not discharged until the mustering out of the three years' men in July, 1864. He went to work at the cigarmaking trade, which he followed until 1875. He then learned the trade of painter, in which he is now engaged. In 1865 he married Miss Kate F. Dick. Their family consists of two daughters and one son, all grown up. He has never entirely recovered from the effects of his wound.

## ADAM STEWART.

Sturdy, genial Adam Stewart was born in Glasgow, Scotland, coming to America when about seventeen years old. He was engaged in clerking at the breaking out of the war, but, being full of love for the country of his adoption, he enlisted in the battery in Chicago, July 16, 1861, as private, serving his full term of enlistment, being mustered out with the company

HENRY H. POND.

July 23, 1864. He had a miraculous escape from death at the siege of Jackson, Miss. His army blouse was torn to pieces by an exploding shell, and his memorandum book and letters in the pockets blown into shreds, hardly a word on a piece of the paper being found. His eyes and ears were filled with cotton and sand, and he was unconscious for several minutes. After the war he followed orange growing for several years in Florida, but a terrible frost a few years ago destroyed that industry for a time, and he abandoned it. He is now in the National Soldier's Home, Virginia.

## MAC. SLOSSER.

Members of the battery will recognize in the name of Mac. Slosser our old comrade enlisted as A. V. Slusser. For good and sufficient reasons he had his name changed as above after the war, and he is now so known legally. He was born in Portage, N. Y., Oct. 12, 1834, and lived there and at Castile, N. Y., while a child and youth. He came to Chicago when about nineteen years of age, and was appointed a clerk in the postoffice there, remaining from 1854 to 1856. He was then is Texas and New Orleans for nearly a year. He returned to Chicago in 1860 and voted for Abraham Lincoln for President. He was not engaged in any business in 1861 and enlisted in the battery as private at Chicago in July of that year. He served five months as postillion and the remainder of his term of enlistment as cannonier, until mustered out July 16, 1864. He again went to work in the Chicago postoffice, where he still remains, being one of the oldest employes. He is afflicted with deafness caused by his army service. He has never married.

## GEORGE M. SCOTT.

G. M. Scott is a native of Canada, where he was born Jan. 11, 1842. He came to Chicago in 1849, before the day of railroads in that city, coming by steamboat around the lakes. He attended the old Dearborn school on Madison street, between State and Dearborn streets. At the breaking out of the war he was working as a clerk. He enlisted in the battery in Chicago, June 16, 1862, and started out on his own account to join the battery, which was on the march across the country from Corinth to Memphis, and was not easily found. He plodded along and, after numerous adventures, overtook it at Memphis. He served with the battery until the three years' men were mustered out, when he was detailed at General John A. Logan's headquarters, Fifteenth Army Corps. He accompanied the corps in the march from Atlanta to the sea and then to Washington. He was mustered out May 25, 1865, his term of enlistment having expired and the war virtually closed. He has been successfully engaged in the bellows manufacturing business for many years, lives at Riverside, and has never married.

CHARLES W. POOLE.

## CHARLES E. SMITH.

The Northwestern University of Evanston, Ill., furnished from the ranks of its students a great many soldiers for the Federal army, and five or six of these were members of Battery "A" during the early part of the war.

The youngest of these was Charles E. Smith, who was scarcely eighteen years old when he enlisted. He was born at Wilbraham, Mass., June 26, 1843, and lived there an orphan, with his guardian, until he was fourteen years old, when he came to Chicago. Leaving the University in 1860, he taught school that winter, being then only just past seventeen. In the early spring of 1861 he entered into arrangements with a friend to cut the grass off 700 acres of land on Blue Island avenue to make hay for the Chicago market. When the war spirit seized the country, realizing that his partner, Mr. Ayres, being married, could not go as well as he, he immediately dropped his plans and all prospective profit, and started and enlisted as a private in Battery "A." After being in Cairo for some time he was, with the company, mustered into the United States service, July 28, 1861, and was with the battery the entire term of his service, excepting only at the battle of Shiloh. Shortly after the battle of Fort Donelson he was sent home on a sick furlough, but immediately after the battle of Shiloh he returned to the battery and from that day until the battery was dismissed from service he lost no more time. He was appointed corporal just before the advance on Vicksburg, and before General Grant made his grand detour, getting in the rear of Vicksburg.

Governor LeRue Harrison, of Arkansas, offered him a commission as First Lieutenant in the First Arkansas Battery, but General Grant refused to muster anyone out until after the charge on Vicksburg. When Vicksburg was captured the commission was offered him again, but he declined it, preferring to remain with the battery until his time of service should expire. When mustered out in 1864 he entered the Chicago postoffice under the postmastership of Mr. Scripps, and with others assisted Mr. Armstrong to inaugurate the railway mail service of the present day. After one year's service there, he entered the employ of Keith Bros., of Chicago, remaining with them until 1867, when he engaged in business for himself, and has so continued since.

He was engaged for ten years in the lumber business both in Chicago and Bay City, Mich. In 1880 he removed to Cincinnati, where he purchased the branch house of Wilson Bros., and has been since then engaged in the men's furnishing goods business, and at the same store. His present address is 49 West Fourth street.

Mr. Smith was married in March, 1868, and has since his marriage become the father of six children. Two sons are now in business with him. Only one of his children is married, but this son has a son, so that Mr. Smith is a happy grandfather.

HARVEY B. RISLEY.

## JAMES H. SHRIGLEY.

The subject of this sketch is a native of Chicago, where he was born Jan. 16, 1838. He lived in and near Chicago during his childhood and youth, and until eleven years old, when not "running away," spent his time in acquiring knowledge at the public schools of the city. He took a course at Bell's and Dyhrenfurth's commercial colleges, from both of which he graduated, after which he worked at bookkeeping and clerking in Chicago and vicinity until 1856, when he moved to Michigan and engaged in the lumber business. He left his business in Manistee and came to Chicago in August, 1862, and enlisted on the 15th of that month, as private in the battery, with which he served until June 24th, 1864, when he was detailed as headquarters clerk in the Adjutant General's office, Second Division, Fifteenth Army Corps, in which capacity he served until the close of the war, being mustered out near Washington, D. C., May 25, 1865. He returned to Michigan and resumed the lumber business, which he has since followed extensively and successfully. He married Miss H. C. Golden and has one married daughter. He lives at Traverse City.

## SILAS COOK STIGER.

New Jersey, though one of the smallest States in the Union, furnished her quota of native sons for Battery "A" membership. Principal in the number is Silas C. Stiger. He was born in Hackettstown, in that State, April 16, 1831, where he lived, attending the schools there, as a youth, and acting as clerk at the close of his school days in Hackettstown and at Mendham. He purchased a farm in Virginia, on which he remained several years, and from there went to Chicago and was working with Wm. Little & Co., wholesale grocers, as shipping clerk, when the war broke out. He enlisted as private in the battery, July 16, 1861, and served with it till July 26, 1864. He was wounded in the fight at Dallas, Ga., May 28, 1864, being shot in the left hip by a sharpshooter, and when discharged was in the hospital at Nashville, Tenn. Returning to Chicago he engaged in the commission business as Little & Stiger. Thinking to better his condition he closed out his business in Chicago, and, turning to the "wild and woolly" West, he established a general merchandise business at Lincoln Gulch, Montana, which he continued for a while, then, closing out, returned to his native State and went into the coal business at Morristown. He retired from active business fifteen years ago. He married Miss Anna E. Walduck, and they have had four children. Mrs. Stiger died in 1896, and the published notice of her death was the means of the Veteran Association locating Comrade Stiger, whose whereabouts had been lost trace of for several years. Of the four children one daughter only survives, and with her father lives at 1207 Grand avenue, Asbury Park, N. J.

HARRISON ROBERTS.

## WILLIAM L. SOUTHWORTH.

One of the most popular and well-known of the three months' men was W. L. Southworth. He served in the battery from April 19, 1861 to July 16, 1861, but his interest in it never ceased. He returned to Chicago at the expiration of his term of enlistment and was one of the most active workers in the Battery Association in looking after the welfare and comfort of the battery boys, especially the sick and wounded, who were sent home to recover. He was born in New York City, Dec. 9, 1837, where his childhood and youth were spent, and his early school education obtained. At the breaking out of the war he was employed as a clerk in Chicago. He was gunner of the gun squad that assisted in the capture of the steamer "Hillman" in the beginning of the war, of which an account is given in the history of the battery's three months' service. He was in the wholesale commission lumber business from 1866 to 1884, in Chicago, and was the first Secretary of the "Chicago Lumbermen's Exchange," acting as such until the business required the more necessary attention of a salaried officer.

He has been a valuable and trustworthy employe in the County Treasurer's and County Clerk's offices in Chicago for many years, and is at present engaged in the County Clerk's office.

## JOHN SCHAFFER.

The veteran among all the veterans of the battery is brave, earnest and loyal old German John Schaffer. He came to this country from his native land in 1848, having previously served three years and nine months in the German army under King William IV. He was born in Alfern, Germany, July 22, 1825. He enlisted in the battery April 19, 1861, for three months, and at the end of that term re-enlisted July 16 for three years. He served the full term of his enlistment, taking part in all the engagements of the battery. He was severely wounded at the battle of Shiloh, but remained with the company and recovered without entering a hospital. When John joined the battery he understood but very little of the English language, owing to the short time he had been in this country, but he set about the task of learning it with eagerness, and under the teaching of such proficient instructors as Johnny Peters and Johnny Irwin, he soon acquired a very fair knowledge of it, although John declares to this day that he was wrongfully and maliciously instructed in regard to the meaning and use of many words and phrases which had no place in genteel society. But his "nit by dam site" was not to be misunderstood when expressing his disapproval of any proposition not in accordance with his ideas of right and wrong. After being mustered out of the service he returned to Chicago and immediately joined the militia battery in the city, and for over thirty years was a regular and

EVERETT H. REXFORD.

active member. He was always ready to answer every call with the battery in turning out to suppress riots or disorder, and he is ready and willing at any time the American flag is threatened, or in danger, to come to the rescue as promptly as he did in 1861. He was married in 1848 and has had seven children, three surviving, and nine grandchildren. He is now a widower, his wife having died Nov. 2, 1897. He has a son, grandson and great-grandson named after him, so his name is not likely to soon become extinct.

### WILLIAM EICHBAUM STOCKTON.

Among the business men of Chicago who, by their enterprise, honesty and integrity, add in no small degree to the general prosperity and good business reputation of the city, is Comrade W. E. Stockton. He is the trusted manager of the Falcon Iron and Nail Co., at 16 to 20 West Lake street. He was born in Pittsburg, Pa., Dec. 18, 1840. He lived there till the breaking out of the war, and at that time was receiving clerk for Clarke & Co., Duquesne depot, Pennsylvania Railroad. He enlisted in Company "I," Twelfth Pennsylvania Infantry, April 25, 1861, and was discharged Aug. 6, 1861. He re-enlisted in Battery "A," Aug. 31, 1861, and served with great credit in that company. He was discharged therefrom Feb. 15, 1863, on surgeon's certificate of disability. Recovering his health he re-enlisted Feb. 25, 1864, in Company "A," Fourteenth Pennsylvania Cavalry, and was discharged Jan. 16, 1865, from a gunshot wound received in action. His rank was sergeant major of his regiment. Few veterans can show a more persistent, patriotic record than can Comrade Stockton. He was married to Eliza L. Cook, of Shields, Pa., and has two grown children living at their home in Evanston, Martha C. and John W. Stockton.

### EDGAR PRAY TOBEY.

Edgar Pray Tobey was born in the city of New York, January 20, 1840. He came to Chicago when six years old, and remained there until his death. He received his schooling in the public schools, and at Warrenville, Ill.; two years were spent at the business college of Bryant & Stratton. When a young man he was a prominent and active member of the Hope Hose Volunteer Fire Company of Chicago. On October 15, 1859, he became a member of the Chicago Light Artillery Association, Captain James Smith commanding, retaining his membership therein until the troops left for the front. April 19, 1861, he was appointed quartermaster sergeant, and left with the battery for Cairo, Ill., for ninety days. The following July 16th he was mustered into the United States service for three years as Junior Second Lieutenant. July 3, 1862, he was mustered out with above rank, at Paducah,

LIEUT. JOHN W. RUMSEY.

Ky., on account of sickness. Returning home on July 20, 1863, he was elected Senior First Lieutenant of the Dearborn Light Artillery, a local militia organization, under the command of Captain James Smith. While not able for active service in the field, he did not lose his interest in the old battery, and was an active worker in the home association in looking after the interests of the company, and made frequent trips to the front, visiting them and bearing the good things contributed for their comfort by friends at home. He took an active interest in militia military matters, and gave freely of his time and money in their support. He was in command of the battery and rendered very efficient service during the railroad riots in 1877, and, although it was not necessary to fire a single shot, the very presence of the battery had a quieting effect on the riotous mob. March 31, 1879, he was elected Captain of Battery "D," Illinois National Guard, and July 17 of the same year he was elected Major of the same command, and he continued in command of the battery until his death, which occurred June 28, 1895, from spinal troubles.

After leaving the United States service he was for many years with the firm of Tobey & Booth Packing and Provision Co.

He was married February 15, 1864, to Arozina L. Hurlbut, who died on Easter Sunday, April 25, 1886. From the time of his wife's death his health began to fail, gradually growing weaker and weaker until his death. The funeral services at his home were conducted by Bishop Charles Edward Cheney. The members of Battery "D" acted as escort, and the body was laid to rest in Rose Hill Cemetery, by members of Home Lodge, A., F. & A. M. At the time of his death he was one of the most active and valuable members of the Battery "A" Veteran Association, his battery armory always being open for their meetings. He was also a member of the Society of the Army of the Tennessee, Abraham Lincoln Post, G. A. R., Fireman's Benevolent Association, Home Lodge, A., F. & A. M., Chevalier Bayard Commandery, Oriental Consistory, and the Mystic Shrine.

Three daughters, living in Chicago, survive him.

## SAMUEL HOBART TALLMADGE.

Chicago had numerous native-born sons in Battery "A," and among them was S. H. Tallmadge. He was born June 8, 1840, and lived in the city of his birth till the breaking out of the civil war. At that time he was salesman in the prominent wholesale dry goods house of Bowen Bros. He enlisted as private April 16, 1861, and served three months with the battery. He re-enlisted in July, 1862, in the Chicago Mercantile Battery and served with that command till the close of the war, ranking as private, gun sergeant and quartermaster sergeant. He was mustered out July 10, 1865. After the war he located in Milwaukee, where he now resides. He is man-

WILLIAM H. RENFRO.

ager of the Milwaukee Pulmonary Sanitarium. He married Miss Jessie M. Johnston, of Milwaukee, in 1868, and they have six children. He has taken an active interest in Grand Army affairs.

He joined E. B. Wolcott Post, No. 1, G. A. R., Milwaukee, in November, 1885, and served as follows: Sergeant major, two years; Adjutant of Post No. 1, seven years; Commander, one year; Assistant Adjutant General's Department of Wisconsin, two years; in all, twelve consecutive years. Was aid on staff of Commander-in-chief T. S. Clarkson in 1897-8.

## WILLIAM BLANDING VERNON.

A noble, true and earnest Christian soldier was personified in William B. Vernon, who died at his home in Chicago, Jan. 22, 1864, of disease contracted in the service with the battery. He was born in Milbrook, Kendall County, Illinois, Sept. 20, 1839. When the war broke out he was living in Chicago, and clerking in O. Kendall's bakery, corner of Washington and Dearborn streets. He enlisted in the battery April 19, 1861, and served with it till his death. He was always a quiet, unassuming gentleman, ever ready and willing to execute his duty, and his death removed one of the most estimable members from our ranks. His remains were buried with military honors from his home, 125 South Green street, Chicago, in beautiful Rose Hill Cemetery. His brother, John M. Vernon, was one of the most prominent and popular members of Battery "B," and lives in Chicago, where he is a successful business man, and takes an active interest in G. A. R. matters.

## FREDERICK OSCAR WHITSON.

The city of Boston, Mass., was the birthplace of Frederick O. Whitson. He first saw the light of day there July 24, 1841, and that city was his home until March, 1848, when he came to Illinois with his parents, who settled in Waukegan. He lived in that city, attending her public schools, until 1854, when he, with his parents, again moved to Woodstock, which city was his home until his death, which occurred Aug. 21, 1878. When the war broke out he was clerking in the Exchange Hotel of that city. He enlisted in the battery as private, Feb. 3, 1862, and served three years with it, taking part in all its marches, campaigns and engagements, with the exception of the battle and siege of Jackson, Miss., in July, 1863, at which time he was confined in the hospital with a severe case of the bloody flux, which he contracted during the siege of Vicksburg, and for which he was later on furloughed and sent home to recover. He was mustered out at the end of his term of enlistment, with the rank of corporal, to which he was appointed when the batteries were consolidated, in July, 1864. He returned to his home in Woodstock, and for a short time resumed work in the same hotel

JEREMIAH N. SHERMAN.

clerk, and later formed a partnership in the same business, with his father and brother, all being practical in that line of business, and they soon became the leading firm in McHenry County, doing an extensive and prosperous business. In the winter of 1877 Oscar, who belonged to the Volunteer Fire Department of Woodstock, while engaged in helping to extinguish a fire in the large building of the well-known seminary for boys conducted by the Rev. R. K. Todd, became thoroughly drenched with water, which froze to his clothing. He took a severe cold, which brought on asthma, and finally resulted in consumption, which resulted in his death. He was never married. He was honored and respected by all who knew him. His funeral was largely attended, and during the services every place of business in the city was closed in respect to his memory.

## CHARLES M. WILLARD.

Charles M. Willard was born in Livingston County, New York, in 1825, and, when old enough, studied law, and was a practicing lawyer when he moved to Richmond, McHenry County, Illinois, in 1853. He remained in Richmond about two years, then removed to Woodstock, Ill., the county seat of McHenry County, and soon became one of the leading lawyers of Northern Illinois. In 1858 he went to Chicago, practicing law there till the breaking out of the war. He left Chicago with the battery as Senior First Lieutenant, was elected Captain to succeed Captain Smith, and resigned Jan. 16, 1863, to accept a commission as Major of the First Illinois Artillery. He was appointed Provost Marshal of Memphis and acted in that capacity till the movement for the advance on Vicksburg, when poor health compelled him to resign. After his army service he returned to Chicago and again resumed the practice of law. He never fully recovered his health, and died in that city in 1870, and was buried there. He was married when he came West, and left a widow surviving him.

## EDWARD ERASTUS WILLIAMS.

Edward E. Williams was born in Homer, N. Y., Dec. 18, 1840. The early years of his life were spent in New York City, Newark, N. J., and a short time in West Point, N. Y. He received his school education in the New York City public schools, and in Hudson Academy, N. Y. At the age of seventeen he went to California, returning East, and, locating in Chicago just before the breaking out of the war, engaging in the news business. He enlisted as private in the battery in Chicago, July 21, 1861, and remained with it, in all its service, until July 23, 1864, when he was mustered out. He was severely wounded at Shiloh, and had an arm broken afterward. He took a leading part in the famous theatrical combination organized in the battery

JOHN STEELE.

at Larkinsville, in the winter of 1864. A portrait taken in costume will be found in the chapter of this history relating to Larkinsville. After the war he went to New York City, where he engaged in the wall paper business, first as salesman and later as partner in the firm of H. Bartholomae & Co., wall paper manufacturers. His health has not been of the best of late, though he hopes for speedy improvement. He is married and resides at 181 West 87th street, New York City. He is a member of Post 607, G. A. R., New York City.

## PETER PRESTON WOOD.

A brave, gallant, tried and true comrade, commander and friend stepped from the ranks of Battery "A" survivors when Captain Peter P. Wood passed away at his home in Chicago, Dec. 13, 1865. He was born in New York City, Nov. 10, 1834, and was therefore but a little past his thirty-first birthday when he died. He came to Chicago with his parents when about eight years old, and was educated in the public schools of the city. While at school he was a bright, intelligent scholar, and was always a favorite with his teachers and schoolmates. In his home life he was a devoted and affectionate son and brother, wholly unselfish in every way and always cheerful and considerate. Throughout his life he was a great reader, and his choice of books was excellent. He left school at the age of fifteen and was employed in the office of Higginson & Co., lumber merchants, and later was bookkeeper for Mears & Co., in the same business. In the spring of 1855 he entered the employ of Hannah, Lay & Co., one of the largest lumber firms in the city, and remained there until April 19, 1861, when he enlisted in Battery "A," in Chicago, and was chosen Junior Second Lieutenant. He was in command of the battery in nearly all its engagements, the exceptions being once or twice when he was at home on sick furlough, and each time he returned before he was recovered, risking his life in doing so. The last time he was at home on sick leave was just before the expiration of the three years' term of the battery, and, though in a weak condition, he went back to the field, that he might have the joy and honor of returning with his brave command to be mustered out, which was done July 23, 1864. Those who witnessed that return will ever remember the triumphal march of the battery, and the glorious reception given by the citizens of Chicago. After the war Captain Wood was inspector of lumber, and he followed this business until about one month before his death, from a disease which he contracted in front of Jackson, Miss., which caused him much suffering, especially during the last year of his life, and finally resulted fatally. He was slightly wounded and had a very narrow escape from death at Jackson, by the fragment of an exploding shell striking his arm and tearing away a portion of the sleeve of his blouse. His reports of several of the important engagements of the battery

GEORGE M. SCOTT

are published in full in this battery's history, also copious extracts from his private letters, all of which speak of his pride in the men of his command and according them full credit for the part they bore. Captain Wood strongly objected to any promotion, except through his own merit, and any outside pressure brought to bear to secure promotion was most distasteful to him. A relative of Captain Wood's was very anxious for his promotion, and for the purpose of securing it wrote to General Sherman for it, without the Captain's knowledge. The reply of General Sherman is given below in full, as it is a deserved tribute to a brave soldier from one of the greatest commanders of the age:

Department of the Tennessee. On the "Diana."
Feb. 29, 1864.

'Dear Sir: Absence in the interior, away from mails for a month, is the reason of the non-receipt of yours of Jan. 26 till to-day. I hasten to assure you that I esteem Captain P. P. Wood, of Company "A," Chicago Light Artillery, as an officer of great merit. He has been with me everywhere, and has always done his whole duty. I have again and again commended him, and he knows I esteem him as an officer of great merit. I have done all in my power to notice and advance him, but it is true that commanders of batteries are only Captains, and it is hard to rise any higher in that service. Congress will not give volunteer officers brevets, and real advancement to them must come by way of promotion from the State of whose volunteer organization they form a part. I will go as far as you or any of Captain Wood's family or friends to advance him, and do him merited honor, but such is the fact, that in all armies of the world the commander of a battery is only a Captain, and brevets are not conferred on volunteers. So, you see, I am powerless. I would be pleased if you would show this to Captain Wood's family, and let this assure them that I have often, very often, stood by Wood's guns when served with a precision and skill which elicited my marked approval, especially at Arkansas Post, at Vicksburg and Jackson. He has always done his duty, and he knows I appreciate him. Truly yours,

W. T. Sherman, Major General."

Captain Wood was a communicant of St. James Episcopal Church, of which the Right Reverend Bishop Robert H. Clarkson, brother of Sergeant T. S. Clarkson, of our battery, was pastor. He wrote a letter to the members of the battery, who went from his church in the beginning of the war, among these being Ed Russell, George McCagg and Captain Wood. The letter was as follows:

St. James Rectory, Chicago, Ill.

"To the gallant men who have gone from St. James Church, Chicago, to defend the Constitution and Laws:

Dear Beloved: We are proud of you, and shall every day have you in our thoughts and in our prayers. May the God of battles bless, protect and keep you. No men on earth were called to a plainer and holier duty than you have been; and we expect to hear that you have done that duty well. The Right must triumph and Treason be overthrown, but it may cost us your precious lives. Be ready, then, for death, as well as victory. Repent of

JAMES H. SHRIGLEY.

your sins, and have faith in Jesus Christ, your Savior, and the way is as short and straight to heaven from the battlefield as from your bed at home. As fast as you depart from us to the scenes of battle your names shall be read in the church, and constant and special prayers shall be offered for your health, your protection and your triumph. And if you fall in battle, I promise you that no efforts or means will be spared to procure your bodies, which shall be brought home and buried, if practicable, under the tower of the church; your names shall be graven upon its walls, to remain there while the stone itself remains, and our children's children shall be taught to revere your memories. * * * That you may return to us in health and safety, with no wound upon your body, no stain upon your valor, and no scar upon your Christian character, shall be the daily prayer of your affectionate friend and pastor. Robert H. Clarkson."

Captain Wood's funeral services were conducted by the Rev. Dr. Clarkson, who paid a loving and glowing tribute to the departed soldier. He said in part: "One more hero has fallen! Long after the last cannon of war has ceased its firing, and the last campaign ended, another martyr has laid his life upon his country's altar. For none of us who have sadly watched the gradual fading away of this young man's life can doubt that he died for this government, for freedom, and for us, as truly as if his soul had gone up from his body amid the storm and crash of battle. When there rises upon yon deep foundation the noble tower which we here have solemnly pledged as a memorial to the valor and the self-sacrifice of our own brave boys, side by side with the names of Russel, Kinzie, Larrabee and DeWolf, et id omne genus, there should be carved in striking capitals that of Peter Preston Wood, our latest, and, we trust, our last martyr. He was among the very foremost of those who on that ever memorable 21st of April left us amid the prayers and tears, the sadness and the gladness of a great congregation, for the perils and endurance of camp and field. How he bore himself in all the years of that conflict, on scores of battlefields; how he led on to victory that famous battery, whose achievements were the pride of our city and a praise throughout the land, I need scarcely here describe. How, though wounded, faint and sick, with an enemy that would not be conquered preying upon his vitals, he never in all those lingering months of disease knew fear or despair, but still always hopeful, sanguine, enthusiastic, and stout-hearted—why should I tell you of these things? Who knew them as well? On his horse when he should have been in the hands of nurses; at the front when almost any one else would have been in the rear, cheering, encouraging, inspiring and commanding others when he himself needed their care and ministrations, he was in every way, and every where, and always a model soldier and officer.

"But his last battle has been fought. An enemy that shall one day conquer us all has at last overcome that resolute, patient, indomitable, and courageous spirit. * * * Triumphant in the hour of death; calm and un-

SILAS C. STIGER.

dismayed, in the certainties of approaching dissolution; cool, collected, thoughtful, and unselfish, as if he had been in his office at his business, instead of on the bed of death; with the solemn services and the gracious aid of the holy communion of a Savior's love still lingering in his ear, and filling his soul with whispered prayers for a pardon and forgiveness, never denied to those who ask in Jesus' name, occupying his latest moments, he was conquering the last enemy even while he was yielding to the inevitable lot of humanity. * * * His last words were: 'I thank God for my sickness; I am ready to go; thy will be done, O Lord; God bless you all,' and gently passed away, carrying himself triumphantly through the last conflict. His memory will ever be cherished by his surviving comrades."

Captain Wood had never married.

## THOMAS WILCOX.

Thomas Wilcox was one of the three Wilcox brothers who served in the battery during the war, all of whom have passed away. He was born in Montgomery County, New York, where his childhood years were spent. The family moved to Chicago and settled on a farm near Blue Island, where they lived for many years. Thomas was engaged in farming at the breaking out of the war, and in August, 1862, enlisted in the battery in Chicago, and went to join his brothers, Willard and Wilber, who had enlisted the year before. He served in the battery till mustered out at the close of the war. He was made a prisoner before Atlanta, and held in Andersonville for eight months. After the war he returned home and engaged in farming at Washington Heights until 1872, when he moved on his farm, near Remington, Ind., where he lived until his death, which occurred June 27, 1895. His remains were buried in the Remington Cemetery. He was married to Miss Lois K. Hastings, July 30, 1865. They had two children and two grandchildren. His widow lives with her daughters at Remington.

## WILLIAM HARRISON YOUNG.

The survivor of over two years of active military service in the civil war, coupled with sixteen months' captivity in rebel prison pens, is the creditable record of William H. Young. The story of his capture and imprisonment is told by himself in Chapter 2 of this history, in the portion relating to the siege of Jackson, in a very interesting and entertaining manner. He was born in the city of Pittsburg, Pa., in July, 1840, where he lived until 1851, when he came to Chicago and has since made that city his home. He attended the public schools until 1858. Aug. 4, 1862, he enlisted in Battery "A," and joined it at Memphis. He took part in all of the marches and en-

WILLIAM L. SOUTHWORTH.

gagements with the battery up to the siege of Jackson, Miss., where, with a number of others of the battery, he was taken prisoner, and held for sixteen months, as before stated. He was paroled Nov. 16, 1864, but having his "fighting mad up," he rejoined the battery in April, 1865, and served till mustered out at the close of the war, and there was no more fighting to be done. He came home and, in 1866, did the next best thing to being a soldier, which was to join the fire department of Chicago, in which he served three years. In 1869 he was appointed letter carrier, and he has been connected with the postoffice department ever since, being at present employed in the Registry Division of the General Postoffice, Chicago. He is, as he says, one of the few privates who, since the close of the civil war, has escaped promotion to any military rank other than private, and is well contented to be known and remembered simply as a private of old Battery "A." He is at present the Vice President of the Battery Veteran Association.

WILLIAM E. STOCKTON.

## OFFICERS OF BATTERY "A," CHICAGO LIGHT ARTILLERY VETERAN ASSOCIATION.

| Year. | President. | Vice Presidents. | Secretary. | Treasurer. | Medical Director | Sergeant-At-Arms. |
|---|---|---|---|---|---|---|
| 1885–86 | Jno. W. Rumsey | 1st, E. P. Tobey. 2d, F. W. Young. 3d, W. H. Johnson. 4th, J. H. Long. 5th, H. W. Chase. 6th, E. Baggot. | C. B. Kimbell. Record. Sec., W. L. Southworth. | S. S. Kimbell. | | L. F. Jacobs. |
| 1886–87 | E. P. Tobey. | 1st, L. F. Jacobs. 2d, F. S. Allen. 3d, W. E. Stockton. 4th, O. C. Foster. 5th, G. M. Scott. 6th, Enoch Colby, Jr. | C. B. Kimbell. Record. Sec., W. L. Southworth. | H. W. Chase. | E. H. Rexford. | J. R. Irwin. |
| 1887–88 | Frank S. Allen. | 1st, W. H. Young. 2d, Jacob Clingman 3d, F. V. Gindele. 4th, Wm. Lowe. 5th, C. W. Poole. 6th, Jas. Phillips. | C. B. Kimbell. Record. Sec., W. L. Southworth. | H. W. Chase. | E. H. Rexford. | Edward Hughes. |
| 1888–89 | Enoch Colby, Jr. | 1st, Ed. Baggot. 2d, J. H. Long. 3d, Geo. King. 4th, A. W. Pendleton. 5th, John Steele. 6th Olof Benson. | C. B. Kimbell. Record. Sec., F. V. Gindele. | H. W. Chase. | E. H. Rexford. | W. H. Young. |

## OFFICERS OF BATTERY "A," CHICAGO LIGHT ARTILLERY VETERAN ASSOCIATION—Continued.

| Year. | President. | Vice Presidents. | Secretary. | Treasurer. | Musical Director | Sergeant-At-Arms. |
|---|---|---|---|---|---|---|
| 1889-90 | Ed. Baggot. | 1st, J. H. Long. 2d, W. E. Stockton. 3d, John Steele. 4th, Olof Benson. 5th, Jas. Phillips. 6th, C. L. Arnold. | C. B. Kimbell. Record. Sec., F. V. Gindele. | H. W. Chase. | E. H. Rexford. | E. D. Clark. |
| 1890-91 | | | | | | |
| 1891-92 | J. H. Long. | 1st, W. E. Stockton. 2d, A. V. Pitts. 3d, Wm. Lowe. 4th, Harry Morgan. 5th, C. L. Arnold. 6th J. W. Kimbell. | C. B. Kimbell. Record. Sec., W. L. Southworth. | H. W. Chase. | E. H. Rexford | C. W. Poole |
| | Incorporated, June 7, 1892. | | | | | |
| 1892 | J. H. Long. | C. L. Arnold. | C. B. Kimbell. | H. W. Chase. | E. H Rexford. | |
| 1893-94 | W. E. Stockton | S. S. Kimbell. | C. B. Kimbell. | Ed. Baggot. | E. H. Rexford. | |
| 1895-96 | S. S. Kimbell. | Geo. M. Scott. | C. B. Kimbell. | Ed. Baggot. | E. H. Rexford. | |
| 1896-97 | M. A. Bartleson. | A. W. Gray. | C. B. Kimbell. | J. H. Long. | E. H. Rexford. | |
| 1897-98 | A. W. Gray. | C. W. Poole. | C. B. Kimbell. | J. H. Long. | E. H. Rexford. | |
| 1898-99 | C. W. Poole. | W. H. Young. | C. B. Kimbell. | J. H. Long. | E. H. Rexford. | |

# REUNIONS OF BATTERY "A," FIRST ILLINOIS ARTILLERY VETERAN ASSOCIATION.

## CHAPTER IV.

The survivors of the battery at the close of the war were then of the age when most men were beginning to find their life's work, and take upon themselves the responsibilities and cares of the world's business, carving out for themselves homes, reputations and fortunes. Having been relieved from the long-continued strain of military life and discipline, they had little inclination and less time to keep up old army associations, in addition to their many other duties. After a number of years, being occasionally called together by the passing away of some of our numbers, the spirit of comradeship began to revive.

The city resident members of the battery, who naturally met each other occasionally, had for many years frequently discussed the subject of holding a reunion, but until 1885 nothing definite was accomplished. On Jan. 15 of that year a call was issued by Comrades J. W. Rumsey, C. B. Kimbell and S. W. Butterfield, for a preliminary meeting, to make arrangements for a reunion. About a dozen members responded, and a committee of arrangements was appointed, consisting of Comrades Frank S. Allen, Chairman, Fred W. Young, W. L. Southworth, S. W. Butterfield, O. Benson, and S. S. Kimbell, with full power to act. Invitations were mailed to every member whose address could be obtained, and hearty responses were returned from all receiving them. The use of Battery "D" Armory was generously donated by Major Tobey, and the meeting was a complete success, and in every way satisfactory to all participants.

# FIRST REUNION.

## Members of Battery "A," First Illinois Light Artillery.

PHOTOGRAPHED AT THEIR FIRST REUNION AT CHICAGO, ILL., FEBRUARY 16, 1885.

W. R. Phillips. H. W. Chase. S. J. Sherwood. F. B. Levitte. A. R. Abbot. John Shaffer. Geo. A. Pratt. C. W. Peale.

A. P. Maddock. Henry H. Pond. Chas. L. Arnold. Wm. R. Page. G. M. Scott. S. G. Williams. G. E. Cowper. O. C. Foster.

W. H. Bailey. Albert Dixon. J. W. Kimbell. W. H. Johnson. John R. Irwin. J. Henry Lorg. C. S. Burdsal, Jr. Geo. R. Beach.

F. V. Gindele. John Steele. H. B. Risley.

W. L. Southworth. Wm. H. Young. A. W. Gray. A. W. Pendleton. William Lowe. Edgar P. Tobey. Enoch Colby. H. S. Foote.

Lew. F. Jacobs. W. H. Leppen. C. E. Clark. Edward Hughes.

John W. Ramey. J. N. Sherman. Edward E. Williams. Moses Hawks. J. J. Rehwoni. Cass. F. Maurer. S. W. Butterfield.

C. B. Kimbell. S. S. Kimbell. F. M. Kuntzler.

Jacob Clingman. James Phillips. E. Baggot. W. E. Stockton. F. T. Sweeue. Fred. W. Young. Frank S. Allen. Obed Benson.

A. V. Pitts. S. N. Pease. E. D. Clark.

The first reunion was held at Chicago, in Battery "D" Armory, Monday, Feb. 16, 1885, the anniversary of the surrender of Fort Donelson, in which battle the battery was for the first time under the fire of rebel guns.

The armory building was thrown open for the use of the members on Sunday and Monday, and many were in attendance. A photographic group was taken Monday afternoon, by the celebrated artist, C. D. Mosher. The weather was very unfavorable, extremely cold and snowing hard a portion of the time. Many members were deterred from attending by the snow blockade of the railroads, which was general throughout the West.

The following members were in attendance and signed the register:

Arnold, Chas. L., Chicago.
Abbott, A. R., Chicago.
Allen, Frank S., Chicago.
Beach, Geo. B., Chicago.
Butterfield, S. W., Chicago.
Bursdal, Jr., C. S., S. Evanston, Ill.
Bailey, W. H., Englewood, Ill.
Benson, Olof, Chicago.
Baggot, Ed., Chicago.
Colby, Enoch, Chicago.
Clark, Chas. E., Chicago.
Clingman, Jacob, Wilmette, Ill.
Clark, E. D., Lincoln Park, Chicago.
Chase, H. W., Chicago.
Dixson, Albert, Highland Park, Ill.
Dutch, J. B., Chicago.
Foote, H. S., Milwaukee.
Foster, O. C., Chicago.
Gindele, F. V., Chicago.
Gray, A. W., Chicago.
Hughes, Ed., Chicago.
Hawks, Moses, Arlington Heights, Ill.
Irwin, Jno. R., Chicago.
Jacobs, L. F., Chicago.
Johnson, W. H., Alpena, Mich.
Kimbell, S. S., Chicago.
Kimbell, C. B., Chicago.
Kimbell, J. W., Chicago.
Kantzler, Fred. M., Chicago.
Kelley, Harrison, Chicago.
Long, J. Henry, Chicago.
Lepperr, W. H., Ottawa, Ill.
Lowe, Wm., Chicago.
Mitchell, L. B., Chicago.
Morgan, Harry, Blue Island, Ill.
Maurer, Cass F., Chicago.
Phillips, Jas., Chicago.
Pitts, A. V., Marseilles, Ill.
Pease, S. N., Chicago.
Poole, C. W., Chicago.
Pendleton, Alfred W., Chicago.
Pond, Henry H., Chicago.
Pratt, Geo. A., Ft. Atkinson, Wis.
Powell, Thos., Chicago.
Phillips, W. B., Marion, Iowa.
Phillips, W. S. Dubois City, Pa.
Redmond, J. J., Chicago.
Rumsey, J. W., Chicago.
Risley, H. B., Joliet, Ill.
Steele, John, Chicago.
Schaffer, John, Chicago.
Slosser, Mac., Chicago.
Sherman, J. N., Chicago.
Stockton, W. E., Chicago.
Swenie, F. T., Lake, Ill.
Smith, Chas. E., Cincinnati, Ohio.
Southworth, W. L., Chicago.
Scott, G. M., Chicago.
Tobey, Edgar P., Chicago.
Williams, Edw. E., New York City.
Williams, S. G., Chicago.
Young, Fred W., Chicago.
Young, Wm. H., Chicago.

EDGAR P. TOBEY.

The meeting was called to order at 8:15 p. m. by W. L. Southworth, in the absence of Frank S. Allen, Chairman of the Committee of Arrangements. S. S. Kimbell officiated as Secretary. The Secretary gave a brief history of the work done in preparing for the reunion, after which J. W. Rumsey was chosen as the presiding officer of the evening. He thanked the comrades for the honor conferred, and congratulated them on the large number in attendance. He said: "When we realize that over twenty years have passed since we were last together, after passing through three years of hard service in the most gigantic war of modern times, and look about this room this evening and see the large number of familiar faces 'of long ago,' we wonder that so little change has occurred to us, and that so many are spared to meet and recall the scenes of those trying times. We have met to effect a permanent organization of our surviving members. When we organize let it be permanent in fact as well as in name. Let it be the treasury of record of the battery's history during the war, and of contributions from every member, of facts and incidents of interest to the members, relating to the battery or the war, which shall form a record worthy of being handed down to our children and generations to come." He then announced the meeting as ready for the business of the evening.

On motion of Comrade C. B. Kimbell, the chairman appointed a committee of nine on permanent organization. He named the committee as follows: Comrades C. B. Kimbell, Enoch Colby, Lew F. Jacobs, Fred. W. Young, Sam. W. Butterfield, F. V. Gindele, W. L. Southworth, J. R. Irwin and C. L. Arnold.

While the committee was preparing its report, the Secretary read the roll call as it was printed in September, 1861, at Paducah, in the "Picket Guard," a paper published by the boys of the company. The committee reported the following Constitution and By-Laws, which was adopted unanimously:

### ARTICLE I.

This organization shall be known as "The Battery 'A' C. L. A. Veteran Association."

### ARTICLE II.

The object of this Association is to preserve and strengthen those kind and fraternal feelings which bound together the members of old Battery "A" who united in suppressing the late rebellion, and to perpetuate the history of the battery and the memory of its noble dead.

SAMUEL H. TALLMADGE.

## ARTICLE III.

Section 1. Regular meetings of this Association shall be held annually, on the call of the President.

Sec. 2. Special meetings may be called at any time by the President, or he shall call such meeting upon the written application of five members.

Sec. 3. Nine members shall constitute a quorum for the transaction of business.

## ARTICLE IV.

Any member of the late Battery "A," First Illinois Artillery, shall be eligible to membership upon signing this constitution. Sons of members may be admitted as full members at the age of twenty-one.

## ARTICLE V.

Section 1. The officers of this Association shall consist of a President, six Vice Presidents, Secretary, Recording Secretary, Treasurer and Sergeant-at-Arms, and they shall constitute the Executive Committee.

Sec. 2. The elective officers shall be chosen by vote at the regular annual meeting, and shall hold office for the term of one year, or until their successors are duly elected. A majority of all votes cast shall be necessary for a choice. If there is no election on the first ballot, the name of the comrade receiving the lowest number of votes shall be dropped, and so on in successive ballots until an election is made.

Sec. 3. The President shall preside at all meetings of the Association.

Sec. 4. The Vice Presidents shall perform such duties as may be required of them by the President, and in his absence shall take his place, in the order of their rank.

Sec. 5. The Secretary shall keep in books properly prepared a journal of the proceedings of the Association.

Sec. 6. The Recording Secretary shall keep a roster, in which he shall enter the names of all members, with their residence and address, with a column for remarks, making such changes from time to time as shall come to his knowledge. He shall also gather and preserve all matters of historical interest connected with the old battery or any of its members.

Sec. 7. The Treasurer shall receive and safely keep all moneys belonging to the Association, and pay the same out only on the order of the President, or in his absence that of the Recording Secretary. He shall make a report at each regular meeting of the amount received since his last report, the amount disbursed, and the amount remaining in the treasury, which shall be entered on the minutes. His books and vouchers shall at all times be subject to inspection by the President and Executive Committee.

Sec. 8. The Executive Committee shall have the management of the general affairs of the Association, and the appropriation of its funds, but

JOHN TACK

shall have no power to make the Association liable for any debt or debts to an amount which shall exceed the amount of cash in the hands of the Treasurer, not otherwise appropriated, and shall report their proceedings at the regular meetings. The Sergeant-at-Arms shall preserve order at all meetings. Vacancies may be filled by the President.

### ARTICLE VI.

The Association will be sustained by the voluntary subscriptions of its members.

### ARTICLE VII.

This Constitution shall only be amended at an annual meeting by a majority present.

### REGULAR MEETING.

1. Association called to order by the President.
2. Roll of Officers and Members called by the Secretary.
3. Reading of Journal of last regular or special meeting.
4. Report of Treasurer and Executive Committee.
5. Reading Miscellaneous Communications.
6. Unfinished and new business.
7. Balloting for Officers.

A committee on nomination of officers was then appointed, consisting of Comrades O. C. Foster, W. H. Young, Chas. E. Smith, John Redmond, Ed. Clark, Mac. Slosser and Ed. Hughes. They reported the following ticket: For President, J. W. Rumsey; First Vice President, E. P. Tobey; Second, F. W. Young, Third, Wm. H. Johnson; Fourth, J. Henry Long; Fifth, H. W. Chase; Sixth, Ed. Baggot; Sergeant-at-Arms, Lew F. Jacobs; Treasurer, S. S. Kimbell; Secretary, C. B. Kimbell; Corresponding Secretary, W. L. Southworth.

The ticket as reported was elected unanimously. After deciding to hold the next reunion July 22, 1886, the meeting adjourned to the upper rooms, where a bountiful spread had been laid on tables arranged in an oblong octagonal shape around a hollow square, the seats facing inward, enabling every face at the table to be seen by the others. A simultaneous attack was made on the viands along the whole line, and after about an hour's easy work, the company resolved itself into a harmonious informal gathering. Comrade Rumsey arose and acknowledged his thanks for the members' kindness in electing him the first President. He proposed a toast to the memories of our departed comrades, which was drank in silence standing. The Secretary then read the following letters, in response to invitations sent, addressed to the Committee of Arrangements:

FREDERICK O. WHITSON.

"Your invitation received; I will be with you in spirit, but not in the flesh, as it will be impossible for me to get off duty. (R. R. mail agent.) Wishing you a pleasant time, I remain, yours truly,
"E. S. Hills, Atlanta, Ga."

"I very much regret not being able to attend on account of my bad health, not being able to work only about a fourth of the time.
"M. A. Chittenden, Atchison, Kan."

"I should be very happy to attend, but, as I am a railroad man, I am out of the city on Feb. 16. Silas G. Williams, Chicago."

"I am very sorry that I cannot accept your invitation; I am so situated that I will not be able to get away. Nothing that I know of would afford me greater pleasure than to see the "old boys." I wish you a splendid time. Send paper, if possible. Yours in F., C. & L..
"Wm. Furness, Ogdensburg, N. Y."

"I regret that it will be impossible for me to 'fall in' at the call of the old bugle on the 16th. My heart will be with you.
"J. G. Eastwood, A. G. O. War Dept., Washington, D. C."

"Gladly would I embrace the opportunity of meeting with my old comrades of Battery "A," C. L. A., but it will be impossible for me to do so, on the 16th inst., the aniversary of the battle of Fort Donelson, where the first real victory of the war was won, and where Battery "A," using double charges (two canisters, then a canister and a shrapnel), held the rebel host in check until our brigade (Lew Wallace's) came up and drove them inside their fortifications, where they surrendered (13,000) the next morning. I well remember how bravely we were supported by the gallant First Nebraska Infantry. I shall think of you during the reunion and at the same time my mind will go over our camp life, as well as the battles of Fort Donelson, Shiloh, Corinth, Chickasaw Bayou, Arkansas Post, Champion Hills, Vicksburg, Jackson, Chattanooga, Resaca, Dallas, Big Shanty and Kennesaw Mountain, in which we participated. I hope it will be so that most of the boys will be able to hear *Rexford's "Bugle Blasts," and that you may have a grand reunion and make them permanent. With kindest regards to each and every member of the battery, as well as to all our noble friends in Chicago, who remembered us in time of need, I am, very truly, your most obedient servant, John T. Connell, Grand Island, Hall County, Neb."

*Rexford fully expected to be on hand with his old bugle to stir up the boys, but was prevented by the serious illness of his aged father. Every one was disappointed, but none more so that brave old "Rex" himself.

MAJ. CHARLES M. WILLARD.

"Thanks for your invitation. I regret that I cannot be there. I should be glad to be called on for my share of the necessary funds.

"G. E. Adams, Washington, D. C."

"I regret exceedingly that my duties here will not permit me to enjoy the first reunion of old Battery 'A.' When I read that Rexford, the old bugler, would be on hand, scenes of the past came to my mind, and I had a pleasant time thinking of my old comrades. I trust I shall be able to attend some of your future meetings. I wish each and every one of you a pleasant reunion and a happy evening together. Don't forget to count me in as a member if you should organize permanently, and what dues there may be I want to pay them, and if any of the boys should visit Florida, don't fail to call on me, and I will try and make it pleasant for them. Your comrade,

"A. Stewart, Sorrento, Orange County, Fla."

"I am very sorry that I cannot be at the meeting Feb. 16, as I leave for New York on the first and will not return in time. You can put me down as one of the 'boys,' and I will be present at next meeting, if in the city.

"S. J. Sherwood, Chicago."

"Mr. J. P. Henry has been dead nearly two years.

"P. L. Henry (son), Arcola, Ill."

"I regret not being able with safety to myself to attend the reunion and meet all my old comrades that may be present. Give my regards to all of them. Wishing all a jolly time, I am, etc.,

"Jas. H. Shrigley, Manistee, Mich."

"I am very sorry that I cannot be with you, but my business is such that I cannot leave it. Although I cannot be there, my heart is with you, and I wish you the greatest success and pleasure in this, your first meeting, and I wish further to say that I feel just as well as I did in the old days of Battery 'A.' I enclose my picture, though a rather poor one, and wish I had the pictures of you all, as the remembrance of you and the old days we passed together are among my dearest recollections. Your sincere friend,

"John Tack (per John Sherman Tack), Syracuse, N. Y."

"I regret my inability to attend the reunion of the company, especially so as I have not been located so as to meet with the 'boys' since the war, being, I think, the only living member of the company located in the South. I shall think of you all on the 16th, and wish you a happy time. Tell John Schaffer I have quit hanging my 'haversack' on his caisson, but often think of the time I did, down on the Tallahatchie.

"John M. Peters, Memphis, Tenn."

CAPT. PETER P. WOOD.

"My Dear Old Comrades: I was in hopes of being able to attend the reunion of the battery, but now find it will be impossible for me to get away. I hope I may be able to take part in future meetings and that I may be put down as one of you in the new organization. My kindest wishes to all the old comrades, and I only wish I could be there and talk over old times and see you all. Williams will be with you, he writes me. I have sent a message to where I thought John Day might be, but have not heard from him. Do not know where Daily is, but will still make efforts to find him. God bless you all.         F. S. Church, 58 East 13th street, New York City."

"Please say to my old comrades I greatly regret that a similar entertainment, of which I am chairman, occurs here the 17th, preventing my attendance at your reunion, which, under other circumstances, I would travel 1,000 miles to attend. I am delighted that the project has been started, and you can count me in for it hereafter. Let us meet and re-cement the old ties of comradeship so long as any of us last, and 'Here's a health to the last man that dies.' May you have as good a time as you anticipate. I shall be with you in spirit if not in the flesh. My warmest regards to all the 'boys.' Very truly,         T. S. Clarkson, Schuyler, Neb.,
"Senior Vice Commander G. A. R., Dept. of Neb."

"As much as I would like to be with you, I have got to forego the pleasure of meeting the boys on account of ill health, but my heart is with you. God bless you all.         Wm. O. Rice, Osseo, Wis."

"I do not know of anything that would please me more than to be with you, but I dare not attempt the trip on account of my health. I hope you will enjoy yourselves and keep up the old company organization, for our ranks are growing thinner annually. I have not seen a member of Battery 'A' since 1868, and would like to see you all, and hope you will enjoy yourselves, as I know I would if I could be with you.
         A. C. Hall (Garibaldi), Des Moines, Iowa."

"I regret that business and family affairs render it impossible for me to be with you on that occasion, but in interest and sympathy I am with you most heartily. I know of no organization that can more consistently meet to perpetuate by fraternal communion the memories of the past. While we all deplore the war, its causes, and the fearful loss of life and treasure incident thereto, I rejoice in the fact that there was a Battery 'A,' and am more than proud of my membership in it. Convey to the members my regrets for absence, and my hope of being present at some future gathering. My best wishes for the health, happiness and prosperity of all. Use my 'mite' (enclosed) for the benefit of the organization. Your friend,
         H. Roberts, Seneca Falls, N. Y."

THOMAS WILCOX.

"It is with most sorrowful regret I am compelled to tell you it is only the condition of my health that prevents me from attending the reunion. It would be a pleasure to meet with those that are left of the old crowd, especially with that gang that stole the roof from the Irishman's shanty at Memphis.
A. P. Maddock, Chicago."

"Greatly do I regret my inability to be present at that time. The name Battery 'A' fills my soul with vivid memories and admiration of your gallant and heroic services. All honor to the brave boys.
"E. P. Wilcox, Yankton, Dakota."

"You cannot imagine how it grieves me to inform you of my inability to be present at the reunion. I should enjoy above all things to mingle once again with my former companions in arms. It has been my desire for years to be permitted to attend a reunion of our old battery, and now that there is an opportunity, I am obliged to remain away on account of sickness. I have never seen a well day since my release from Andersonville. I hope your efforts to get the boys together will be successful, and that in recounting the incidents connected with army life, the names of our gallant dead, who answered the last summons, and have crossed to the 'other shore' in advance of those who are left yet a little while, may not be forgotten. Your friend,
Wm. H. Cowlin, Woodstock, Ill."

"Nothing would afford me more pleasure than to meet with Battery 'A' once more. Of all my associations during the late 'unpleasantness,' there are none more highly treasured than with 'the' battery, but my business is such now that it will be impossible for me to leave home. Hoping you may have an enjoyable time and many more of them, I am very truly.
"James R. Ross, Indianapolis, Ind."

"I am sorry I cannot be with you at your reunion of Wood's Battery on the 16th inst. I have good reason to remember that battery at Shiloh and Vicksburg, and am glad enough remain to meet and celebrate their devotion to the cause and country. Truly your friend,
"W. T. Sherman, St. Louis."

"I am so situated here that it will be impossible for me to accept your kind invitation for the 16th inst. Please convey to your comrades my sincere regards and my best wishes for their success.
"John A. Logan, Springfield, Ill."

"In answer to your very cordial invitation, I reply for General Wallace, he being at his post in Constantinople. Were he at home I am sure he would greatly enjoy fighting the old battles over again, at the coming reunion.

WILLIAM H. YOUNG.

And your expression of good feeling (for which let me thank you heartily), is all the more grateful, coming as it does when the accusations over the disputed field of Shiloh are being brought forward with fresh vigor and warmth. It will give me sincere pleasure to forward your letter to my husband, and have you convey to his friends and especially to the members of 'Wood's Battery' the unfailing interest and friendship of their old comrade in arms. Very truly yours, Susan E. Wallace, Crawfordsville, Ind."

"It would be a great pleasure to take again by the hand the survivors of that glorious old battery, whose gallant services in the field it was my good fortune on several occasions to witness. I regret that my arrangements to go to New York City before that event are already made, and cannot be postponed without inconveniencing others that I am not at liberty to do. Please present to them my best wishes for their prosperity, hoping you will organize permanently, that you may have the satisfaction of standing by one another in the every day battle of life as manfully as you used to do on the field of danger, I am your friend and comrade,

"John McArthur, Chicago."

After the reading of the letters, a condensed history of the battery, by Comrades Gindele, C. B. Kimbell and Enoch Colby was read by Comrade Foster, after which the banquet closed, and the boys gathered in a group at the end of the hall and had a genuine old-fashioned Battery 'A' love feast, singing all the old songs, telling stories and jokes on one another, and at midnight they regretfully dispersed, all feeling well repaid for braving the cold and storm to attend, and urging one another to not fail to attend the next reunion, July 28, 1886, and all bring their wives and babies, large and small.

The second annual reunion of the association was held at Battery "D" Armory, July 28, 1886. Members in attendance were: John W. Rumsey, President; E. P. Tobey, F. W. Young, J. H. Long, H. W. Chase, E. Baggot, C. B. Kimbell, W. L. Southworth, S. S. Kimbell, L. F. Jacobs, F. V. Gindele, M. N. Kimbell Sr., G. M. Scott, George King, J. N. Sherman, James Phillips, C. W. Poole, S. G. Williams, H. H. Pond, L. B. Mitchell, J. J. Redmond, F. S. Allen, A. C. Hall, E. Colby Jr., E. R. Howard, John Steele, E. H. Rexford, John Schaffer, Olof Benson, S. N. Pease, James F. Crocker, F. M. Kantzler, A. W. Pendleton, J. R. Irwin, J. W. Kimbell, G. M. Brown, Ed Hughes, W. E. Stockton, C. E. Clark, A. V. Pitts, Harry Morgan, J. B. Dutch, Mac. Slosser, Jerry Maloney, G. A. Pratt, O. C. Foster. The Sec-

FREDERICK W. YOUNG.

retary submitted a printed report in pamphlet form, as the minutes of proceedings of first reunion, which was received and approved as such. The following was also submitted, in addition to the printed report, which was also approved: "Since our first reunion two of our number have passed away: Augustine P. Maddock, in Chicago, May 16, 1885, and Willard I. Wilcox, in San Francisco, in the fall of 1885. Maddock left no family that is known of. Wilcox left a wife and three children in comfortable circumstances."

A copy of the Reunion and Battery History was sent the Chicago Historical Society, which was acknowledged as follows: "The Society has received and entered on catalogue a copy of the Battery History, for which I have the honor to return the Society's grateful acknowledgment." (Signed.) A. D. Hager, Secretary, Feb. 19, 1886.

One hundred and two notices of the second reunion were mailed to members, to which fifty-four responses were received. The Treasurer's report was read and approved. On motion of Comrade Colby, M. N. Kimbell Sr., and John L. Stockton were elected honorary members. The following sons of members who had reached the age of twenty-one years, were added to the list of membership: John Schaffer, Ethan A. Gray, George T. Phillips, James E. Baggot and Richard L. Powell.

There being no further new or unfinished business, the election of officers was proceeded with. The Chair appointed as Nominating Committee, Comrades J. H. Long, S. S. Kimbell, Ed Hughes, James Phillips and A. C. Hall. The committee reported the following ticket, which, on motion, was elected unanimously, the Secretary being instructed to cast one ballot for same: E. P. Tobey, President; F. S. Allen, First Vice President; L. F. Jacobs, Second Vice President; W. E. Stockton, Third Vice President; O. C. Foster, Fourth Vice President; G. M. Scott, Fifth Vice President; Enoch Colby, Sixth Vice President; C. B. Kimbell, Secretary; W. L. Southworth, Recording Secretary; H. W. Chase, Treasurer; J. R. Irwin, Sergeant-at-Arms; E. H. Rexford, Musical Director. The business meeting then adjourned to meet in September, 1887, or on call of the Executive Committee. The comrades then proceeded to the upper room, where a sumptuous banquet was spread, the bill of fare containing, among other things: "Spring (1861) Chicken," which reminded the "boys" of the days when they would have been glad to get a piece of even a more antique fowl than that. A large number of letters of regret were read from absent comrades, and brief ones

CAPT. E. P. WILCOX.

from Generals Sherman, Logan and Lew Wallace were read. Short speeches, music and singing of old war songs concluded the second reunion and evening's entertainment.

A special meeting of the association was held at "D" Battery Armory, April 10, 1887, twenty-three members being present. The following resolutions were unanimously passed: "Comrade Samuel W. Butterfield died April 7, 1887, at his residence, 296 Elm street, Chicago. He has finished his labors on earth, and has been suddenly called to enter the eternal and better life. It is fitting that we, his intimate associates and comrades in arms should bear testimony to the manner in which he discharged his duties here. Therefore, we declare that by his death we have sustained a severe loss. During his entire career as a citizen he has always shown himself to be an upright, honorable man, possessed of many virtues. His modest but firm deportment marked him as a gentleman. Whatever he undertook he did well, and every duty he assumed was faithfully discharged. As a soldier he was true and loyal, and he was excelled by none in his courage and fidelity to the cause of his country in her hour of peril. As a husband he was kind, affectionate and true, and altogether he left a record well worthy of imitation. We tender to the wife of our departed comrade our deepest sympathy in this her great bereavement and affliction." The minutes of the regular and special meetings having been read and approved, the Treasurer, Comrade Chase, presented his report:

| | |
|---|---|
| Cash on hand from second reunion (including receipts for badges) | $71.43 |
| Paid out during the year—Mourning Badges | 25.00 |
| Carriages for Comrade Butterfield's funeral | 16.20 |
| Repairing monument | 15.00—56.20 |
| Leaving balance on hand Oct. 4, 1887 | $15.23 |

The Secretary, Comrade C. B. Kimbell, read the report of the Executive Committee as follows: The committee would report that during the year three of our comrades have passed away: Samuel W. Butterfield, Francis Morgan and Jeremiah Maloney. A large number of comrades were in attendance at Comrade Butterfield's funeral. Very short notice was had of Comrade Morgan's death, and but few could attend. Comrade Maloney's death was not known by any of the committee until some time after his funeral. Our monument and the graves at Rose Hill were appropriately decorated on Decoration Day, twelve of our comrades being on hand. We had the monument treated to a coating of preservative, and it is now in good condition to stand for many years without any additional expense. One hundred and four notices of this reunion were mailed to comrades, many of whom responded.

The following sons of veterans, having attained their majority, were admitted as members of the association:

Henry King, son of George King.

Sherman T. Kimbell, son of C. B. Kimbell.

Louis A. Gray, son of A. W. Gray.

The names of George Anderson, father of Alex. Anderson, and John Alston, father of James Alston, were ordered placed on the honorary membership list.

A committee on obituary notices was appointed to draft resolutions on the deaths of Comrades Morgan and Maloney, consisting of Comrades Enoch Colby, A. W. Pendleton and F. V. Gindele.

The election of officers for the ensuing year being next in order, the Chair appointed as Nominating Committee, Comrades J. H. Long, George M. Scott, A. V. Pitts, Fred W. Young and S. S. Kimbell.

The committee submitted the following names for the offices for 1887-8: President, Frank S. Allen; First Vice President, Wm. H. Young; Second Vice President, Jacob Clingman; Third Vice President, Ferd. V. Gindele; Fourth Vice President, Wm. Lowe; Fifth Vice President, C. W. Poole; Sixth Vice President, James Phillips; Secretary, C. B. Kimbell; Recording Secretary, W. L. Southworth; Treasurer, H. W. Chase; Sergeant-at-Arms, Ed. Hughes; Musical Director, E. H. Rexford. The Secretary was instructed to cast one ballot for the association for the officers named, and the Chair declared them duly elected. This closed the business meeting. The members then adjourned to the parlors, where the wives, daughters and sisters of many of the comrades were in waiting. After a short time spent in introductions and conversation, the entire party proceeded to the upper hall, where tables had been spread for the accommodation of about eighty, which was as many as the Committee of Arrangements felt warranted in providing for, judging from the number of responses received to invitations sent out. Over one hundred were in attendance, which somewhat disturbed the caterers and interfered with the prompt and satisfactory service which they expected to render; but all exerted themselves to the utmost to "bridge over the difficulty," and all enjoyed the banquet.

The third annual reunion of the Veteran Association was held at Chicago, in Battery "D" Armory, Tuesday, Oct. 4, 1887. An informal reception was held during the day, the following comrades acting as the Reception Committee: W. H. Young, J. W. Kimbell, George M. Scott, John R. Irwin, Ed. Hughes and John Schaffer.

The managers of the Shiloh Panorama kindly invited the comrades to visit the panorama in the afternoon, many of whom availed themselves of the opportunity to inspect this wonderful and life-like painting.

The following comrades registered during the day:

| | | |
|---|---|---|
| Wm. Furness. | H. W. Chase. | A. W. Pendleton. |
| Thos. Wilcox. | W. H. Lepperr. | E. Baggot. |
| J. W. Kimbell. | G. M. Brown. | J. L. Haslett. |
| H. B. Risley. | L. F. Jacobs. | Stephen N. Pease. |
| S. S. Kimbell. | E. P. Tobey. | John Schaffer. |
| Geo. M. Scott. | F. V. Gindele. | J. J. Redmond. |
| Ed. Hughes. | John R. Irwin. | A. M. Kinzie. |
| W. H. Young. | George King. | Chas. J. Sauter. |
| J. N. Sherman. | Ed Mendsen. | C. W. Poole. |
| Jas. Phillips. | C. E. Clark. | E. D. Clark. |
| M. N. Kimbell, Sr. | W. L. Southworth. | E. H. Rexford. |
| W. E. Stockton. | A. V. Pitts. | James Crocker. |
| Will Lowe. | Henry H. Handy. | Allen W. Gray. |
| E. S. Hills. | J. Clingman. | Thomas Powell. |
| F. W. Young. | George E. Adams. | Cass F. Maurer. |
| C. B. Kimbell. | Mac. Slosser. | F. M. Kantzler. |
| Enoch Colby. | John Steele. | Harry Morgan. |
| J. H. Long. | P. P. Powell. | |

Comrade Rumsey was unavoidably absent in Dakota and Comrade Allen was confined to his house by sickness, with which he had been afflicted several months.

A relic of the war in the shape of a genuine hardtack, one of the last meals issued to the battery by Commissary Chase in 1864, was on exhibition, having been contributed by Comrade John Tack, of Syracuse.

A copy of the play bill of the Battery Theatrical Co. at Larkinsville, in 1864, was contributed by a friend, and as an interesting and valuable relic of those days, attracted considerable attention from the "boys." It is given in full in Chapter II. of this history, in the portion relating to Larkinsville.

After the banquet letters of regret were read from the following absent comrades: J. H. Shrigley, Harry Roberts, C. L. Church, A. R. Abbott, E. P. Fish, Charles E. Smith, John Tack, W. H. Bailey, W. O. Rice, W. H. Cowlin, A. C. Hall (Garabaldi), Adam Stewart, Meric Gould, John T. Connell, Edward Johnson, John H. Page, E. E. Williams, T. A. McKnight, Charles A. Lamb, and George A. Pratt. Letters were also read from Generals Sherman and Lew Wallace, Commissioner of Pensions John C. Black and Mrs. S. W. Butterfield. A fine selection of instrumental war music was rendered by Comrade Rexford, cornet; his daughter Laura, violin, and Miss Sarah M. Kimbell, piano. Prof. McCosh's orchestra discoursed appropriate music during the evening, and aided materially in drowning any discords the "boys" may have produced in bringing out the old war songs which had not been rehearsed for a concert since the war. Many comrades who were noted as singers of special pieces during the war, were called upon for songs, but invariably declined, though Comrades Handy and Southworth promised to rehearse "Larboard Watch" during the coming year, and Jake Clingman was warned to be prepared with "Fairy Bell" for the next reunion. M. N. Kimbell, Sr., was called upon, and made a few feeling remarks, and congratulated the "boys" on the records they had made since, as well as during, the war; and he heartily approved of their plan of adding the presence of their lady relatives to their reunions, there being between thirty and forty present.

The Executive Committee was authorized to fix the date for the reunion for next year, as in their judgment would be best. It was midnight when the meeting finally dispersed, and the good-bys for another year were spoken.

The fourth annual reunion of the association was held at Battery "D" Armory, Oct. 4, 1888. President Comrade Frank S. Allen presiding. After the roll call the minutes of the last meeting were read and approved. Treasurer Comrade H. W. Chase read his report showing:

Receipts from members for preceding year......................$177.23
Payments as per vouchers........................................146.75

Leaving balance on hand..................................$30.48

Which report was approved and placed on file. The Executive Committee, through Secretary C. B. Kimbell, submitted their annual report, as follows:

The committee has had occasion to hold but one meeting during the past year, which was on July 27, and was for the purpose of arranging for this, our fourth annual reunion. The following committees were appointed:

Reception, George M. Scott, Wm. H. Young, J. W. Kimbell, James Phillips, Ed. Hughes; Entertainment, S. S. Kimbell, Jacob Clingman, O. C. Foster; Banquet, H. W. Chase, W. L. Southworth; Music, E. H. Rexford.

One hundred and twenty-three notices were mailed to members and responses were received from fifty-seven only, twenty sending regrets, and thirty-seven acceptances. Since our last reunion one member has passed away. George E. Cooper died December 17, 1887, in Chicago. One honorary member, George Anderson, father of Alex. Anderson, died in October last, one month after his admission into our association. The additional addresses of six of our old comrades were received by the Secretary during the year, to whom copies of the history and reunion pamphlets were mailed. Copies of same were also sent to Judge Advocate of Department of Iowa, G. A. R., George M. Van Louven, who wished to obtain a list of our members for the purpose of assisting a former member of our battery, name not given, to get a pension. The Secretary was able to furnish an affidavit for Comrade Merie Gould, of Monroe (now of Brest), Michigan, which assisted him in securing a pension of $6 per month, which he acknowledged in a very appreciative letter. Comrade Fred S. Church was expected to furnish an illustrated "bill of fare" for this occasion, but, being absent from home, did not receive our letter in time. He promises to show the boys at our next reunion that he has not forgotten them. Our roster now contains 123 names. Our ranks are gradually being thinned and but a few years will elapse before it will be necessary to have the name of every survivor in order to make a quorum. We would urge the members to show their remembrance of our departed comrades by decorating the monument at Rose Hill each Decoration Day as far as possible. The report as read was received and ordered on file. Letters of regret were read from Comrades C. E. Smith, C. L. Church, W. O. Rice, John Tack, E. P. Fish, W. H. Bailey, Hoxie L. Hoffman, Ed. E. Williams, Adam Stewart, J. H. Shrigley, H. H. Handy, J. B. Day, Harry Roberts, Moses Hawks and W. H. Johnson. Comrade F. V. Gindele read the following resolutions on the death of Comrades Frances Morgan and Jeremiah Maloney:

"Whereas, Death has removed from our midst Comrade Frances Morgan, who was in command of our battery in the early part of the war, in 1862, and was obliged to resign his commission on account of ill health; Resolved, That by his death another name has been added to the list of those who have joined the silent majority of our country's defenders. Capt. Morgan possessed fine ability as a drillmaster, and much of the efficiency of our battery during the war was due to the instruction given by him during the three months' service; Resolved, That this association deeply sympathize with the bereaved family of the deceased, and that a copy of these resolutions be spread upon the records of our association. And, Whereas, It has pleased Almighty God to remove from our ranks Comrade Jeremiah Maloney, a faithful and brave soldier, and one of the youngest in the battery, therefore be it Resolved, That in his death we mourn the loss of a comrade who, though young in years, faithfully stood by us in many battles in the face of the enemy, a true and courageous soldier, always ready when duty called, and never lagging in zeal and enthusiasm in the cause of his country; Resolved, That we sincerely sympathize with the family of our late comrade in their bereavement, and that a copy of these resolutions be sent to them, and also spread upon the records of the association." Signed by Enoch Colby and F. V. Gindele, Committee. The resolutions were adopted unanimously by a rising vote.

A Nominating Committee appointed by the Chair, consisting of Comrades W. L. Southworth, F. W. Young, George King, James Phillips, W. H. Young, S. S. Kimbell and P. P. Powell, reported and recommended the names of Enoch Colby, Jr., for President; Ed. Baggot, J. Henry Long, George King, A. W. Pendleton, John Steele and Olaf Benson, Vice Presidents unmbered in the order named; C. B. Kimbell., Secretary; F. V. Gindele, Recording Secretary; H. W. Chase, Treasurer; W. H. Young, Sergeant-at-Arms; and E. H. Rexford, Musical Director. The Secretary was instructed to cast one ballot for the names as reported, which, being done, the President declared them duly elected as officers of the association for the ensuing year. Comrade Pitts asked for information as to how a proper discharge could be obtained for service during the three months' service, no discharges ever having been issued. After some discussion, the following resolution, offered by Comrade Jacobs, was adopted: "Resolved, That the Executive Committee be empowered to communicate with the proper authorities, either of the State or the United States, to the end that the members of three months' service should receive an honorable discharge signed by the Adjutant General of the State or United States.

Comrade Allen, in behalf of the members, in a neat speech presented Secretary Kimbell with an elegant gold-headed cane, suitably inscribed, as a token of their esteem and appreciation of his services to the association.

The event, with the well-chosen remarks of the President, completely unnerved the recipient, who attempted to express his thanks as best he could for the unexpected gift.

M. N. Kimbell, Jr., and John F. Powell, of Waukegan, Ill., brother of Comrade P. P. Powell, were elected honorary members. James M. Baggot, son of Comrade Ed. Baggot, was admitted to membership as such. The meeting then adjourned to the upper rooms of the armory, where tables were spread and a substantial banquet served, after which an adjournment was had for one year.

The fifth annual reunion of the association was held was held at Battery "D" Armory, August 26, 1889, President Enoch Colby, Jr., in the Chair. In the absence on account of sickness of Secretary C. B. Kimbell, the minutes of the last annual meeting were read by Recording Secretary F. V. Gindele, which were approved. He made a verbal report for the Executive Committee, stating that no business had been transacted by them during the year. The report of Treasurer Chase was read and approved and ordered on file. The Chair appointed a Committee on Resolutions, consisting of Comrades W. E. Stockton, C. L. Arnold and E. D. Clark, on the death of Comrades Jacob Clingman and Francis T. Sweenie. Comrades P. P. Powell, W. S. Southworth, S. S. Kimbell, W. H. Young and Charles W. Poole were appointed a committee to nominate officers for the association for the ensuing year. They reported the following nominations: President, Ed. Baggot; Vice Presidents, in the order named, J. Henry Long, W. E. Stockton, John Steele, Olaf Benson, James Phillips and C. L. Arnold; Secretary, C. B. Kimbell; Recording Secretary, F. V. Gindele; Treasurer, H. W. Chase; Sergeant-at-Arms, E. D. Clark; Musical Director, E. H. Rexford. The Secretary was instructed to cast one ballot for the names submitted, which, being done, the Chair declared the comrades duly elected as officers for the association for the ensuing year. The names of Walter K. Clark and —— Pease, sons of Comrades E. D. Clark and S. N. Pease, were enrolled among the "Sons of Veterans" of the Battery Association. Comrade Allen reported regarding the condition of Comrade Jacobs, that he was still in the hospital and was desirous of seeing any of the boys whenever they could conveniently call on him. The members then adjourned to the supper room, where a tempting and substantial spread awaited them. After the banquet, letters of regret were read from Comrades Ed. Baggot, C. B. Kimbell, H. S.

Foote, S. G. Williams, J. B. Day, S. H. Tallmadge, John Tack, E. S. Hill, C. L. Church, A. W. Pendleton, E. E. Williams, Wm. Furness, George M. Brown and Harry Roberts. The reunion then closed, adjourning till 1890.

A special meeting of the association was held at Battery "D" Armory, November 4, 1889. There were present: Comrades E. Baggot, F. V. Gindele, George M. Scott, H. W. Chase, W. L. Southworth, E. D. Clark, Fred W. Young, H. W. Young, Ed. Hughes, James Phillips, Wm. Lowe, John Steele and C. W. Poole. The object of the meeting was to take action on the death at the hospital of Comrade Lewis F. Jacobs, also to secure information regarding the graves of comrades at Rose Hill, in the battery lot, and not marked. A committee consisting of Comrades W. L. Southworth, Frank S. Allen and C. W. Poole was appointed to draft suitable resolutions on the death of Comrade Jacobs, which occurred in this city Oct. 21, 1889. He had willed some property to the association, and proper action to place the same in trust was taken under advisement, and the question of incorporating the association was referred to the Executive Committee, with power to act. A meeting of the Executive Committee was held at the office of Comrade Baggot, Nov. 21, 1889. There were present Comrades E. Baggot, F. V. Gindele, James Phillips, O. Benson and H. W. Chase. C. B. Kimbell was absent in New York on account of sickness. Comrade Allen reported that the lot willed to the association by Comrade Jacobs was subject to his personal debts, which were not of very large amount, and unpaid taxes and special assessments. Comrade Allen is the executor of the estate and has probated the will. An offer has already been made for the lot, through Bowes & Cruikshank, for $1,000, part cash and balance on time. Committees were appointed on headstones, consisting of Comrades Allen, H. W. Chase and Gindele, and on charter of Allen, Redmond and E. D. Clark. The committee then adjourned and held a subsequent meeting May 21, 1890, at the office of Comrade Baggot, 171 Adams street, at which were present Ed. Baggot, F. V. Gindele, Harry Morgan, John Steele, James Phillips, F. S. Allen, Enoch Colby, Jr., H. W. Chase, and C. B. Kimbell. Chairman Allen, of the Committee on Headstones, reported that he could get no definite information of the Rose Hill Cemetery Company regarding the location of graves; although they had promised to do what they could, they had failed to accomplish anything definite. Chairman Gindele, of the Monument Committee, reported that the iron rust spots in the monument had been cut out and stone plugs inserted in the holes. Painting the monument was recommended. A general discussion was had regarding the lot donated by Comrade Jacobs, and various plans and suggestions were made for raising money to pay the debts of Jacobs, for which the lot was held, also to meet taxes and special assessments which stand against it. On motion of Comrade Chase, Comrade Allen was authorized to receive subscriptions in the nature of a loan, to be repaid when the lot was sold, for the purpose of meeting the estate's indebtedness, which amount, so far as known, to not less than $500. The Committee on Headstones asked for and were granted further time. Thereupon the meeting adjourned.

The sixth annual meeting of the association was held at Battery "D" Armory, October 1, 1890.

There were present at this meeting: Ed. Baggot, E. D. Clark, James Phillips, Charles E. Clark, Wm. H. Young, George King, Moses Hawks, E. P. Tobey, Mac. Slosser, H. W. Chase, F. S. Allen, Wm. Lowe, P. P. Powell, Enoch Colby, and C. B. Kimbell. The minutes of the last regular and all special meetings were read and approved.

Treasurer H. W. Chase reported:

Receipts on account of last reunion..............................$149.98
Payments on account of same as per voucher submitted............ 117.50

  Leaving balance on hand.................................. $32.48

Which report was approved and ordered on file. Comrade Allen made a verbal report regarding the Jacobs lot. Comrades Ed. Baggot, H. W. Chase and C. B. Kimbell had each responded with $50, under resolution of May 21. The election of officers for the ensuing year was discussed, and, on motion of Comrade Colby, Comrade Tobey was authorized to cast one ballot for the present officers of the association. It was done, and Comrade Tobey announced their election in due form. The death of Comrade John J. Redmond, on June 8, 1890, was announced, and a Committee on Resolutions on his death was appointed, consisting of Comrades C. B. Kimbell, Enoch Colby and W. L. Southworth. The meeting then adjourned, a large number of the members accepting the invitation of Comrade Baggot to proceed to the Wellington Hotel, where oysters, etc., were "set up" in generous style. The officers as re-elected for 1890-91 were: President, Ed. Baggot; Vice Presidents, in order named, J. H. Long, W. E. Stockton, John Steele, Olof Benson, James Phillips, C. L. Arnold; Secretary, C. B. Kimbell;

Recording Secretary, F. V. Gindele; Treasurer, H. W. Chase; Sergeant-at-Arms, E. D. Clark; Musical Director, E. H. Rexford.

Seventh annual reunion, October 7, 1891.

The members met at Battery "D" Armory, at 10 o'clock a. m. The time was spent until noon in hearty greetings, talking and lunching, coffee, sandwiches, biscuits and doughnuts having been liberally provided, and the boys demonstrated that their joviality and appetites were as lively and vigorous as during the times of war. At noon they formed into line and marched to the Lake Front, where, with many other veteran organizations, all formed into column and marched to Lincoln Park, to take part in the unveiling of the Grant monument. An immense concourse of people was present. Our company had a fine position during the ceremonies, close to the monument. After the unveiling ceremonies, the members assembled at the Germania Mannerchor Club rooms, where Comrade Baggot had arranged for our entertainment. There were present during the day and evening, Comrades:

| | | |
|---|---|---|
| F. W. Young. | E. P. Tobey. | W. E. Stockton. |
| A. V. Pitts. | John Schaffer. | Olof Benson. |
| W. R. Page. | Harry Morgan. | C. L. Arnold. |
| Henry Burdick. | Chas. E. Clark. | W. H. Johnson. |
| M. N. Kimbell, Sr. | P. P. Powell. | J. W. Kimbell. |
| F. S. Allen. | W. H. Young. | S. S. Kimbell. |
| J. H. Long. | E. D. Clark. | S. G. Williams. |
| John B. Day. | J. S. Anderson. | H. W. Chase. |
| E. Colby, Jr. | Thos. Wilcox. | Ed Hughes. |
| Mac. Slosser. | Jas. Phillips. | C. W. Poole. |
| John D. Dyer. | T. S. Clarkson. | J. R. Irwin. |
| Ed. S. Hills. | John Steele. | E. D. Clark. |
| G. M. Brown. | Will Lowe. | C. B. Kimbell. |
| W. H. Lepperr. | E. H. Rexford. | |

After roll-call the minutes of last meeting were read and approved. Resolutions were read and adopted on the death of Comrades John J. Redmond and Lewis F. Jacobs. Comrade Redmond died at Chicago, June 8, 1890, and was buried at Calvary. Comrade Jacobs died in hospital at Chicago, Oct. 21, 1889, and was buried in the battery lot at Rose Hill. Both funerals were well attended by comrades of the battery.

Comrade Stockton was appointed a committee of one to obtain, if possible, of Mr. Larrabee and others, such original documents of Captain

Wood's as they might have in their possession, for the purpose of getting them in our records and incorporating such as would be valuable in the history of the battery. It was decided to postpone the reunion for 1893, during the World's Fair. The election of officers was held, resulting as follows: For President, J. Henry Long; Vice Presidents, in the order named, W. E. Stockton, A. V. Pitts, Wm. Lowe, Henry Morgan, C. L. Arnold and J. W. Kimbell; Secretary, C. B. Kimbell; Recording Secretary, W. L. Southworth; Treasurer, H. W. Chase; Sergeant-at-Arms, C. W. Poole; Musical Director, E. H. Rexford. The thanks of the association were tendered to President Baggot and Secretary Kimbell for their services to the association during their terms of office. The banquet which followed the business meeting was attended by a number of the comrades, wives, sons and daughters, and a very pleasant occasion was enjoyed by all. The banquet was followed by reading letters and regrets from absent comrades. Comrade Parson Risley's letter from Seattle was so characteristic that it is given in full, and we have no doubt all the boys will enjoy reading a communication direct from the "Old Parson."

"Seattle, Washington, July 17, 1893.
"C. B. Kimbell, Secretary Battery 'A' C. L. A. Vet. Assn.:

"Dear Comrade: Your very kind invitation to the grand reunion of the old Battery 'A' is received, and in reply would say that I deeply regret my inability to be present on that occasion, but in heart and hand I am always with you. I am at the present writing enjoying the delightful climate and scenery of Puget Sound, in the city of Seattle, where I have been for the last four years, having as good a time as possible so far away from old comrades, friends and associates.

"Say to the girls and boys of Battery 'A' that 'Old Parson' is still on deck, and often, while in company with Jack Rumsey, we talk over those pleasant recollections of bygone days. Jack and myself are in all probability farther away from that beautiful city of Chicago than any other members of Battery 'A,' still our love for her and her kind-hearted and patriotic citizens that were so generous to us in those dark days, grows no less. We still cling to her and her good people, as we do to our country and the dear old flag.

"Seattle, the queen city of the Sound, is well stocked with all kinds of choicest fruits and berries of the season, while the shores of her lovely bays are filled with delicious clams, and her waters, with all kinds of salt water fish, the mountain streams alive with trout, all of which afford abundance of sport for the angler these delightful summer days.

"Still Jack and myself have been sitting down so long waiting for 'suckers' that we will soon need re-enforcements to make us presentable to our families. It recalls to memory a scene in '61, way down in Egypt, when Lou Mitchell was crucified for being in camp with a whole pair of pants. But such is life in the wild and woolly West.

"Mrs. Risley wishes to be kindly remembered to all the girls of Battery 'A,' especially to Mrs. Spencer Kimbell, Mrs. Chase and others.

"Wishing you all a good time and a full house, and my kind regards to all the girls and boys, is the prayer of the only private on the Sound. Yours fraternally, H. B. Risley."

Comrade Rexford gave all the bugle calls, which were enthusiastically received by the boys. Short speeches were made by Comrades Clarkson, Day, Rexford and others, and at 8:30 p. m. the meeting adjourned.

June 4, 1892, a meeting of the association was held at the office of Comrade J. H. Long, for the purpose of incorporating the association under the State law. Comrades present at this meeting were J. H. Long, H. W. Chase, A. W. Gray, Mac. Slosser, F. S. Allen, Harry Morgan, E. D. Clark, C. L. Arnold, C. B. Kimbell, P. P. Powell and James Phillips. It was decided that we should incorporate, and Comrades J. H. Long, H. W. Chase, C. B. Kimbell, C. L. Arnold and Harry Morgan were instructed to procure the necessary papers from the Secretary of State, and they were appointed as a Board of Directors, to serve for the first year. The Constitution and By-Laws adopted were as follows:

## ARTICLE I.

This organization shall be known as "The Battery 'A,' Chicago Light Artillery, Association."

## ARTICLE II.

The object of this association is to preserve and strengthen those kind and fraternal feelings, which bound together the members of old Battery "A," who united to assist in suppressing the late rebellion, and to perpetuate the history of the battery and the memory of its noble dead.

## ARTICLE III.

Section 1. Regular meetings of this association shall be held annually, on the call of the President.

Sec. 2. Special meetings may be called at any time by the President, or he shall call such meeting upon the written application of five members.

Sec. 3. Nine members shall constitute a quorum for the transaction of business.

## ARTICLE IV.

Any member of the late Battery "A," First Illinois Artillery, shall be eligible to membership upon signing the Constitution.

## ARTICLE V.

Section 1. The affairs of this association shall be under the management of five directors, to be elected by ballot, at the annual meeting of the members of the association.

Sec. 2. The directors shall choose from their own number a President, Vice President, Secretary and Treasurer, and they shall hold their respective offices for the period of one year next following their election, and until their successors shall be elected and qualified.

Sec. 3. Vacancies in the offices of the association or Board of Directors may be filled for the unexpired term at any regular or special meeting of the Board of Directors.

Sec. 4. The Board of Directors may require from the several officers, from time to time, such bond as in their discretion they shall deem best for the faithful performance of their respective duties of said offices.

## ARTICLE VI.

Section 1. The President shall preside at all meetings of the association.

Sec. 2. The Vice President shall perform such duties as may be required of him by the President, and in his absence shall take his place.

Sec. 3. The Secretary shall attend all meetings of the Directors and keep a record of the proceedings of said meetings. He shall keep, or cause to be kept, proper books of account of the association. He shall have custody of all books, documents and papers of said association, and its corporate seal. He shall annually furnish a detailed statement of the receipts and expenditures of the association.

Sec. 4. The Treasurer shall keep all moneys of the association, and shall disburse the same on the order of the President, countersigned by the Secretary.

Sec. 5. All bonds, contracts and other instruments to be made on behalf of the association shall be executed by the President and Secretary, after having been approved by the Board of Directors.

## ARTICLE VII.

This association will be sustained by the voluntary subscriptions of its members.

## ARTICLE VIII.

This Constitution shall be amended only at an annual meeting, by a majority present.

## ORDER OF BUSINESS.

1. Association called to order by the President.
2. Roll of officers and members called by the Secretary.
3. Reading of journal of last regular and special meeting.
4. Report of Treasurer and Executive Committee.
5. Reading miscellaneous communications.
6. Unfinished and new business.
7. Balloting for officers.

The license for incorporation which was granted reads:

"State of Illinois, Department of State.
"Isaac N. Pearson, Secretary of State.

"To All Whom These Presents Shall Come—Greeting:

"Whereas, A certificate, duly signed and acknowledged, having been filed in the office of the Secretary of State, on the 7th day of June, A. D. 1892, for the organization of the Battery 'A,' Chicago Light Artillery, Association, under and in accordance with the provisions of 'An Act concerning corporations, approved April 18, 1872, and in force July 1, 1872, and all acts amendatory thereof, a copy of which certificate is hereto attached. Now, therefore, I, Isaac N. Pearson, Secretary of State of Illinois, by virtue of the powers and duties vested in me by law, do hereby certify that the said Battery 'A,' Chicago Light Artillery, Association, is a legally organized corporation under the laws of the State of Illinois. In testimony whereof I hereto set my hand and cause to be affixed the great Seal of State.

Done at the city of Springfield, this 7th day of June, in the year of our Lord 1892, and of the Independence of the United States the 116th.

"Seal. Isaac N. Pearson, Secretary of State."

June 20 following the Board of Directors met at the office of Comrade J. H. Long. There were present Comrades J. H. Long, H. W. Chase and C. B. Kimbell. Comrade Frank S. Allen was also present unofficially. An election of officers to serve for one year was held. J. H. Long was elected President; C. L. Arnold, Vice President; C. B. Kimbell, Secretary; H. W. Chase, Treasurer. Comrade Allen made a verbal statement regarding the condition of the Jacobs lot matter, he being the executor of the estate. It was decided by the Board that if an advantageous offer for the purchase of the lot could be obtained, it would be for the best interests of the association to sell it, and with the proceeds pay off the debts against the Jacobs estate and have the balance for a fund to keep the battery cemetery lot at Rose Hill in proper condition, procure headstones for comrades buried on the lot, and for such uses as the association should deem best.

The eighth annual reunion of the association was held during the World's Fair, Sept. 9, 1893, at the Sheridan Club House, in Chicago. The Executive Committee having the arrangements for this meeting in charge were: J. H. Long, H. W. Chase, C. L. Arnold, Harry Morgan and C. B. Kimbell. The last circular letter issued by the committee to the members, setting the date for the meeting, was Aug. 18, 1893, at which time all the members of the committee were in their usual health and vigor. Before the date of the reunion Comrades Chase and Morgan were called suddenly to their final rest. Their sudden taking off cast a gloom over the boys, and all realized more than ever before that we were rapidly nearing the end of our earthly career. Members in attendance as registered were:

| | | |
|---|---|---|
| Edgar P. Tobey, | P. P. Powell, | Fred. B. Leavitt. |
| Enoch Colby, Jr. | John T. Connell, | O. C. Foster. |
| J. H. Long. | Wm. E. Stockton. | M. N. Kimbell, Sr. |
| E. D. Clark, | John Schaffer. | Will Lowe. |
| John Steele, | F. M. Kantzler. | W. H. Renfro. |
| G. M. Scott. | Wm. H. Young. | Olof Benson. |
| Ed. Baggot. | S. S. Kimbell. | G. M. Brown. |
| Chas. C. Briggs. | M. A. Bartelson. | Wm. L. Southworth. |
| E. H. Rexford. | Albert Dixson. | Frank S. Allen. |
| A. W. Gray. | Moses Hawks, | Thos. Powell. |
| C. B. Kimbell. | Sam. M. Fargo. | Thad. S. Clarkson. |
| J. W. Kimbell. | C. W. Poole. | Mac. Slosser. |
| Ed S. Hills. | Ed. Mendsen. | Chas. A. Lamb. |
| Henry Burdick. | John L. Haslett. | |

President J. H. Long presided. Many of the members were accompanied by their wives, sons and daughters. The rooms were patriotically decorated with flags and bunting, and at 9 a. m. were opened for the reception of the company. Before noon nearly every member had arrived. Until 2:30 p. m., when the company adjourned to the banquet hall, the time was spent in greetings and sociability. A sumptuous banquet excellently served was enjoyed by all. After the banquet followed the reading of letters of regret from absent comrades. Those who had responded were: Wm. O. Rice, John B. Day, Parson Risley, Ed. E. Williams, Wm. H. Cowlin, Nathan T. Cox, Charles E. Smith, E. P. Fish, Clarence L. Church, Sam. Kennedy, J. M. Dusenberry, B. Burdick, J. F. Dunlap, J. S. Anderson, Harry Roberts, and J. N. Sherman. After the banquet the comrades and their guests repaired to the Assembly Hall, where the business meeting was held. The

Secretary called the roll of the entire battery. The minutes of the last meeting were read and approved. The Secretary, in the absence of Treasurer Comrade Chase, who died so recently, made a verbal statement of the financial condition of the association, which was approved. The Committee on Resolutions, through Comrade W. E. Stockton, reported and read the following resolutions, which were adopted by a rising vote:

"Comrades: Since our last meeting it has pleased Almighty God to relieve from their duties here, that they may enter upon their rest, our Comrades and friends, George B. Beach, Laurin H. Beach, Caleb S. Birdsall, Horace W. Chase, James Phillips, Harry Morgan and Fred W. Young, all well-known as tried and true comrades, soldiers and friends, never found wanting in the hour of peril and privation, and ever ready to brighten the lot of those around them by their kindly counsel and assistance. Therefore, we, their comrades, who are left to mourn their absence from their places here with us to-day, would offer the following as a slight token of our respect and love; be it

"Resolved, That in the death of our comrades, Geo. B. Beach, Laurin H. Beach, Caleb S. Birdsall, Horace W. Chase, James Phillips, Harry Morgan and Fred W. Young, we bow to the will of Him who has led our friends safely through the hum of battle and privation, and who has brought them to the everlasting peace and rest of those who, knowing their duty, do not flinch from its performance. 'He doeth all things well.'

"Resolved, That the memory of their gallant deeds and kindly actions can never be effaced from our hearts.

"Resolved, That these resolutions be inscribed on the records of our association, that those who shall stand in our places may learn how they were mourned and loved by those who knew them well and found them true. And be it further

"Resolved, That copies of these resolutions be suitably prepared and sent to the families or sorrowing friends of the deceased."

Next in order was the nomination and election of officers. A Board of Directors was elected, consisting of Comrades Wm. E. Stockton, Spencer S. Kimbell, Charles B. Kimbell, Edward Baggot and E. H. Rexford. There being no further unfinished or new business the meeting resolved itself into an informal gathering, various members making interesting short talks. Major T. S. Clarkson made a particularly happy and interesting speech. All the bugle calls were given by Comrade Rexford, each call bringing out rousing cheers from the boys as the old familiar notes brought back the memories of bygone days. Comrade Rexford also furnished sentimental

and patriotic music, ably assisted by his daughter Laura, with the violin, in fine, artistic style. Prof. Burmeister, of the First Nebraska, the support of our battery at Fort Donelson, gave a fine recitation. After all joined in singing "America," the reunion adjourned. Immediately after adjournment a meeting of the newly-elected Board of Directors was held; E. H. Rexford was chosen Chairman and C. B. Kimbell Secretary. The election for officers resulted in choosing: President, Wm. E. Stockton; Vice President, S. S. Kimbell; Secretary, C. B. Kimbell; Treasurer, Ed. Baggot; Musical Director, E. H. Rexford.

A photographer was on hand and a very fine group of the members was taken. Copies were sent to many of the nonresident comrades. One sent to Mrs. Charles A. Lamb, whose husband was present and only survived two weeks after the reunion, brought forth the following grateful acknowledgment.

"404 Cass Street, Albion, Mich., Dec. 12, 1893.
"C. B. Kimbell, Secretary:

"Dear Sir: The photograph of group is received. Many thanks for your kindness in mailing it to me. It is a very fine group, indeed, and I shall prize it highly, both on account of the picture of my beloved husband and of the comrades he loved to mention so often. I am very proud of it, as Mr. Lamb would have been could he have lived to see it, and show it to his friends. With kind regards to all the comrades, I am, very truly yours,
"Mrs. Charles A. Lamb."

"The Timberman," the lumber trade journal of Chicago, of date of Sept. 9, 1893, the day of our eighth reunion, contained a very eulogistic article on the life of Comrade Horace W. Chase, who was an old and honored member of the lumber trade of the city.

The ninth annual reunion was held Sept. 7, 1895, at the home of Comrade S. S. Kimbell, 1527 Kimbell avenue, Chicago. Members in attendance as registered were: W. H. Bailey, Edward Johnson, Charles E. Clark, C. B. Kimbell, S. S. Kimbell, George M. Brown, W. H. Renfro, George M. Scott, P. P. Powell, C. L. Arnold, John Schaffer, W. L. Southworth, J. D. Dyer, C. W. Poole, S. N. Pease, J. W. Kimbell, E. H. Rexford, Henry Burdick, Edward Baggot, A. W. Gray, W. E. Stockton, E. P. Fish, Moses Hawks, E. Colby, Jr., Olof Benson, Ed. Mendsen, J. H. Long. Comrade A. C. Waterhouse, of Waterhouse's Battery, made a short call, which was entirely unexpected and very much enjoyed.

A large number of the wives, sons and daughters of members were present, also many of our deceased members' near relatives. A season of sociability, music, etc., was enjoyed, and at 1 o'clock the tables, set in form of a letter "A." under a spacious tent on the lawn, and well filled with substantial and tempting viands, were filled, and an hour spent in disposing of them. The business meeting then opened, President Comrade Stockton presiding.

The roll of the entire battery was then called, after which the minutes of the last meeting were read and approved. The Treasurer's report was next read and approved and ordered placed on file. Letters of regret were read from absent comrades, followed by a bugle solo, "The Soldier's Farewell," by Comrade Rexford.

Resolutions on the death of comrades passing away since our last reunion, also on the death of Martin N. Kimbell, Sr., were read by Comrade Stockton, and passed by a rising vote. The resolutions were as follows:

"Comrades, since our last meeting the following comrades have entered into their rest: Charles A. Lamb, Edgar P. Tobey, Edgar D. Clark, Aurelius V. Pitts, Silas G. Williams, M. W. Axtell.

"Those of us who knew these comrades intimately, who stood beside them in battle, who endured with them the trials and privations of the long and weary marches, and the monotony of camp life away from home and its attractions, learned to feel a bond that endeared them as brothers, and which we doubt is felt or sustained in any other path of life, and its full significance is known to us, when their names are called on this, their last roll call, and we know we shall see them and hear their voices no more until we, too, shall enter into the future life; therefore, be it

"Resolved, That in the loss to us of these comrades who have passed from this life since our last meeting, we feel that bereavement which comes to them who lose from their lives those who stood tried and true in the hour of danger, and in whose pleasant friendship the care and trials of a soldier's life were made bright and endurable, and we feel their loss all the more as our roll call grows shorter, for we know that their places can never again be filled in our hearts. And be it

"Resolved, That these resolutions be spread on the minutes of this meeting, and suitably engrossed copies be sent to the families of each departed comrade by the Secretary."

"Since our last meeting we are called upon to mourn the loss of one who, while known as an associated member of Battery "A" on our records, was recognized and loved by every member of our organization as Battery "A's" father. I allude to our dear friend, Martin N. Kimbell, Sr. He gave his brave boys to help fill our ranks, and, not satisfied with that, his great heart overflowing with patriotism and love for Battery "A" brought him to our camp again and again, always with the same bright presence, always brave and helpful, believing in the justice and success of our cause as he believed in his God; such a man was an inspiration to every soldier who was honored by his friendship. We speak of the spirit of 1776, and we understand the devotion of those trying days, and so we would speak of Father Kimbell as the spirit of Battery "A." He was fearless in the hour of danger, tender and true to comrades always. In testimony of our love and regard, we offer the following:

"Be it resolved, That in the departure of our good friend, Martin N. Kimbell, Sr., this association has lost one who at all times has held our Battery 'A' close to his heart, giving his sons to fill its ranks. He gave his heart and all that went with it to comfort and sustain its members and to instill in their minds a sense of patriotism and duty. We can never repay his kindness, but we will love and keep green his memory. He has passed away full of years and honors, living to see the consummation of his dearest hope in the wonderful growth of a reunited country. And, in the love and regard of every soldier, and of every one who knew him, reaping his well-won reward. As long as a name is answered to our roll call, so long will his good life and kind deeds be remembered by Battery 'A.' Be it

"Resolved, That our Secretary be instructed to send to each member of Mr. Kimbell's family a copy of these resolutions."

After the reading of the resolutions, "Home, Sweet Home" was beautifully rendered on the cornet by Comrade Rexford.

The election of Directors followed. Five Directors were nominated and unanimously elected by ballot cast by the Secretary as follows: S. S. Kimbell, George M. Scott, Edward Baggot, C. B. Kimbell and E. H. Rexford.

The Directors imediately met and elected officers for the ensuing year as follows: S. S. Kimbell, President; George M. Scott, Vice President; Edward Baggot, Treasurer; C. B. Kimbell, Secretary; E. H. Rexford, Musical Director; Miss Laura Rexford, Assistant Musical Director.

A vote of thanks was passed to the Kimbell family for their part of the entertainment. Two national salutes were fired by Comrade S. M. Tyrrell with Comrade Baggot's gun, which were vigorously cheered by the comrades, and created havoc with horses in the neighborhood.

After singing and music, the meeting adjourned subject to the call of the officers.

The tenth annual reunion of the association was held Sept. 5, 1896, at the residence of S. S. Kimbell, 1527 Kimbell avenue, Chicago. The meeting was in the form of a basket picnic. Twenty-nine members were present, many of them with their wives, sons and daughters. The near relatives of several of our deceased comrades were present, making a total of about 200 in attendance. The day was all that could be asked for, and it was greatly enjoyed by all. Tables were spread under spacious tents on the lawn. The boys were mostly on hand at 10 o'clock, and spent the time till noon in greetings and general sociability. At 12 o'clock dinner was announced. All fell in with all the ardor of old war tines, and ample justice was done to the meal. After dinner the meeting was called to order by Comrade President S. S. Kimbell. The roll of the entire battery was called by Secretary C. B. Kimbell, followed by reading the journal of the last annual meeting. The reports of the Treasurer and of the Executive Committee were also read, and all were approved and ordered placed on file.

The annual report of the officers of the association for 1895-6, as submitted, was as follows:

"We have great cause for thankfulness that since our last reunion on these grounds, September 7, 1895, we have held unbroken ranks. Not a single member of our association (so far as we know) has crossed over the river of life. In view of the physical condition of many of us, and the advancing years of all, this is a record which we could hardly hope to maintain for any great length of time. We are pleased to report the financial affairs of our association in a comfortable condition. The first note in payment of the lot bequeathed to us by our late Comrade Jacobs was promptly paid with interest. Also interest on the two remaining notes, which notes we hold, and are due in one and two years, and are amply secured against any possible depreciation. The payment of this note has enabled us to pay all the bequests of Comrade Jacobs, so far as we have been able to find the beneficiaries, and to liquidate all of the debts incurred by the association in carrying the lot until sold, and the interest on the remainder of the fund is ample to meet our current expenses, which are not large, and probably leave a small amount which can be placed in a sinking fund to meet any future emergencies of the association. A few of our members met on Decoration Day at our monument in Rose Hill, and decorated the gun and the graves with flowers and flags. Members should make special efforts to gather there on that day, as other associations are doing so more generally each year, and we do not want to be behind our brother comrades in this respect. The large oak tree standing in the center of our lot was found to have several large decayed branches overhanging the monument, endangering it in case of their falling during a high wind. These branches have been removed, and the tall, straight trunk of the tree stands covered with vines, and is much improved in appearance, and is a very appropriate ornament to the last resting place of our departing comrades. The Cemetery Association has been communicated with regarding terms for the "perpetual care" of our lot. In reply the following was received:

"Chicago, Sept. 1, 1896.

"C. B. Kimbell, City:

"Dear Sir: Our greenhouse manager informs us that a principal sum of $200 would be needed for the proper care of the Battery 'A,' Chicago Light Artillery, Association lots (one to six, section A). The lots need grading, but if the sum named is deposited this fall, we will do that without any extra charge. The trimming of the tree you called attention to has been done, for which there will be no charge. The sum named cares for and preserves the lot and memorials forever. Yours truly,

"Eugene C. Long, Secretary."

We would recommend that favorable action be taken by the association on this proposition whenever our finances will warrant it. We have been placed in possession of a very valuable relic of the early days of the old battery through the kindness of Comrade Southworth, which is the first record of the battery organization before the war, from Dec. 2, 1857, to Aug. 7, 1863. If the full history of our battery is ever published this will be a very appropriate and useful starter for it.

Notices and invitations of this meeting were fairly well responded to, and regrets were received from twenty-eight members. The national encampment of the G. A. R. closed its session at St. Paul yesterday. A number of our comrades were prevented from being present here to-day on account of attendance there, but we have great consolation therefor in learning from the dispatches that our loved and respected comrade, Thaddeus S. Clarkson, was unanimously elected to the high office of Commander-in-Chief of that grand and noble organization, a fit recognition of his long, faithful and valuable services to it, and of which we may all well be proud."

Letters of regret were read from absent comrades. New business being next announced, it was resolved to send a telegram to Comrade T. S. Clarkson, congratulating him on his election to the office of Commander-in-Chief of the G. A. R. at the national encampment then in session at St. Paul. The following dispatch was forwarded and reply returned:

"Chicago, Sept. 5, 1896.

"Major T. S. Clarkson, Commander-in-Chief G. A. R., Omaha, Neb.:

"Your original comrades, in annual reunion assembled, are proud of the honor and distinction of furnishing from our ranks the highest officer for the grandest soldier organization on earth. We know the honor so worthily bestowed will be faithfully and creditably executed.

"Battery 'A,' Chicago Light Artillery, Veteran Association,
"C. B. Kimbell, Secretary."

"Headquarters Grand Army of the Republic,
"Office of the Commander-in-Chief,
"Omaha, Neb., Sept. 18, 1896.

"C. B. Kimbell, Secretary:

"The message of congratulation from Battery 'A' Veteran Association conveyed to me by you has touched me beyond expression. No word received has meant so much to me, or touched me so deeply, as that coming from the grand men with whom I immediately touched elbows during that awful struggle. Three members of Battery 'A' were present at St. Paul, and participated in the great honor conferred upon me, and I believe that honor carried no greater satisfaction to any of the thousands present than to those splendid fellows, Page, Gray and Sam. Tallmadge. Please convey to the 'boys' my hearty thanks and my best wishes for their success, and my sincere hope that I shall meet them personally at an early official visit to Chicago. Very truly yours, T. S. Clarkson, Commander-in-Chief."

The election of officers of the association then followed, resulting in the election of: Comrade Martin A. Bartleson, President; Dr. Allen W. Gray, Vice President; C. B. Kimbell, Secretary; J. H. Long, Treasurer; E. H. Rexford, Musical Director. These five comrades also constitute the directory. A fine musical program was rendered by Comrade Rexford, assisted by his daughter Laura, Miss Sarah M. Kimbell, daughter of C. B. Kimbell; and Mrs. Pratt, sister of Enoch Colby, interspersed with songs, less classical but fully as musical to the old boys, by the boys themselves. A photographer was present and took pictures of a group of the boys on the porch and lawn, and one of the boys and their families. The meeting then adjourned subject to the call of the officers.

The eleventh annual reunion occurred at the Union League Club, Chicago, Oct. 1, 1897, beginning at 5 p. m. Lunch was served at 6 p. m., after which the business meeting was held. Twenty-nine members were present, viz., J. H. Long, A. W. Gray, Ed. Baggot, C. B. Kimbell, S. S. Kimbell,

**Members of Battery "A," 1st I. L. A., 10th Reunion, Chicago, Sept. 5th, 1896.**

1. Enoch Colby, Jr.
2. Geo. M. Sevit,
3. O. C. Foster,
4. W. R. Page,
5. W. H. Young,
6. Chas. E. Smith,
7. Wm. Lowe,
8. W. H. Renfrn,
9. M. A. Bartleson,
10. C. Kemdall,
11. Harrison Kelley,
12. W. L. Smithworth
13. C. W. Poole,
14. S. S. Kimball,
15. G. M. Brown,
16. E. H. Renkord,
17. W. F. Stockton,
18. A. W. Gray,
19. T. P. Powel,
20. O'ef Benson,
21. F. N. Gimbeler,
22. J. W. Kimbell,
23. J. W. Kimbell,
24. W. E. Beecham
25. C. A. Church,
26. C. B. Kimbell,
27. W. H Bailey,
28. J. D. Dyer,

George M. Brown, W. H. Young, W. H. Bailey, A. W. Pendleton, Harrison Kelley, Enoch Colby Jr, W. L. Southworth, Henry Burdick, Fred B. Leavitt, W. E. Stockton, W. H. Reniro, W. E. Beecham, Charles E. Clark, W. R. Page, P. P. Powell, Ed. Mendsen, John Steele, Wm. Lowe, C. W. Poole, O. C. Foster, F. V. Gindele, John D. Dyer, E. H. Rexford and W. H. Johnson. President Comrade Bartleson being absent on account of a serious accident, Comrade A. W. Gray, Vice President, presided. The roll of all members was called by the Secretary. The minutes of the last annual meeting were read and approved, as were also the reports of the Treasurer and Directors. Cards of regret were read from W. H. Cowlin, of Woodstock, "prevented by sickness;" T. S. Clarkson, Omaha, "prevented by official business;" C. L. Church, Wellington, Ohio, "kind remembrances;" Edward Johnson, National Soldiers' Home, Leavenworth, "best wishes;" J. P. Brown, Florin, Cal., "too much labor;" Moses Hawks, Phenix, N. Y., "poor health;" M. A. Bartleson, Utica, N. Y., "injury from accident;" E. S. Hills, Atlanta, Ga.; Wm. Taylor, Chicago. Letters were read from C. C. Briggs, Pittsburg; S. H. Tallmadge, Milwaukee; Nathan T. Cox, Denver; M. A. Chittenden, Atchison, Kan.; C. L. Arnold, Chicago; George A. Pratt, Ft. Atkinson, Wis.; W. B. Phillips, Marion, Ohio; Ed E. Williams, New York; E. P. Fish, Pueblo, Colo.; Wm. Furness, Ogdensburg, N. Y.; F. A. Emory, Magnolia, Va.; J. T. Connell, Grand Island, Neb.; J. N. Sherman, Soldiers' Home, Quincy, Ill.; John B. Day, Bedford, N. Y.; H. E. Brewster, Marlboro, N. H.; Meric Gould, Brest, Mich.; A. C. Hall, Des Moines, Iowa. A memorial on the death of Comrade Julius W. Kimbell was offered by Comrade W. E. Stockton and adopted unanimously by a rising vote. (The memorial is found in his biography.)

Officers for the ensuing year were elected, with Dr. A. W. Gray, C. B. Kimbell, C. W. Poole, J. H. Long and E. H. Rexford as Directors. The Directors met and elected: A. W. Gray, President; C. W. Poole, Vice President; J. H. Long, Treasurer; C. B. Kimbell, Secretary; E. H. Rexford, Musical Director. The bugle calls were given by Comrade Rexford, with all his usual vigor and old-time skill. Excellent music was furnished by Miss Laura Rexford and Miss Bacon. The meeting then adjourned for one year.

The twelfth reunion was held in Hinsdale, a beautiful suburb of Chicago, at the home of C. B. Kimbell, Sept. 10, 1898. The Hinsdale Doings, the local paper, published an account of it, which is given in full below:

## VETERANS GATHERED AGAIN.

Battery "A" Remembers the Battles of 1861-5 at C. B. Kimbell's.—Magnificent Entertainment Enjoyed by the Soldiers and Their Families—Special Cars Provided—The Fun.

Probably no other village in this State was so aglow with evidences of earnest patriotism last Saturday as was Hinsdale. In addition to the royal reception accorded by the entire people of this vicinity, to the returning Naval Reserve Corps, the surviving veterans of the famous Battery "A," Chicago Light Artillery, of 1861 to 1865, held their twelfth annual reunion, with their wives and families, at the pleasant home of C. B. Kimbell, who, with two brothers, were members of that battery during the civil war. Upwards of one hundred and fifty were present, among them being several of deceased members' families, and a livelier, pleasanter time could not have been had. The commodious grounds and all the buildings were profusely and tastefully decorated with flags and bunting. An immense flag was hung across Elm street, in front of the house, and a large white banner was stretched over the front of the lawn with a red border and blue letters, inscribed, "Welcome Battery 'A' Veterans." An immense tent on the lawn covered tables fifty-four feet long, set to form the letter "A." These were loaded with toothsome viands, to which all did ample justice, as the cool, crisp air was very conducive to a keen appetite, and the "old boys" demonstrated their ability in that direction as well as when they were thirty-seven years younger and had better teeth than they now have.

George Bohlander's orchestra perched up in the barn balcony, covered with woodbine and draped with bunting, furnished patriotic airs during the forenoon and until after dinner, when he was ordered by the young people to "come down off his perch" to the first floor, which had been covered with canvas and prepared for dancing, and they kept things lively and warm for about three hours. Many of the older ones declared they had not seen dancing "on the old barn floor" for forty years, and the seats were filled with amused spectators of the young folks' antics.

From 12:30 to 1:30 p. m. was occupied in disposing of the picnic dinner, which was announced by ringing the old farm bell, and the sounding of "Grub Call" by E. H. Rexford, the battery bugler, on his old war bugle. All the old battery calls were blown by him, at intervals during the day, and the stirring notes awakened memories of war days in the hearts of the old veterans. After dinner the business meeting of the veterans' association was held under the tent, all remaining seated at the tables. The first thing after being called to order, Comrade W. E. Stockton offered a resolution, extending greetings and congratulations to the young soldiers of the Naval Reserve Corps on their safe return home, and thanking them for the splendid record they had made during their short term of service. In acknowledgment of the courtesy the entire procession, with their martial band of eighteen pieces, paraded past the grounds, halting for fifteen minutes in front. The veterans lined up on the pavement and their families formed a background on the grass plat and sidewalk. The scene was very effective and touching. President Dr. A. W. Gray, in behalf of the veterans, made a short and stirring address of welcome to the naval boys, who were seated in carriages directly in front of the veterans. The band played "America" and the "Star Spangled Banner," and all joined in singing one verse of "America," when the whole procession passed on amid cheers in review of the battery veterans.

The whole affair was a pleasant and unexpected feature, and one never to be forgotten. The roll of the entire battery was called, first of the survivors, then of those who had passed away. The total number of enlistments from the beginning to the closing of the war, including fifty that served for three months only, was 262. Survivors known at this date, 115. Killed, dead and missing, 147. Many that served three months only in this battery, served with distinction in other commands through the war. Most of the members of the battery have made as good records in their various lines since the war as they did during the war, and have been prominent in business, professional and political circles. Ex-Congressman George E. Adams, of Chicago; General Thad. S. Clarkson, ex-postmaster of Omaha and Past Commander-in-Chief of the G. A. R.; Col. J. H. Page, of the Third United States Infantry, now at Santiago, and many of the leading and successful business men of Chicago were members of this battery. The Directors' report showed the finances of the association to be in a flourishing condition.

Permanent badges of a neat and tasty design had been procured and were worn for the first time on this occasion.

The Directors' report, as follows, for 1897-8 was read and approved: "Since our last annual meeting, your Directors have had little to do except to carry out the instructions of the members at that meeting. A beautiful granite headstone in memory of Comrade Lewis F. Jacobs was erected on the battery lot at Rose Hill. It was inscribed with his name and "Noble Patriot, Brave Soldier, True Friend." We have also supplied the permanent badges, which we trust will be satisfactory, as they were to all with whom we had an opportunity of consulting. In the matter of government headstones for those buried in our lot, little has been done, owing to difficulty in obtaining definite, correct data in regard to the names and number buried there. We would recommend that the new Board of Directors take the matter in hand and do the best they can during the coming year to get it finished up. The final payment on the Lewis Jacobs lot has been made and the money is in the hands of the Treasurer. One of our members, George King, passed away at Elgin, Ill., Thursday, July 14, 1898. Owing to the shortness of the time of receiving notice of it, none of our members were present."

The following resolutions on the death of Comrade George King, who died in Elgin last July, and of honorary member John L. Stockton, who died in Chicago, were passed by a rising vote:

"It is our sorrowful duty to announce the passing away of one of our loved and honorary members, John L. Stockton, brother of Comrade Wm. E. Stockton. His death occurred at his home in Chicago, Oct. 31, 1897. Of delicate physical frame, he was incapacitated from entering active service in the army, but his patriotism was proved beyond a question by his untiring zeal and devotion to the care and comfort of the soldiers in the field, especially the sick and wounded of our battery. He was the most active in keeping up the home organization of our battery during the war, and none of our sick and wounded reached the city without being under his watchful care, and several times he visited us while in the field, bringing things of comfort and words of cheer. He was chiefly instrumental in securing the necessary funds for the erecting of our beautiful monument at Rose Hill, and was one of the most active and helpful members of the Monument Committee. His memory will ever remain as bright with us as the flowers that blossom over his silent grave.

"We are called upon to mourn the death of one whose name revives memories of all that went to make camp life more endurable and to brighten and cheer the hard lot of the soldier.

"Comrade George King died at his home in Elgin on Thursday, July 14 last (1898).

"We knew him as a brave and gallant soldier, one of the most active and untiring men in the battery. Kind and generous to his comrades, and one of the most proficient in the drill, not only in the battery but in the 'manual of arms,' probably, in the corps to which we were attached. Who does not remember how he won honor for the battery by defeating the best-drilled infantryman the division afforded? The following notice is taken from Comrade Wm. H. Cowlin's paper, and fitly expresses what we all feel:

" 'The death of an old comrade, even so many years after the war, who has touched elbows with us in the ranks, or who has marched or rode by our side over countless miles of country, being with us in battle and in camp, sharing all the hardships and vicissitudes of war, cannot but help to carry sadness and sorrow, though we may not have met that old comrade since the close of the war.

" "The Elgin Courier of July 15, a marked copy of which we recently received, contained this announcement:

" ' "George King died, Thursday evening, at his home, 323 Orange street, aged sixty-two years. He was born at Niagara Falls, and had been a resident of this State thirty-six years. He was formerly an employe of the gas company, and had recently been janitor of a school building."

" 'Comrade King was an exceptionally good soldier, brave and true as steel. He served three years in our company—A, Chicago Light Artillery—and was with our battery on all its long and weary marches, in every battle from its first, Fort Donelson and Shiloh, to Kenesaw Mountain, Ga., in the summer of 1864, when his term of service expired. He marched thousands of miles and was carried by steamboat other thousands, participated in eighteen battles and dozens of skirmishes, always ready and willing for any and every kind of hazardous and hard service. He was admired for his soldierly bearing and kind and genial companionship by every officer and man in the battery. There was no better soldier—there could not be—hence we regret and are sad to hear that he has been summoned to join the silent majority, and our sympathies are extended to the sorrowing wife and family of our deceased comrade.' "

Letters and cards of regret were read from absent members, their addresses showing how widely they had separated since the war. They were from New Hampshire, New York, Pennsylvania, Virginia, Ohio, Georgia, Tennessee, Michigan, Illinois, Wisconsin, Kansas, Nebraska, Colorado, Washington, New Mexico, Iowa and California.

The business meeting closed after electing as officers for the ensuing year: President, C. W. Poole, of Lawndale; Vice President, W. H. Young; Treasurer, J. H. Long, Chicago; Secretary, C. B. Kimbell, Hinsdale; Musical Director, E. H. Rexford, Blue Island. After an hour spent in five-minute entertaining talks by the members and a few invited guests, among whom was Mr. C. F. Elliott, came the contest and award of prizes. For the oldest member present, John Shaffer, of Chicago, aged 74, captured a silver mounted hickory cane, cut from the battlefield of Shiloh. The youngest member present, P. P. Powell, of Winfield, Kansas, took a silver-plated bugle. For the member present with the largest family, Mr. C. B. Kimbell showing up with eleven was awarded the first prize, which he at first declined to receive, being the host for the occasion, but his objections were overruled and he was forced to accept. The prize was a beautiful small silk flag, representing the "banner" family member. The member with the smallest family, George M. Brown, of Conneaut, Ohio, who is a happy old bachelor, captured a small steel toy cannon. The awarding of prizes occasioned much merriment.

Fine music was rendered by some of the veterans' daughters, among them Miss Laura Rexford and Miss Sarah M. Kimbell. A hearty and unanimous vote of thanks was passed for the entire Kimbell family for their work and efforts in furnishing so successful an entertainment. The 5 o'clock train, with two special cars, carried the entire party back to the city, all declaring they would ever remember the day spent in "beautiful Hinsdale."

The battery veterans who were present were: Wm. E. Stockton, Evanston; Dr. A. W. Gray, Chicago; C. W. Poole, Lawndale; E. Colby Jr., Chicago.; W. H. Renfro, Blue Island; Wm. Lowe, Chicago; E. H. Rexford, Blue Island; G. M. Brown, Conneaut, Ohio; John Shaffer, Chicago; S. S. Kimbell, Chicago; W. E. Beecham, Chicago; Charles E. Clark, Chicago; Olof Benson, Chicago; W. L. Southworth, W. H. Young, Chicago; J. D. Dyer, Ravenswood; W. H. Bailey, Chicago; Edward Hughes, Chicago; P. P. Powell, Winfield, Kan.; H. S. Foote, Milwaukee; S. H. Tallmadge, Milwaukee; Ed. Mendsen, Evanston; Harrison Kelley, Chicago; George A. Pratt, Ft. Atkinson, Wis.

The veteran guests were Rev. C. F. Elliott, cavalry; Abe Harris, Mercantile Battery; Ed. Simons, Mercantile Battery; A. H. Townsend, Hinsdale; Colonel W. B. Keeler; Henry M. Matthews, Chicago.

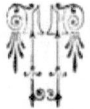

# HONORARY MEMBERS

### Of Battery "A" Chicago Light Artillery Veteran Association.

M. N. Kimbell Sr., Maplewood, Ill. Elected July 28, 1886; died Feb. 13, 1895
John L. Stockton, Chicago, Ill....Elected July 28, 1886; died Oct. 31, 1897
John Alston, Chicago, Ill..........................Elected Oct. 4, 1887
George Anderson, Chicago, Ill....Elected Oct. 4, 1887; died October, 1887
    M. N. Kimbell, Jr., admitted Oct. 4, 1888.
    John F. Powell, Waukegan, admitted Oct. 4, 1888.

---

# SONS OF VETERANS

### Admitted to Membership.

John Schaffer Jr., son of John Schaffer, Chicago, admitted July 28, 1886.
Ethan A. Gray, son of Allen W. Gray, Chicago, admitted July 28, 1886.
George T. Phillips, son of Jas. Phillips, Chicago, admitted July 28, 1886.
Jas. E. Baggot, son of Ed. Baggot, Chicago, admitted July 28, 1886.
Richard L. Powell, son of Thos. Powell, Chicago, admitted July 28, 1886.
Henry King, son of Geo. King, Elgin, Ill., admitted October 4, 1887.
Sherman T. Kimbell, son of C. B. Kimbell, admitted Oct. 4, 1887.
Louis A. Gray, son of Allen W. Gray, Chicago, admitted Oct. 4, 1887.
Walter K. Clark, son of E. D. Clark, admitted Aug. 26, 1889.

# TABLE OF CONTENTS.

### CHAPTER I

| | PAGE |
|---|---|
| History of early organization of the Battery | 9 |
| Battery responds to President Lincoln's first call for troops | 10 |
| Battery leaving Chicago for the front | 13 |
| Roster of Company in three months' service | 14 |
| Arrival of Battery at Cairo and occupation of the City | 16 |
| Capture of steamer "Baltic," "First shot of the war" | 19 |
| Capture of steamer "C. E. Hillman" | 19 |
| Occupation of "Camp Smith" | 19 |
| Expedition to Mexico, Missouri | 20 |
| Battery "Home Association" organized | 20 |
| Re-enlistment of Battery for three years | 20 |
| Presentation of flag to Battery by Miss Katie Sturges | 23 |

### CHAPTER II.

| | |
|---|---|
| Battery mustered into U. S. service | 23 |
| Number of enlistments in Battery | 23 |
| Roster of three years members of Battery | 24 |
| Battery left Cairo and occupied Paducah, Ky | 35 |
| Expedition making feint on Columbus, Ky | 35 |
| "Calloway March" Expedition | 36 |
| Raid on Mayfield, Ky | 36 |
| First Deaths in Battery | 36 |
| Incidents in camp at Paducah, Ky | 36 |
| First regulation uniforms received | 37 |

## CHAPTER II.—Continued.

|                                                                              | PAGE |
|------------------------------------------------------------------------------|------|
| Departure from Paducah                                                       | 37   |
| Capture of Fort Heiman                                                       | 37   |
| March to Fort Donelson and first battle                                      | 38   |
| Chicago Board of Trade sends vote of thanks to Battery                       | 39   |
| Left Fort Heiman for advance up Tennessee River                              | 40   |
| Arrival at Crump's Landing and advance to Pittsbug Landing                   | 40   |
| Battle of Shiloh                                                             | 40   |
| Captain Wood's official report of battle of Shiloh                           | 46   |
| Stand of colors presented by "Friends at Home"                               | 48   |
| Battery held in reserve at Pea Ridge                                         | 49   |
| Capture of W. M. Pratt at Pea Ridge                                          | 49   |
| March from Pea Ridge to Memphis                                              | 50   |
| Occupation of Memphis                                                        | 51   |
| Incidents in camp at Memphis                                                 | 51   |
| Departure from Memphis in advance on Vicksburg                               | 55   |
| Captain Wood's official report of advance on Vicksburg                       | 55   |
| Battle of Chickasaw Bayou                                                    | 56   |
| Advance up Arkansas River to Arkansas Post                                   | 59   |
| Captain Wood's official report of battle of Arkansas Post                    | 60   |
| Incidents of battle of Arkansas Post                                         | 61   |
| Battery moved to Young's Point                                               | 62   |
| Expedition up Sunflower River and Black Bayou                                | 62   |
| Expedition up the Yazoo                                                      | 62   |
| Battle of Champion Hills                                                     | 62   |
| Siege of Vicksburg                                                           | 63   |
| March from Vicksburg to Jackson, Mississippi                                 | 64   |
| Siege of Jackson, Mississippi                                                | 64   |
| Capture of eight men, and story of their captivity                           | 64   |
| Exciting episode to Squad I during siege of Jackson                          | 70   |
| From Jackson to Big Black                                                    | 71   |
| Advance on Chattanooga                                                       | 71   |
| Occupation of Missionary Ridge                                               | 71   |
| Battery moved to Bellfont, Alabama                                           | 72   |
| In winter camp at Larkinsville, Alabama                                      | 72   |
| "Larvinsville Theatre Company" organized                                     | 76   |
| Loss of Battery "mascot"                                                     | 80   |
| Leaving camp at Larkinsville                                                 | 82   |
| Start for Chattanooga on Atlanta Campaign                                    | 82   |
| Fight at Resaca                                                              | 83   |
| From Resaca to Kenesaw Mountain                                              | 84   |
| Letters of Geo. Gates and General W. T. Sherman                              | 85   |
| Return of three years men at expiration of term of service                   | 86   |
| Consolidation of Batteries "A" and "B"                                       | 86   |
| Advance on Atlanta                                                           | 86   |
| Battle of Atlanta                                                            | 87   |
| List of captured and killed at Atlanta                                       | 87   |
| Battle of Jonesborough                                                       | 87   |
| Surrender of Atlanta                                                         | 88   |
| Last months of service at Chattanooga                                        | 88   |
| Return home and welcomed by friends                                          | 88   |
| Condensed Battery's Record                                                   | 89   |

## CHAPTER III.

|   | BIOGRAPHICAL SKETCHES PAGE | PORTRAITS PAGE |
|---|---|---|
| Captain James Smith | 91 | 92 |
| Allen, Frank S. | 93 | — |
| Arnold, Charles L. | 95 | 94 |
| Adams, Abbott L. | 97 | — |
| Adams, George E. | 97 | 98 |
| Benson, Olof | 97 | 100 |
| Baggot, Edward | 101 | 102 |
| Brewster, Henry E. | 103 | 104 |
| Brown, John P. | 103 | 106 |
| Bailey, William H. | 103 | 108 |
| Briggs, Charles C. | 105 | 110 |
| Brown, George M. | 105 | 112 |
| Bartleson, Martin A. | 107 | 114 |
| Briggs, Jerome P. | 109 | 116 |
| Butterfield, Samuel W. | 109 | 118 |
| Botsford, John R. | — | 18 |
| Burdick, Henry | 111 | 120 |
| Clingman, Jacob | 113 | 122 |
| Clark, Edwin D. | 113 | 124 |
| Clarke, John H. | 115 | — |
| Clark, Charles E. | 117 | — |
| Cox, Nathan T. | 117 | 126 |
| Chase, Horace W. | 119 | 128 |
| Chittenden, Morris A. | 121 | 130 |
| Cowlin, William H. | 123 | 132 |
| Connell, John T. | 127 | 134 |
| Connell, Mrs. John T. | — | 136 |
| Clarkson, Thaddeus S. | 129 | 138 |
| Crocker, James F. | 131 | — |
| Cooper, George | 131 | — |
| Colby, Enoch Jr. | 133 | 140 |
| Dyer, John D. | 133 | 142 |
| Dusenberry, James M. | 135 | — |
| Dixson, Albert | 135 | 144 |
| Dutch, James B. | 137 | 146 |
| Day, John B. | 137 | — |
| Eastwood, James G. | 137 | 148 |
| Emory, Fred A. | 139 | — |
| Farnham, Daniel R. | 141 | — |
| Follansbee, William P. | 141 | 150 |
| Foster, Orrington C. | 143 | — |
| Furness, William | 145 | — |
| Fish, Edward P. | 145 | 152 |
| Gindele, Ferdinand V. | 147 | 154 |
| Gould, Meric | 149 | 156 |
| Gray, Allen W. | 149 | 158 |
| Hall, Adam C. | 151 | 160 |
| Handy, Henry H. | — | 162 |
| Hills, Edward S. | 153 | 164 |
| Hoffman, Hoxie L. | 155 | 166 |
| Hawks, Moses | 157 | 168 |

## CHAPTER III.—CONTINUED.

|  | BIOGRAPHICAL SKETCHES PAGE | PORTRAITS PAGE |
|---|---|---|
| Hughes, Edward | 157 | 170 |
| Johnson, Edward | 159 | 172 |
| Jacobs, Lewis P. | 159 | 174 |
| Johnson, Wm. H. | 161 | 176 |
| Kantz'er, Fred M. | 163 | — |
| Kelley, Harrison | 163 | 178 |
| Kendall, Cornelius | 165 | 180 |
| Kennedy, Theo. W. | 165 | 182 |
| Kennedy, Sampson | 167 | 184 |
| Kinzie, Arthur M. | 167 | — |
| King, George | 169 | 186 |
| Kimbell, Mr. and Mrs. M. N. | 169 | 188 |
| Kimbell, Chas. B. | 173 | 190 |
| Kimbell, Julius W. | 177 | 192 |
| Kimbell, Spencer S. | 181 | 194 |
| Leavitt, Fred B. | 183 | 196 |
| Long, Jas. Henry | 183 | 198 |
| Lowe, William | 185 | 200 |
| Lamb, Charles A. | 185 | 202 |
| Morgan, Francis | 187 | 204 |
| McKnight, Thos. A. | 189 | — |
| McCagg, George | 189 | 206 |
| Milner, Jas. W. | 191 | 208 |
| Mendsen, Edward | 193 | 210 |
| Mitchell, Lewis B. | 195 | 212 |
| Morgan, Harry | — | 214 |
| Nelson, Conant C. | 195 | 216 |
| Pendleton, Alfred W. | 197 | 218 |
| Phillips, James | 197 | 220 |
| Pitts, Aurelius V. | 199 | 222 |
| Page, William R. | 201 | — |
| Page, John H. | 203 | — |
| Powell, Jeremiah D. | 205 | 224 |
| Peters, John M. | 207 | — |
| Pratt, George A. | 207 | 226 |
| Powell, Perry P. | 209 | — |
| Pease, Stephen N. | 211 | 228 |
| Pond, Henry H. | 211 | 230 |
| Phillips, Wm. B. | 213 | — |
| Paddock, James O. | 213 | — |
| Poole, Charles W. | 215 | 232 |
| Risley, Harvey B. | 215 | 234 |
| Rice, William O. | 221 | — |
| Roberts, Harrison | 221 | 236 |
| Rexford, Roscoe E. | 223 | — |
| Rexford, Everett H | 223 | 238 |
| Rumsey, John W. | 227 | 240 |
| Renfro, Wm. H. | — | 242 |
| Sherman, Jeremiah N. | 229 | 244 |
| Steele, John | 229 | 246 |
| Stewart, Adam | 229 | — |

## CHAPTER III.—CONTINUED.

| | BIOGRAPHICAL SKETCHES PAGE | PORTRAITS PAGE |
|---|---|---|
| Slosser, Mac | 231 | — |
| Scott, George M. | | 248 |
| Smith, Charles E. | 233 | — |
| Shrigley, James H. | 235 | 250 |
| Stiger, Silas C. | 235 | 252 |
| Southworth, Wm. L. | 237 | 254 |
| Schaffer, John | 237 | — |
| Stockton, Wm. E. | 239 | 256 |
| Tack, John | — | 268 |
| Tobey, Edgar P. | 239 | 364 |
| Tallmadge, Sam. H. | 241 | 266 |
| Vernon, Wm. B. | 243 | — |
| Whitson, Frederick O. | 243 | 270 |
| Willard, Charles M. | 245 | 272 |
| Williams, Edward E. | 245 | 77 |
| Wood, Peter P. | 247 | 274 |
| Wilcox, Thomas | 253 | 276 |
| Young, William H. | 253 | 278 |
| Young, Fred W. | — | 280 |
| Wilcox, Edward P. | — | 282 |

## CHAPTER IV.

| | PAGE |
|---|---|
| Officers of Battery Veteran Association | 257 |
| First Reunion | 259 |
| Constitution and By-Laws of Association | 265 |
| Second Reunion | 279 |
| Third Reunion | 285 |
| Fourth Reunion | 286 |
| Fifth Reunion | 289 |
| Sixth Reunion | 291 |
| Seventh Reunion | 292 |
| New Constitution and By-Laws | 294 |
| Eighth Reunion | 297 |
| Ninth Reunion | 301 |
| Tenth Reunion | 304 |
| Eleventh Reunion | 306 |
| Twelfth Reunion | 309 |
| List of Honorary Members | 315 |
| List of Sons of Veterans Members | 315 |

## ILLUSTRATIONS

| | PAGE |
|---|---|
| MONUMENT | FRONTISPIECE |
| View of Camp Smith | 11 |
| View "In Battery," Camp Smith | 17 |
| Gun Squad, Camp Smith | 21 |
| Dining Hall, Camp Smith | 25 |
| Battle of Chickasaw Bayou | 57 |
| History of Pitt's Laurel Root Gun | 73 |
| Group First Reunion | 262 |
| Group Eighth Reunion | 299 |
| Group Tenth Reunion | 307 |

# HISTORY OF BATTERY "A"

The sixteenth annual reunion of Battery "A," First Illinois Light Artillery Veteran Association, was held in Kimbell Hall, 1527 Kimbell avenue, Chicago, Saturday, September 6, 1902. It being the forty-first anniversary of the battery's leaving Cairo, where we had been stationed the first four and a half months of the war, and occupying Paducah, Ky., where we remained about five months, added a special interest to the meeting to all of the original members of the battery present.

A beautiful Fall day, an attendance of eighteen veterans of the battery, with more than sixty members of their families and a few invited neighboring veteran comrades, all combined to furnish a very pleasant and enjoyable occasion. The hall and dining-room were profusely and appropriately decorated with flags, bunting and flowers, and all present entered into the enjoyment of the occasion with hearty spirit and good cheer. The meeting was called for 12 o'clock noon and continued till nearly 6 o'clock P. M. The President of the Association, W. L. Southworth, presided, and the following members registered, all of Chicago, unless otherwise indicated: Edward Hughes, C. B. Kimbell, Enoch Colby, Barrington, Ill.; W. H. Bailey, Wm. L. Southworth, E. H. Rexford, Blue Island, Ill.; S. S. Kimbell, W. E. Beecham, A. W. Gray, John D. Dyer, P. P. Powell, David Butts, Momence, Ill.; John Schaffer, W. H. Renfro, Blue Island, Ill.; Fred B. Leavitt, Austin, Ill.; Geo. M. Brown, Conneaut, O.; Olof Benson and W. E. Stockton, Evanston, Ill. The widows and relatives of our deceased comrades A. V. Pitts, Jacob Clingman, J. W. Kimbell, Geo. King and Jerome P. Briggs were also present. After the roll call the minutes of the fifteenth annual reunion, which follow, were read and approved:

"The fifteenth annual reunion of Battery "A," C. L. A. Veteran Association, took place September 7, 1901, at Kimbell Hall, Chicago. President Wm. H. Young presided. The following members were present and registered: Edwd. Mendsen, C. B. Kimbell, W. H. Bailey, Wm. Lowe, Edwd. Hughes, John D. Dyer, Enoch Colby, Jr., W. E. Beecham, Thos. McKnight, S. S. Kimbell, E. H. Rexford, W. L. Southworth, John Schaffer, W. H. Young, David Butts, A. W. Gray, Henry Burdick, W. H. Renfro, C. J. Sauter, John Steele, J. H. Long; total, 21. Fifty-six members of families of the comrades were also present. A picnic dinner was served and good fellowship prevailed throughout the entire meeting, with plenty of music and some dancing. The business meeting was held at 3 o'clock. The attempted assassination of our noble President, Comrade William McKinley, at Buffalo yesterday, was denounced in strongest terms by many of the comrades, and the following preamble and resolution was unanimously adopted by a rising vote: "For the third time within the memory of the veterans of the Civil War we are dumfounded by the startling intelligence of the attempted assassination of our nation's Chief. As long as our government sanctions the forming and continuing of anarchistic societies, which are boldly and brazenly announced and published in the daily press, just so long may such events as occurred yesterday be expected. The life of one such man as our noble President is worth more to our nation than all the ignorant, bristle-haired anarchists that could be stowed in a line of emigrant steamers reaching from Liverpool to New York. It is to be hoped that the people of this enlightened nation will now arouse themselves to a proper appreciation of this most vital question. Resolved, that the Secretary be directed to forward the following message of sympathy

"CHICAGO, Sept. 7, 1901.
"To Mrs. Wm. McKinley, Washington, D. C.:

"The veterans of Battery "A," First Illinois Artillery, assembled in annual reunion, deplore with horror the attempt by a miserable, worthless anarchist to assassinate our noble President. We hereby extend our profound sympathy to you and him in this terrible national calamity, and in unison with the entire people of our nation will fervently pray that he may be spared for the long life of usefulness he is so ably qualified to fill.

(Signed) BATTERY 'A,' C, L. A. VETERAN ASSN.
C. B. KIMBELL, Secy."

Letters of regret were read from many of the absent comrades. The reports of the Treasurer and of the Executive Committee were received and ordered placed on file. A communication from Comrade E. D. Howland regarding the publishing of a second volume of Battery history and offering some valuable suggestions, was informally discussed and the Secretary was instructed to communicate with all the members of the battery and obtain their views as to the advisability of undertaking it. It was voted that at future reunions, instead of a picnic dinner a regular one be furnished and paid for at a given price per plate, any deficiency from inability of comrades to attend or pay to be met by funds from the Association. The use of Kimbell Hall for next year's meeting was offered and accepted with thanks.

A communication from the National Military Park Commission of Vicksburg was received, asking for information which would enable it to locate the positions of our battery during the siege of that place, that they could be designated by appropriate markers on the spots, and also be shown upon the map to be made for that purpose. It was referred to the directors of the Association with a committee of Comrades Enoch Colby, John D. Dyer and Geo. M. Brown, with instructions to get all the data obtainable and forward same to the commission. Notice was read of the death of Comrade

C. C. Nelson, who died at his home near Washington, D. C., January 31, 1901. The sketch of his life was read from the History.

The secretary reported the number of Histories on hand August 25, 1900, 84 copies; Histories delivered and sold in past year, 12; total, 72.

The election of officers for ensuing year was then held, with the following result:

1901-2 directors elected were W. L. Southworth, J. D. Dyer, A. W. Gray, C. B. Kimbell and E. H. Rexford. These elected officers as follows: President, W. L. Southworth; Vice-President, J. D. Dyer; Treasurer, A. W. Gray; Secretary, C. B. Kimbell; Musical Director, E. H. Rexford; Assistant Musical Director, Mrs. Laura R. Pettijohn.

The meeting then adjourned for one year, subject to call by the officers.

C. B. KIMBELL, *Secy.*"

The Treasurer's report was read, showing a balance of $40.77 on hand and all bills and indebtedness paid. Approved and ordered on file.

The Secretary then read the following report of the Executive Committee, which was acted upon in same manner.

### REPORT OF EXECUTIVE COMMITTEE, SEPT. 6, 1902.

The business of our Association for the past year has been somewhat limited; the only special meeting being held to arrange for this reunion. The matter of locating the positions of the battery during the Siege of Vicksburg, for use of the National Military Park Commission, which was referred at the last meeting to the directors and a committee consisting of Comrades Colby, Dyer and Geo. M. Brown, was attended to, and sketches and explanations, as far as obtainable, were forwarded to the Commission, and their receipt was acknowledged with thanks. One name has been added to our roster, that of A. C. Bristow, an usher at the Joliet Penitentiary, who was detailed to the battery from the 127th Illinois July 23, 1864, serving till January 18, 1865. Death has invaded our ranks since our last meeting and claimed four of our members. Edward Baggot died in this city January 23d last. Arthur M. Kinzie died at Riverside May 10th Chas. C. Briggs died at Pittsburg this Spring, and Chas. W. Poole in this city, July 13, 1902. These leave us a net loss on our list of three during the year. Little was accomplished by the Secretary in regard to a second volume of our History, owing to an absence of three months from the country, limited time and strength, and the slight encouragement received from the few members consulted. All were willing it should be done, but few were able to or could promise any material help in any direction, so the matter is open for your further action. In the report of our last meeting there were seventy-two copies of our History on hand, eight of which have been disposed of, leaving sixty-four copies, which at cost price would amount to $160. Respectfully submitted.

C. B. KIMBELL, *Secy.*

Letters and cards of regret, all conveying expressions of good wishes and fraternal feelings, were received from comrades who were unable to be present, were read from A. L. & Geo. E. Adams (the latter in Europe); MacSlosser, Chicago; John Marder, Chicago (with remittance); W. H. Young, Chicago; Albert Dixson, Rochester, N. Y.; A. C. Hall, Des Moines, Ia.; Mrs. H. W. Chase (widow), Chicago; W. D. Logan, Poland, Ohio, announcing death of his sister, Mrs. John M. Clark (widow), May 19, 1901; H. H. Pond, Chicago; Chas. R. Poole (son), Chicago; Al. W. Pendleton, Chicago; Jas. H. Shrigley, Traverse City, Mich.; John B. Day, Bedford, N. Y.; S. C. Stiger, Asbury, N. J.; Wm. Furness, Ogdensburg, N. Y.; Henry A. Spaulding, Lowell, Mass.; J. N. Sherman, Soldiers' Home, Quincy, Ill.; B. Burdick, Waterloo, Kan.; Wm. H. Cowlin, Woodstock, Ill.; Mrs. Thos. Wilcox (widow), Remington, Ind.; Col. J. H. Page, 3d U. S. Infty., Ft. Thomas, Ky.; John P Brown, Florin, Cal.; Morris A. Chittenden, Atchison, Kan.; Fred A. Emory, Magnolia, Va.; Mrs. E. D. Clark (widow), Chicago, notice returned; Mrs. Harry Morgan (widow), notice returned; E. P. Fish, Pueblo, Col.; M. A. Bartleson, Nogales, Ariz.; Harrison Kelley, Chicago; J. S. Anderson, Waterloo, Ia.; Jno. T. Connell, Carthage, N. Y.; J. M. Dusenberry, San Francisco, Cal. (returned uncalled for); H. H. Handy, Chicago (remittance); E. D. Howland, New York City; Harrison Roberts, Seneca Falls, N. Y.; Henry Burdick, Woodstock, Ill.; L. M. Farnham (sister of Dan'l R.), Chicago, and O. C. Foster, Chicago. Those sending acceptances intending to attend and being unavoidably absent were J. Henry Long (remittance), Chicago; L. B. Mitchell, Chicago; Cornelius Kendall, Toledo, O.; Geo. B. Burns, Austin, Ill.; W. R. Page, Chicago, and Mrs. Sam'l W. Butterfield (widow), Chicago. Notices sent of this reunion, 114; acceptances (eight failing to attend), 26; regrets received, 37; returned uncalled for, 3; no responses from, 48—114.

It was voted to create the office of Assistant Secretary. A committee consisting of Comrades S. S. Kimbell, Dr. A. W. Gray and C. B. Kimbell was appointed, with power to act, to place our monument in good condition and have it treated to a process to arrest the decay which is showing in some places, and recut any names which may require it. A vote of thanks was given to Comrade W. E. Stockton for the pains he has taken each Decoration day in having our battery monument nicely decorated. The ladies of the Kimbell families were also voted the thanks of the meeting for the excellent dinner furnished for the occasion, which was disposed of with the appetite of true soldiers and highly complimented by all. The comrades formed in a semi-circle in front of the platform and the "Loving Cup." which was presented to Comrade C. B. Kimbell, Secretary, at a former reunion, was filled with clear army coffee and passed by him, all comrades drinking in turn. The entertainment exercises which followed were thoroughly enjoyed by all and consisted of singing of old army and patriotic songs, with piano accompaniment by Mrs. Sarah Kimbell Webster and Miss Mabel Kimbell, with "Rex" and his indispensable old war bugle. Mrs. Rexford was a great help as leader in singing. A patriotic recitation by Miss Virginia T. Kimbell, granddaughter of the Secretary, and a humorous one by Elizabeth M. Kimbell, daughter of our deceased Comrade J. W. Kimbell, were very creditably rendered. Col. W. B. Keeler, of the 35th Iowa, an old friend, was a visitor, and treated the boys to "The Old Canteen" and several other recitations, which were enthusiastically encored. Comrade Colby read an interesting relic of the war, a general order issued by Gen. Sherman after the fall of Vicksburg in 1863. It recalled vividly the events of those trying times and the voice of the reader was frequently tremulous with emotion, and many of the comrades' eyes moistened in listening to some of the stirring words. Comments were made by Comrade Benson.

After the singing of "Old John Brown" Mrs. Henrietta Harris, wife of Comrade Abraham Harris, of the Mercantile Battery, who was also present, gave a short and interesting reminiscence of thoughts suggested whenever she heard that song. An old schoolmate and friend was a member of John Brown's party in his raid on Harper's Ferry, where he was executed and buried. His name was Edward Coppick. His body was secretly taken up in the night by friends and brought back to his old home in Salem, Ohio, and buried. Mrs. Harris' father, a member of the Underground Railway, being one of the party assisting in doing it. The song naturally awakens tender memories to her mind and she could not refrain from speaking of it. A copy of the Battery History was procured by Comrade W. E. Stockton for his grandson, Stockton Russell, and at his request all the comrades present inscribed their names on the fly leaf as a memento, which the youth will probably prize very highly. The Secretary read from the History the sketches of the lives of the four comrades who passed away during the past year. Feeling eulogies were spoken by Comrades A. W. Gray, C. B. Kimbell and others for the deceased members, Comrades Baggot, Kinzie, Poole and Briggs.

Election for officers for the ensuing year then followed and resulted in the choosing of John D. Dyer, Fred B. Leavitt, C. B. Kimbell, A. W. Gray and E. H. Rexford as directors. These met and elected John D. Dyer, President; Fred B. Leavitt, Vice-President; C. B. Kimbell, Secretary; Ed. D. Howland, Assistant Secretary; Dr. A. W. Gray, Treasurer; E. H. Rexford, Musical Director, Mrs. Laura Rexford Pettijohn, Assistant Musical Director. All joined in singing "Auld Lang Syne" and closed by singing "America," after which it was voted to meet next year at about same time and place, and the meeting adjourned.

C. B. KIMBELL, Secy.

*To the Members of Battery "A," C. L. A. Veteran Association:*

DEAR COMRADES—This pamphlet is issued and sent out to you with the hope that its perusal will tend to keep up the interest of the members who have so faithfully stood by our organization since it was formed and to stimulate the interest of those who have failed to give it the countenance which so many think it deserves. Those who have kept in touch with our Association can testify to the great pleasure and enjoyment derived from attendance at our reunions, and the comfort and consolation of the presence of comrades in times of bereavement, and those who attend our reunions feel and experience the incompleteness of the enjoyment and pleasure when we realize that many of our comrades are not with us, and some do not even evince sufficient interest to respond to notices sent, with regrets. I esteem it one of the highest honors of my life that I belonged to such a gallant command in the army and to have served with such brave and patriotic comrades that composed it. Only a few, comparatively, remain to give each other the hearty handshake of comradeship. As the years roll by still fewer of our comrades will assemble at our annual reunions. The soldierly love and fraternity of comradeship which binds us together can not be found in any other organization. If any further perpetuation of our History is ever produced it must be by the hearty co-operation of our members. The feeble efforts of a few will not be sufficient to warrant it. The office of Assistant Secretary was created at this reunion to lighten the task of the Secretary, and our most worthy comrade, E. D. Howland, No. 7 E. Forty-second street, New York, was unanimously elected to the position. Any communications addressed to him or to me will receive careful and prompt attention. I will close by quoting the words so fittingly expressed by some poet:

"Comrades! you who in the battle
   Stood together firm and true,
At the shrine of each reunion,
   Dedicate your lives anew.

"You are like the trees left standing
   When the fierce tornado's past;
Let the boughs of those remaining
   Twine together firm and fast.

"Grand old army! Brave old comrades!
   Grim survivors of the fight,
Warm your hearts at memory's altar,
   Press each other's hand till night.

"And when sounds the last assembly,
   When the guard has gone his round,
We shall pitch our tents together,
   On some happier camping ground."

       Fraternally,
              C. B. KIMBELL, *Secy.*

---

This pamphlet will fit in back part of the History.

Please acknowledge receipt.

CHICAGO, June 20th, 1899.

TO THE MEMBERS AND FRIENDS OF BATTERY "A,"
VETERAN ASSOCIATION:

I desire to make the following statement for the information of the members and friends of the Association who may require extra copies of our History.

When the Association decided to publish a history, the first work was to ascertain the cost of doing so. This was done by obtaining figures from three reliable publishing concerns on the basis of two hundred and fifty books of two hundred pages 9 x 6, to include fifty half-tone cuts of members. This size book was as large as we thought safe in undertaking, and the best figures we obtained was $400.00 for two hundred and fifty books, which was $1.60 each. This was given on a sliding scale, however, to be increased or diminished in proportion as circumstances might require. Circulars and blanks were sent to all our members and friends whose addresses were known, and such general interest was taken and responses so numerously returned, that instead of a book of two hundred pages and fifty half-tone cuts, we have one of three hundred and twenty pages and ninety-three half-tone cuts; five large cuts of views of camp and battery scenes, three reunion groups and three pages of Fred S. Church's illustrations; heavier and enameled paper than was specified in the contract was used, and various other items for the betterment of the book were incorporated, which, with the increased size, brought the cost of the two hundred and fifty books to $3.23 each. Any one familiar with such work knows that the expense per copy on a limited edition, is much greater in proportion than for a large one, and the committee did not feel warranted in going into any publishing venture, and only provided for what they felt would be a reasonable demand for extra copies. The Secretary, however, on his own account, contracted for one hundred and fifty additional copies, which reduced the cost of the whole number to $2.50 each.

Any one desiring extra copies can procure them from the Secretary at Room 302 Chamber of Commerce Building, Chicago, or of J. Henry Long, Treasurer, 1425 Old Colony Building.

Any book sent by mail will require 16 cts. postage. I will be in my office Tuesdays and Fridays from 11 to 12 o'clock, and will be pleased to have city members call for the copy of the book they are entitled to.

C. B. KIMBELL, Secretary.

www.ingramcontent.com/pod-product-compliance
Lightning Source LLC
Chambersburg PA
CBHW021206230426
43667CB00006B/582